Facing Limits

Ethics and Health Care for the Elderly

EDITED BY

Gerald R. Winslow
and James W. Walters

Westview Press

BOULDER • SAN FRANCISCO • OXFORD

Published in 1993 in the United States of America by Westview Press, Inc., 5500 Central Avenue, Boulder, Colorado 80301-2877, and in the United Kingdom by Westview Press, 36 Lonsdale Road, Summertown, Oxford OX2 7EW

Library of Congress Cataloging-in-Publication Data
Facing limits : ethics and health care for the elderly / edited by
    Gerald R. Winslow and James W. Walters.
       p.   cm.
    Includes bibliographical references and index.
    ISBN 0-8133-8504-0
    1. Aged—Medical care—Moral and ethical aspects.   2. Medical
care, Cost of—United States.   3. Right to health care.
I. Winslow, Gerald R.   II. Walters, James W. (James William), 1945–   .
RA564.8.F333   1993
362.1'9897—dc20   92-7153
                                                                                                CIP

Printed and bound in the United States of America

The paper used in this publication meets the requirements
of the American National Standard for Permanence of Paper
for Printed Library Materials Z39.48-1984.

10   9   8   7   6   5   4   3   2   1

For our parents

Mildred and Chester Walters
Elsie and Arthur Winslow

Contents

Tables and Figures

Tables

Figures

Preface

There is abundant evidence that medical breakthroughs, lifestyle changes, and the 1950s baby boom will produce an unprecedented number of elderly citizens in the near future. The rapidly increasing population of older Americans and the ever higher levels of medical technology raise difficult questions about the ethical limits of life-extending interventions. Is there a point beyond which we should no longer attempt to extend life through medicine? Is that point related in any significant way to a person's age? Are the financial burdens of caring for the health of the elderly falling unfairly on younger Americans? Will such burdens be bearable in the future? What are the limits we must face? And what are the limits we should set?

The United States outstrips all nations in spending for health care, about two billion dollars each day, and costs are rising rapidly. An increasingly large percentage of these dollars goes for the care of the elderly. At the same time the proportion of the population working to foot the bill is shrinking. Today there are four workers for every retiree; a third of the way into the next century there will be just over two employees for every retired person.

How is our society to care properly for the health-care needs of the elderly? Probably no individuals have done more to ignite debate over this question than Richard Lamm, former governor of Colorado, and philosopher Daniel Callahan. While he was governor, Lamm caused a national uproar with his public suggestion that life-extending care for the elderly should be limited. Callahan's 1987 book, *Setting Limits: Medical Goals in an Aging Society*, did the same with its call for age-based rationing of health care.

According to Callahan, a "natural life-span" is about 80 years. During this time a person may be expected to have partaken of life's basic goods. After this time, medical resources aimed at extending life should not be used. The elderly, acknowledging their mortality, should be willing to accept a "tolerable death." This attitude toward death and dying entails a significant shift in social policy: governmental health programs would no longer fund any life-extending medical interventions for the very elderly. Priority would be given to making dying as comfortable as possible. Funds saved would be reallocated to enhance the quality of life for the elderly and thereby help to justify withholding life-extending modalities.

It was Callahan's *Setting Limits* that prompted us to apply to the National Endowment for the Humanities for funding of the Ethics and Aging Project. The Project, a broad public discussion of ethics and health care for the aged, was held in the autumn of 1990 in the greater Los Angeles area. It consisted of two conferences, a series of public lectures, a number of community discussions, and production of several publications.

The entire Project proceeded from the conviction that the issue of care for our burgeoning population of the elderly needs to be addressed thoughtfully before it becomes a national crisis. The goal was to provide an opportunity for the insights of the humanities to be brought to bear on the medical and policy choices that we face. The issues are not merely medical or economic. At stake is a vision of a good and just society. As an advanced technological society, what perspectives may be drawn from the study of the humanities to aid us in developing a vision suitable for the twenty-first century? How may these perspectives be related to the issues of health policy for the elderly?

The essays in this volume bring together the work of twenty participants in the Ethics and Aging Project's inaugural conference. Because of the nature of the Project, leading scholars from the areas of health care, economics, public policy, and the humanities were invited to contribute. The book begins with new essays from Daniel Callahan and Richard D. Lamm in which they extend their arguments for age-based rationing and intergenerational equity. For the most part, the essays which follow are evaluative responses to the ideas set forth in Part I.

In Part II, foundational questions of philosophy are explored. Edmund D. Pellegrino considers a wide range of literature in search of a helpful philosophy of finitude. J. Wesley Robb considers basic ethical principles that should guide the discussions of health care for the elderly. And Anthony Battaglia places the discussion of a natural life-span within the context of the tradition of natural law ethics.

Three health-care professionals provide the essays in Part III. Jeanie Kayser-Jones, a nurse, looks at the way decisions are made for nursing home patients and finds serious defects. Donald J. Murphy, a physician, considers ways to establish the medical and economic appropriateness of such interventions as cardiopulmonary resuscitation and hemodialysis for the elderly. He contends that a careful study of patient preferences, costs, and medical effectiveness should lead to reasonable decisions about which interventions are worth providing. Lawrence J. Schneiderman asks whether there is reason to hope that significant cuts in unnecessary medical costs would be achieved if patients' preferences for less aggressive medical treatments were honored more consistently. He concludes that the evidence is still uncertain, but the question is worth pursuing.

The essays in Part IV take up questions of economics and public policy. Michael D. Reagan, a political scientist, questions whether "global budgeting" with a single payer and a set budget would be a politically feasible way to control health-care costs equitably in the United States. His answer is negative, but he suggests that there are other ways to gain health-care efficiency and equity in our culture. Paul T. Menzel looks at the way we count the costs of medical interventions and argues that we should not shrink from counting all of the costs of life-extending medical interventions, including such costs as additional pension expenditures. As Menzel does the counting, an apparently inexpensive and medically effective intervention such as treatment of pneumonia with antibiotics may, in fact, cost thousands of dollars in subsequent expenditures. In Menzel's view, we cannot make reasonable decisions about medical trade-offs if we are unwilling to count the true costs. Charles E. Begley considers the economics and ethics of profit-sharing incentives for physicians in settings such as health maintenance organizations. He concludes that there is little reason to think that such incentives create any greater potential for unethical conflicts of interests than are present in the more traditional fee-for-service arrangements. After outlining the demographic and economic challenges of providing health care for an increasing elderly population, Edward L. Schneider rejects the notion of age-based rationing. Instead, he proposes a program of increased research in the most costly diseases prevalent among the elderly. Schneider argues that money spent on searching for treatments of such diseases as Alzheimer's could cause the costs of health care for the elderly to drop significantly and thus eliminate the need for rationing.

Part V focuses on questions of justice in health care for the elderly. The first two authors consider the impact of age-based rationing on women. Bethany Spielman challenges Callahan's proposal that the elderly relinquish claims to life-extending treatments and devote more of their time in service to the young. The burdens of such service would fall disproportionately on women who would already have given much of their earlier life to serving others. Emily Erwin Culpepper also offers a feminist analysis of our current health-care system and calls for activism to change radically a system that has failed to empower older women. Robert M. Veatch considers the arguments for and against using age as a criterion in the distribution of health care. He argues that age can legitimately be one of the considerations in the allocation of health care when based on a proper understanding of justice. Gerald Winslow ponders the problem that exceptional cases create for

Callahan's proposal for age-based, categorical limits to life-extending medical care. Winslow argues that any system of limits should be prepared to accommodate exceptions that can meet appropriate burdens of proof.

The essays in Part VI explore further the relationship between personal choices and social policy. Judith Wilson Ross considers the cultural stories that inform American health care and finds that the dominant stories do not fit well with the notion of limits unless they are personally chosen. She goes on to search for other possible stories that might support the acknowledgment of limits. Marilyn Moon argues that rather than impose limits we should support such programs as hospice, the use of advanced directives, and reforms in the way health-care professionals are paid. By changing attitudes toward the way health care is delivered, she contends that drastic measures such as age-based rationing may turn out to be unnecessary. Theologian John C. Bennett offers some personal and theological reflections on the ultimate question of autonomy, as it relates to both passive and active euthanasia. Bennett concludes that active euthanasia can be supported in some cases, and social policies should be changed carefully to accommodate this possibility and to guard against its abuse. Finally, James W. Walters suggests ways in which we may build on what he considers to be Callahan's valuable insights in ways that enhance personal autonomy and protect important community values.

A common complaint about edited volumes, like this one, is that the nature, scope, and quality of the chapters are "uneven." Such is the price of bringing together scholars from different fields to discuss a significant social issue from vastly different perspectives. Inevitably, different readers will find some chapters far more valuable than others. Nevertheless, there is good reason to believe that the kind of interaction represented by these twenty contributors is what we will continue to need if we are to establish a more just and efficient health-care system that serves the needs of our entire society, including the elderly.

Gerald R. Winslow
James W. Walters

Acknowledgments

The papers which now appear as essays in this volume were first presented at the National Conference on Ethics and Health Care for the Elderly held in San Bernardino in the autumn of 1990. The conference was part of the Ethics and Aging Project sponsored by the Center for Christian Bioethics at Loma Linda University and funded by a grant from the National Endowment for the Humanities. We wish to thank the Endowment for its financial support and David Larson, director of the Center for Christian Bioethics, for his help with the project. We also acknowledge the invaluable assistance of Shalagh Houghton, administrative associate for the Ethics and Aging Project.

The authors revised their manuscripts during 1991. We thank them for their patience and careful work. We also thank Elaine Walker for copyediting and Lucy Beck for outstanding efforts in managing the final preparation of the manuscripts. Clerical support was also provided by Nancy Miller, Beth Schietzelt, and Lisa Winslow.

Finally, we wish to express gratitude to our colleagues at Pacific Union College and Loma Linda University for their encouragement to finish this project.

G.R.W.
J.W.W.

PART ONE

Proposals to Limit Care

1

Intolerable Necessity:
Limiting Health Care for the Elderly

Daniel Callahan

Introduction

Few subjects seem to make Americans as uncomfortable as that
of the possible need to limit health care for the elderly. I say
"uncomfortable" deliberately, though I might also have said "angry"
or "indignant" or "outraged." I have heard those sentiments
expressed as well, but "uncomfortable" better catches the more
common reaction. Most people seem to understand well enough
that, as the number of elderly increases, as the consequent tax
burden escalates, and as medical progress marches on, it is perfectly
plausible that not everything possible in the name of health care
might forever be feasible. That is an understandable, even if not
necessarily attractive, picture of the future.

Far less tolerable is the thought of just how the lines might be
drawn and the limits set. At that point just about everyone balks.
It is, for many people, unimaginable that we might deliberately deny
to an elderly person medical care that might save life or provide
significant benefit. The result is enormous discomfort. The
troubling truth about the possible need for limits directly clashes
with the even more troubling implications of what it would mean to
do something about setting them.

The most common reaction to this discomfort is to temporize.
That can take many forms. The most common is indignation that
we could ever deny beneficial care to the elderly. That possibility is
rejected out of hand and the potential contradiction that stance poses
for fiscal realism is just left hanging in the air. A more
sophisticated response is to argue that if the American health-care

system can be reformed--the waste eliminated--we might never have a day of reckoning, or at least it would be put so far off in the future as to be irrelevant for all practical purposes. A part of this response often sees an invocation of the benefits of technology assessment: We can find out what actually works for patient benefit and what is useless. The presumption is that if only efficacious treatments are deployed with the elderly, we will be able to pay for those treatments.

Choice, Efficacy, and Individual Treatment Standards

It is sometimes also said that, if we could give elderly people more of a choice about their treatment, many would reject expensive life-extending treatment, thus obviating the need for limits. Yet while the number of those who have signed advance directives grows each year, there is no evidence so far that that trend has made any great impact on health-care costs. In any case, the problem is not only whether elderly patients get to reject expensive treatment in a final illness. The problem also involves the cost of other expensive treatments prior to that time. Signing an advance directive does not guarantee that someone will be inexpensive for the health-care system. It only guarantees that the last illness may be inexpensive; but, even then, a person could be very costly to the system before deciding it was time to invoke the advance directive.

I have long been dubious about those approaches. They may well work for a time, but it is an act of the sheerest faith to think that efficiency alone will be sufficient to help us avoid a crisis. The number and proportion of the elderly grow inexorably. Even the Europeans and Japanese, who already have in place most of the reforms being touted as a way to avoid serious future problems in the United States, have begun to quietly discuss the coming need for limits on health care for the elderly. Our country has failed for two decades to even come close to succeeding in the reduction of cost.

In any case, I have felt that the course of prudence and caution is one that looks down the road, takes the demographic projections seriously, and works with the premise that we are most likely going to have a serious problem in the future. My own guess is that it will begin appearing in a potent form within the next decade or so, and surely within the next 20 years. The problem is coming--but we also have time to think about it and, if necessary, to change our values so as to be ready for it.

I have been among those who have tried to imagine how we might best set limits in the future on elderly health care. In my approach, I have specified some important preconditions, among them: (1) the establishment of national health insurance; (2) a greatly improved program of long-term and home care, achieving a better balance than at present between an emphasis on caring and curing; (3) enhanced efforts to improve the daily quality of life of the elderly; (4) restriction of any government limitations on health care to federal entitlement programs (e.g., Medicare); and (5) limitation of expensive high-technology medicine only.

Assuming those preconditions could be met, how might limits best be set? The great difficulty here is that there are not many feasible ways to do so, and all of them would be both difficult and distasteful to implement. The possibility that many find most tolerable would be to use some kind of individual benefit standard-- that is, some treatment outcome standard that would apply to everyone, regardless of age, and that could be used for reimbursement entitlement. Then it might be decided, for instance, that the elderly would not be eligible for Medicare reimbursement for any treatment that did not provide the possibility of a good and long-lasting (say five-year) outcome. This method, it is argued, would not directly discriminate against the elderly even if it might be recognized that, *de facto*, the burden of such a standard would more likely fall on them than on other age groups. Even so, it would in principle be an age-blind standard.

There are three serious problems with this approach, in addition to its *de facto* discriminatory implications. One of them might be termed the "affordability fallacy," that is, the unsupported belief that if we provide people only beneficial treatments we can societally afford the costs. But why does that follow? As medical technology advances, it may well be that there will be more and more expensively efficacious treatments (as is the present trend and pattern). Many of the most expensive therapies now available are efficacious, such as kidney dialysis and open heart surgery. More and more such treatments are discovered. Why should a continuing and growing pattern be indefinitely affordable?

There may also be some unpleasant surprises. There is much discussion, for example, of the advantages of finding a cure for Alzheimer's disease. That would indeed be a great triumph. But if the recent history of medical progress is any guide--and it usually is--there is a good or even greater chance of a very different research outcome.

What if a discovery was made that offered an expensive treatment for Alzheimer's--one that did not cure the disease but lessened its course of development and spread its lethal effect out over a few more years? That is exactly what AZT has done with AIDS--turned it into an expensive chronic disease. Why could that not happen also with Alzheimer's: change it from a disease that now kills a person in about seven years on average into a disease that killed a person in about ten to twelve years--at a cost of say $10,000 a year? This would be "beneficial" treatment, of a sort, but not necessarily affordable treatment.

A second problem here is that there is a kind of strange injustice in saying that someone should have unlimited expensive care as long as it was efficacious care. Why should the fact that a treatment will work qualify as grounds for providing that treatment? Why should the public, as part of Medicare, be willing to spend thousands of dollars on repeated efficacious treatments simply because they are efficacious? Some lucky people, who repeatedly became sick with expensively treatable illnesses, could be allotted huge amounts of health-care dollars. It would be a perfect case of the "rich getting richer": someone lucky enough to live to old age is then given repeated expensive treatments simply because that person is lucky enough to have illnesses that can be treated. Her neighbor, who may have an untreatable disease, gets nothing, with treatment efficacy being the only difference between the funds lavished on them.

The third serious problem is that behind an individual treatment standard is an unexamined assumption. That assumption is that it is somehow good, and an unlimited good, to keep people alive at public expense as long as possible. But why is that necessarily a good? It needs at least to be shown that there is some direct correlation between a longer life and a happier life, or increased longevity and the public interest. That has never been shown or argued; it is just taken for granted. But since there are many other valuable things conducive to human welfare that public money could be spent on other than efforts to extend and improve the life of the elderly indefinitely, it is a case that must be made, not simply assumed. The fact that some people want to live for an indefinitely long period (surely their right as an aspiration) does not entail that we, as their fellow citizens, should respond without restraint to that desire with our public funds.

For my part, at least, I do not believe it would make much sense to use some kind of treatment efficacy standard with the elderly. It would be unfair, not necessarily affordable, and beg a number of questions about what we owe the elderly. More broadly, if limits are to be set I do not think that can be done on a case-by-case basis. There is too much room for dispute, too great a possibility for injustice, and too much space for endless disputes over individual cases.[1] I doubt, for instance, that any doctor could confidently predict (supported by good data) that a certain expensive medical procedure would almost certainly result in another five years of life on average, or even three years for, as an example, someone over the age of 82.

Categorical Limits

If we are to have fair, meaningful, and feasible limits, they must be what I have called "categorical" limits; that is, they must apply to everyone equally, threaten everyone alike, and be useable in a simple and straightforward way. Thus have I been drawn to age as a standard--and thus have I had to take a certain amount of heat as a result. I have, moreover, been attracted to the idea of what I called in my book, *Setting Limits: Medical Goals in an Aging Society*, a "natural life-span" as a standard for allocating resources. By that I meant an effort to determine when, in general, it can be said that a person has lived a full life and whose claim upon public assistance for more life at high cost can thus be said to be limited. The question I put was this: Granting that the elderly have a powerful claim upon public respect and assistance, what is the reasonable extent of that claim?

To have a powerful claim is not to have an unlimited claim. To agree that we may someday have to set limits is, at the least, to say two things. First, it is to say that the claims of the elderly must, in fairness, be balanced against the legitimate claims of other age groups with their health needs (and their non-health needs as well). Second, it is to say that the claims of the elderly cannot be unlimited, open-ended claims; e.g., that whatever technology develops that could help the elderly, however expensive, should be theirs to have. The obvious problem here is that there are potentially an infinite number of ways to spend large amounts of money to find ways to extend the life of the elderly. Why is it an *obligation* to the elderly to seek out, and then to provide, all those ways?

At this point, laying out the structure of the problem as I have just done, it seems sensible to want to know where we could draw a line on what counts as a "reasonable" claim. In a fine essay a few years ago, Norman Daniels noted that it is just impossible for doctors to say "no" to expensive patient demands in this country, because there are no fixed economic limits and no incentives to say no.[2] In those countries with global budgeting for their health-care system, however, it is much easier to say no: everyone understands that there is a fixed and limited budget and no way to get around that reality. My approach is analogous to Daniels'. I believe we need, in the realm of our concepts, the equivalent of global budgeting--that is, a concept of the limits of reasonable care.[3] For me, the idea of a "natural" life-span plays the same kind of role, but at a conceptual level, that global budgeting does at the economic level. Each allows us to establish a boundary, to have a common and understandable way of saying "no."

The line I think most plausible to draw to establish that boundary is that of age itself, and age calculated by thinking about the human life-cycle. My general proposition is this. We have a societal obligation to help everyone become an elderly person, that is, to live into old age; but we do not have an unlimited public obligation to extend old age as far as either the individual or science might want it to go. We owe each other a long and decent life, a full life, but it is unreasonable for anyone to claim as long a life as might be theoretically possible regardless of the cost. Put another way, we owe each other a "natural" life-span, not immortality.

A "Natural" Life-Span

I use the term "natural" life-span for three reasons. One of them is that all organic creatures, including humans, go through a biological life-cycle that ends with aging and death. It is in that sense "natural" to die at the end of a long life. If it is an evil to die, it is nonetheless our fate as human beings. By using the word "natural" I mean to indicate "within the biological order of things."[4]

A second reason for using the word "natural" is because, at least in my upbringing, it was a word commonly used and commonly understood. It was taken for granted that the death of a person in old age was a "natural" event (save for an accidental or violent death); that is, it was seen as not out of the way, or untoward, not the occasion for muttering or raging against the human condition. I believe this usage reflected a common belief that death in old age is part of the biological order of things. In fact, I got the idea for using the word "natural" not from philosophers (the term makes them nervous), but from the way ordinary people regularly talked about death when I was growing up. I have discovered, interestingly, that those with a rural, agricultural background are most at ease in talking this way, probably because they have a lively sense of biological rhythms and patterns.

A third reason for using "natural" is that I have been unable to find a better word. I concede its ambiguity, and the philosophical problems associated with it. But the fact that so many ordinary people could use it in a meaningful way--could give it a general, and accessible, reference--seemed to me to commend its use. I wish I had a better word, even now, but I do not.

What should be made clear, however, is that in using the word "natural" I am not claiming to be deducing a moral "ought" from a biological "is." Nor, in talking about a "natural" life-span, am I referring to some fixed biological state of affairs. I am not saying, for instance, that because the average life expectancy in the United States is 75 years that this is a "natural" life-span. We do not know, scientifically speaking, what the real limits or possibilities for the average life-span might be. Science might well make it possible for us to live to an average age of 100 (even though 85 is a more common estimate). That does not mean we will therefore owe everyone such an average life-span.

My use of the word "natural" is an attempt to capture a cultural sense, expressed in ordinary language, of a *biographical* life, *not* a biological life. I am trying to work here less with philosophical concepts than with human experience and common modes of discourse. I take it that a common notion of a full life is one that has seen the ordinary possibilities of life realized, if not fully then at least adequately--marriage, love, family, work, travel, and a wide range of experience. I ask myself why it is that the funerals of the very old are different from the funerals of children, why it is that we have in our society the notion of a "premature" death, and why it is that all cultures seem to have the notion of a life cycle tied to achieving different things at different stages of life. To speak, then, of a "natural" life-span is to attempt to capture those cultural features common in our society but in most others as well. I want to fashion my standard of limits from those cultural ingredients.

Keep in mind that my basic question is this: What is a reasonable demand by the elderly for public resources for their health care in old age? My answer, then, is whatever resources it takes to live a full life, a "natural" life-span. I want to make a distinction between what might be scientifically or medically possible (the claiming of which may not be reasonable at public expense) and what makes societal sense. If we could make certain that everyone had a chance to live out a full life, a natural life-span, then it seems to me we would have done them a great service. We owe them only that, not everything that might be possible.

In my book, I left open the question of what that age might be. I said, probably the "late 70s or early 80s." But what I really wanted to convey by that indeterminacy was the necessity of reaching a public consensus. This is a standard we would put together as a people, young and old, not one to be unilaterally imposed by government. There is no magic age in that respect, but only a range within which it might be reasonable to look and to work. For me personally, 80 would be a perfectly reasonable cut-off point; but, perhaps after debate and discussion, the general public might be happier with a different age.

Age and Policy

The most common objection to this approach is the way it systematically ignores individual variations among the old. The old, it is said, are the most heterogeneous of all age groups, and one person of 80 can be very different from another person at age 80. Of course that is perfectly true, and I have said so many times. But, for policy purposes, I want to argue that those differences are irrelevant. For policy purposes, firm and visible boundaries must be set, and they must in general be fair boundaries, even if they do not apply perfectly to all individuals. [It is not now considered unreasonable to start Medicare at age 65, even though we know that some individuals will show signs of old age much earlier, and some much later.] We do not consider it unreasonable to require that drivers be a minimum of 16 years of age, even though we know that some portion of young people have the emotional maturity and physical skills to drive at an earlier age. My view is that *most* people will, by age 80, have lived a full life and done most of what life offers people a chance to do. Some may not have--but policy should be designed for the generality of cases. It is, I think, almost axiomatic that a policy must work with generalities; it cannot be tailored to individual cases and still be a "policy," at least not a coherent one.

Another common objection is that to set an age limit with the elderly is to imply that they are, after that age, less worthy of our support and respect than before. I do not see that such a conclusion need be drawn at all. If our *reasons* for setting an age limit have to do with assuring justice across the age groups, and a desire to avoid giving health care a disproportionate share of resources, then that motive says nothing whatever about the human worth and value of the elderly. It is simply making a statement about the need to achieve an overall balance of goods and resources to all groups in a society. Indeed, those who think an age limit would somehow suggest a lessened value for the elderly commit a simple fallacy: that the only acceptable way of respecting the elderly is to provide them with unlimited medical resources equal to those given every other age group--as if fairness requires that we give a person of 100 years as extensive care as someone of 100 days. We can perfectly respect different age groups by giving them what will assure a decent life course, not a limitless one. What we can offer people is support for a full life, as children, older adults, and elderly. *[* To say that there must be a limit for the elderly is not to say that the elderly years are less precious than the younger years, but that the elderly years are uniquely different from those other years.*]* For one thing, the elderly have already achieved the goal of a long life; for another there is no necessary scientific limit to how much we can spend to extend those years. Indeed, to say that the elderly should be supported wherever science and medicine might take them would be to give a special privilege to the elderly. It would say that that group (and only that group) is subject to no boundaries whatever simply because, unlike other age groups, there are no age boundaries.

Since my scheme specifies as a precondition the effort to achieve a better balance in our health-care system between caring and curing, I am looking as well for a more balanced health-care plan for the elderly. Our present system makes available almost unlimited funds for acute care medicine for the elderly, but poorly supports long-term care and home care. Length of life, not quality of life, is thus the practical outcome of our national health-care programs for the elderly. That makes no sense, particularly since one ironic outcome of the emphasis on acute care medicine is to create a larger group of people needing long-term and home care--those whom medicine has saved but has not cured, itself a growing group of people. The present system does not give the elderly a coherent, rounded set of services. Why not, then, just add the needed additional services and pay for both? But, if it is the case (as it seems to be) that continued curative treatment will simply generate more people who will need long care, then there will be no way to control what will, of necessity, be spiraling and uncontrollable costs. We cannot afford in the long run *both* expensive curative medicine and other forms of health care. I want to limit the former to guarantee the latter.

It has been argued, regarding high technology care for the elderly that an age limit will not save any significant amount of money. However, to say this ignores a central point of my argument--that we face a problem in the future, not now. I indicated in my book that we can muddle along for a number of years more. It is only in 20-30 years that we are likely to have a really serious problem, but the problem could surface perhaps as soon as a decade from now. My anxiety is based upon the *trend* of spending for the elderly, and what that will mean in the future. That is why my book was addressed principally to those not yet old, in order that they may begin thinking in advance about the problems they will encounter later, when the Medicare system will have bankrupted itself and no greater tax burden can be imposed on younger people. At present, somewhere between 25 to 40 percent of the inflationary increase in health-care costs for the elderly is traceable to technological developments. Those developments become more and more costly. The combination of a doubling in the size of the elderly age group and constant, expensive technological progress is the trend that will generate the problem in the future. It will generate it, that is, unless we scale down our expectations.

Conclusion

My proposal to use age as a limit is not a proposal to scale down benefits to the elderly or to cut back on them. It is, rather, to find a way to slow down, or stop, the *constant increase* in costs-- that is, to find a way to get those costs to plateau. Only if we set a firm outer limit on where we will allow medical progress to take us will that be possible. The real, and ultimate, limits I am proposing are on unlimited medical progress. After all, by suggesting that somewhere around the age of 80 would be a reasonable cut-off point, I am proposing an age that is five years *beyond* our average life expectancy at present; that is not to go backwards.

The resistance against the idea of an age limit stems from some profound mistakes we are prone to make in thinking about the elderly. The first mistake is that the only way to respect the elderly is to provide them with the fruits of limitless medical progress. The second is to pretend that the elderly are not old, that age should not count for public policy. The third is to think that to set a boundary on claims and demands is to demean and disrespect the people who make them.

Notes and References

1. For a discussion of exceptional cases see Gerald Winslow's essay in this volume.

2. Norman Daniels, "Why Saying No to Patients in the United States Is So Hard," *The New England Journal of Medicine*, Vol. 314 (May 22, 1986), pp. 1381-1383.

3. For a critique of the global budgeting, see Michael Reagan's essay in this volume.

4. For a discussion of the normative use of the "natural" see Anthony Battaglia's essay in this volume.

2

Intergenerational Equity in an Age of Limits: Confessions of of a Prodigal Parent

Richard D. Lamm

Prodigal Parents

I am a prodigal parent. The Bible tells of the prodigal son, but my generation has turned the biblical story on its head. We inherited wealth and a competitive nation, and we leave debt and an economy that is a pale imitation of that which we inherited. For ten generations American mothers and fathers left a richer and more productive country to their children, but my generation broke the link of trust. Our parents saved; we spent. Our parents invested; we divested.

I brood long on the morality of what my generation has done. My generation has not been good trustees for America. We have not met the most basic of history's tests: we have not left our children a sustainable society. We have improved and are improving our standard of living at the expense of our children. We have inserted into their future a large number of fiscal time bombs. We have not maintained strong, vigorous and sustainable institutions.

Let me give the evidence. When I graduated from high school in 1953, I inherited the world's largest creditor nation. I leave to my children the world's largest debtor nation. I inherited an economy that was supreme in everything, yet I leave an economy that is supreme in practically nothing. When I graduated from high school, almost all of the world's largest corporations were American. Now a small percentage of them are American. I inherited a world where

the largest financial institutions were American. Now they are
Japanese. The world I inherited had its epicenter of finance in Wall
Street. Today it is in Tokyo. History has few examples of a
profligate people losing wealth and national prestige as fast as my
generation of Americans.

My generation has hung an albatross of debt around the necks
of our children. Not only have we amassed the $3 trillion federal
debt (which is equivalent to a $10,000 mortgage on each of us), but
a wide range of unfunded and contingent liabilities which the
current S&L crisis shows often come due. When we pierce all the
"creative accounting" of the federal government, I suggest that our
children will have to pay off between $10 and $14 trillion of our
federal debt--plus interest. Under the most optimistic scenario, our
children will have to take approximately 25 cents out of every tax
dollar they spend just to pay the interest on our federal debt.
Already interest on the federal debt is the third largest item in the
federal budget, behind defense and Social Security. My generation
of politicians has run deficits for twenty-nine of the last thirty years.
Rather than pay for the governmental programs we wanted, we put
them on our children's credit card. I once heard it called fiscal child
abuse.

But by no means have I mentioned all of the debt that my
generation and I have accumulated. The feeding frenzy of leveraged
buy-outs has run up corporate debt to a recent all-time high and
today consumes almost half of corporate income. Total U.S. debt,
public and private, is approximately 230 percent of the Gross
National Product, a level the nation previously experienced only well
into the Great Depression.[1] We have used our political power to
pick our children's pockets. Social Security, Medicare, military
pensions, federal civil service pensions, state and local pensions--all
these (and more)--are chain letters to the future. Medicare is one
recession away from bankruptcy. The average person retiring today
will receive back in Social Security three to five times what he or
she paid in, while our children will be lucky even to get their own
money back. Programs that worked and were good social policy
(when we had a growing economy, many children, and died at 70)
do not make economic sense in a society with far fewer children, a
less productive economy, and with people living to 80 and beyond.

The elderly are 12 percent of America yet they get 61 percent of
federal social spending.[2] This continues to be true despite the fact
that the elderly are no longer disproportionately poor. It is political
power, not social justice, that sets our priorities; and money
desperately needed to prepare the next generation is being

transferred to the last generation, whether they need it or not. Money desperately needed by poor children in St. Paul is transferred instead to wealthy retirees in St. Petersburg.

In public policy, profligacy is a time bomb. Too often a society's sins are pushed off into the future. We build for our children and we inherit the work of our parents. Consider for example the shattering deterioration of our educational system. Today's educational level is tomorrow's social and economic health. Today's education is tomorrow's GNP; it is tomorrow's standard of living. America's current place in the sun is reaping the work, the infrastructure, the sweat, the productivity of another generation.

Today's realties are not the result of today's policies; they are the consequence of yesterday's policies. We daily reap the benefit of yesterday's policies while planting the seeds of tomorrow. Our fathers and mothers planted well, but we laid waste the public policy landscape.

Like the spendthrift children of wealth, we received a rich inheritance and, first, we mortgaged our inheritance, then we started to sell it to maintain our excesses. The percentage of our assets owned by foreign investors has grown proportionately, and America is in danger of losing its economic sovereignty. One has to go back to seventh-century Spain to find a historical example of a country that has lost as much wealth as fast as we have in the last twenty years.

A nation that imports more than it exports will someday be required to export more than it imports. A nation that spends more than it earns will someday be required to earn more than it spends. A nation that borrows to consume reduces the ability of its children to consume. A nation that lives off of accumulated wealth can do so only so long. Ultimately it is our children who will pay for our profligacy.

Given this profligacy, I should like to give a new set of Ten Commandments that I think must be part of restoring the balance.

The First Commandment: "Honor Thy Mother and Father, But Also Honor Thy Children"

U.S. public policy has made tremendous gains in lifting the elderly as a class out of poverty. In 1970, 24 percent of our elderly and 16 percent of our young lived in poverty; today only 14 percent of the elderly live in poverty, but 23 percent of the young live in poverty. Some studies suggest that the elderly as a demographic group have the most disposable income. When all forms of income (including health-care programs of the federal government) are counted, the poverty rate among the senior citizens may be as low as 3 percent. We do know that families over 65 have twice the assets, on the average, as people under 30. This is not to say that there are not many poor elderly. There are. But *as a group* the elderly are doing quite well.

Clearly those over the age of 65 have the highest discretionary income of any age group in the nation. Yet the elderly, who got 2 percent of the federal spending in 1940, today get 28 percent of the federal spending and they get well over half of all federal, social spending. We thus have to insure that our policies toward the elderly do not impoverish our children, and we must make sure they do not create a burden for upcoming generations.

The Second Commandment: "Thou Shalt Not Distribute What Thou Hast Not Earned"

There is a direct correlation between the future of the economy and the future of social justice. A growing economy will allow us to meet these growing demands, and a static economy makes it very difficult to meet the expectations our society has built up. We can fight wars and depressions on borrowed money, but we cannot create long-term social justice on borrowed money.

The Third Commandment: "Do Unto the Next Generation As Thou Wouldst Have Them Do Unto Thy Generation"

Let me give you the evidence that we are being unfair to our children.

First we have not paid our way. We leave to our children a federal deficit which is already over $3 trillion. This year we will have to use the equivalent of all the individual income taxes from everyone living west of the Mississippi River just to pay the interest on the federal debt. Interest alone on the debt that my generation accumulated amounts to 15 percent of all federal spending. Recently we have been borrowing almost 20 cents of every federal dollar we collect and we have been adding $150 to $200 billion a year to the federal debt, plus a cost to future budgets of interest to service this debt.

We then have pressured our politicians to give this generation a disproportionate share of the federal budget. Experts estimate that the federal government spends six times more per capita on the elderly than on children. If you look at all governmental spending (federal, state, local) spending for the elderly is three times what we spend on children. We have all the foresight of Louis XVI.

Let us also consider Social Security. This was a great program for our grandparents and our parents, but is it fair to our children? Someone retiring today will get their entire lifetime contributions to the system back in approximately thirty months. But the system assumed that each generation would be larger and richer than the last generation. Given the new economic and demographic realities, it is likely that those entering the work force today and in the future will have to provide for our generation's retirement and for most of their own retirement. A society whose elderly live significantly longer, and which has significantly fewer children and grandchildren, sails into uncharted demographic waters. We cannot accurately predict the exact size of the storm but we know it will be serious.

For the first thirteen years of my father's career his total annual Social Security payments were $30. When I graduated from college in 1957, Social Security payments were $90 a year. For those entering the work force today maximum payments are $4,000 a year. Social Security will still be profitable for my generation, but it takes almost blind faith to estimate that it will not shortchange my children. If Social Security were actually an annuity, as is sometimes claimed, today's retirees would be entitled to only about one-seventh of what they are actually getting.

It seems overwhelmingly likely that our children will be in a double crunch, with rising numbers of elderly to support and far fewer children to support them when their retirement comes. Today's college students will likely be supporting federal programs which pay benefits to both their parents and their grandparents-- benefits which will be far more generous than they themselves can hope to receive. And looming over these two is an economy which is not meeting its international competition.

We have not kept our industries competitive. We have not fought hard enough or imaginatively enough to keep our goods competitive on the international marketplace. We have allowed industry after industry to move their factories offshore, transferring those jobs from our children to our competitors. We had the opportunity to go to work at U.S. Steel and General Motors. Our

children will have Wendy's or McDonald's, unless they are lucky
enough to work for a Japanese company.

We were upwardly mobile. Our children and grandchildren are
downwardly mobile. In 1961 when I graduated from law school,
households headed by persons age 25-34 spent on the average 61
percent of their after-tax income on the basic necessities of food,
shelter, fuel, utilities, transportation, and health care. Today these
same necessities consume approximately 75 percent of the after-tax
income of households in this age group. It will not be news to this
readership that most young couples must have two paychecks to live
as well as my generation did on one.

The Fourth Commandment: "Thou Shalt Not Steal, Neither Shalt Thou Commit Intergenerational Larceny"

We simply must examine some of the programs for the elderly,
not to abolish them, but to see if they make sense for the next
generation.

Take Social Security. People think they are getting their money
back when they receive a Social Security check. They are really
getting someone else's money back. Social Security is a promise to
our children that they can, in turn, tax their children. The money
that today's retirees paid into Social Security over their lifetimes,
invested at a normal rate of return, would pay for less than one-
sixth of the benefits that a typical retiree actually enjoys. The
Department of Health and Human Services estimates that a retiree
can expect to receive about $28,255 in Medicare benefits before he or
she dies. This is after having paid only $2,640 in Medicare taxes.
Some retirees (those with dependent spouses) will receive 25 times
more in benefits than they paid in. Many elderly have received
back more in Social Security and Medicare than they ever paid in
federal taxes in *all* categories.

We have to understand better this demographic revolution and
its implications. Before 1935 there had never been fewer than 10
working age adults for every American over the age of 65; during
the 1940s there were nine. Yet today there are only five, and in
another 50 years, projections tell us that there will be barely more
than two.

Let's look at military pensions, which carry a $500 billion
unfunded liability. The average enlisted man and woman retire
from the military at the age of 40, the average officer at 43. All
retire with indexed pensions and health benefits. Nine out of ten

military pensioners are of working age and most of these are employed in other jobs and are drawing retirement. Federal civil service pensions also carry a $500 billion unfunded liability and are arguably overly generous. A career civil service worker can retire at 55 with no reduction in pension. While this is older than most military retirees, it still sticks the taxpayer with decades of inflation protected payout, and four out of five federal workers ultimately get two pension checks--one from their federal civil service pension and a second from Social Security, both fully hedged against inflation. The federal government spends more on the retirement of its employees than it does on all of the programs for the needy. From 1970 to 1981, federal pensions went up 240 percent while inflation went up 147 percent.

We could also consider veterans' benefits. Sixty-five percent of the patients receiving free care in the Veterans Administration's 172 hospitals have "non-service connected disabilities" that have nothing to do with past military service. This after a very loose definition of "service connected ailments," with such diseases as peptic ulcers and cirrhosis of the liver automatically presumed to be related to military service.

We simply must find the political courage to examine these sacred cows and streamline and amend them so that they do not steal from our children.

The Fifth Commandment: "Thou Shalt Honor All the Elderly, But Not Base Aid on Age"

I would suggest that we cease to use age as a consideration in the distribution of benefits but instead go to need. Public policy should transfer money from the rich to the poor, not from the young to the old. Age-based programs set up systems whereby young people pay a significant portion of their income to seniors, some of whom are richer than they are. This is also a system which inadequately deals with those elderly who are desperately in need. We cannot continue to subsidize old age without regard to need. There is something terribly inappropriate about a society which does not even provide basic health care to millions of people and yet amends its Medicare regulations to pay for heart transplants, a number of which go to the wealthy elderly. We must stop thinking of the elderly as a monolithic group. It is a mistake to consider the elderly a single, monolithic group; they are too diverse, too variable.

The Sixth Commandment: "Just As a Person Cannot Live by Bread Alone, so Society Cannot Live by Health Care Alone"

We have desperately important functions, other than health care, in which we must invest in order to leave the kind of world we want for our children and grandchildren. We must invest in education, infrastructure, and retooling America. Where are we going to get the jobs for our kids? Yet our whole system is tilting toward health care and toward the military.

When I entered high school in 1950, health care was about 46 percent of what our society spent on education. This last year it was over 100 percent. In 1950, we spent $1 billion a month on health care; in 1990 it is almost $2 billion a day. We have many important things to do with our limited societal resources. Health care is one of them, no question. But it is not the only one. Yet it is the one that we seem to give precedence to, so much so that it almost dominates all of the others. One governor calls health care the "PACMAN of his budget." If you want to build up a great university, you want to build up your infrastructure, you want to help retool your industries, then here comes PACMAN, coming through your budget, eating up your flexibility. In my opinion, like the fading southern family in one of William Faulkner's novel who takes sick and ceases to work, we are treating our illness at the expense of our livelihood.

While we spend almost $2 billion a day for health care, our bridges are falling down, our teachers are underpaid, our industrial plants are rusty. This simply cannot continue. There is something fundamentally unsustainable about a society that moves its basic value-producing industries offshore, yet continues to manufacture artificial hearts onshore. We have money to give smokers heart transplants, but no money to retool our steel mills. We train more doctors and lawyers than we need, and fewer teachers. On any given day, 30 to 40 percent of the hospital beds in America are empty, but our school rooms are overcrowded, our transportation systems are deteriorating. We are great at treating sick people, but we are not great at treating a sick economy. We are not succeeding in international trade. In the last six years we have imported goods worth half a trillion dollars more than we have sold abroad.

One of the challenges of America's future is how to invest our scarce resources wisely. To do this, we must be realistic, we must ask heretical questions, we must question sacred cows. We cannot simply stand back and let one segment of our economy, no matter which one it is, dominate all the others.

The Seventh Commandment: "Thou Shalt Not Lie About the Rationing of Medicine"

We already ration medicine. We all know (though we must remind ourselves again) that about 35 million Americans do not have access to full health benefits. In 1987, the Robert Wood Johnson Foundation found that 12 percent of all Americans (or one in eight) had serious problems with access to health care and, in that year, one million families had at least one member who was refused health care.

On page one of every economics textbook is the truism that resources are limited relative to wants. My life's experience suggests that it is not so much a question of "setting limits" as "making choices." We are careening unavoidably into a brave new world of trade offs. The explicit decision to spend resources on person A with disease B is an implicit decision not to spend those resources on person Z with disease Y.

But we should be honest about the need to make such trade-offs. Any nation that misses 35 million people from its health-care system, that has 600,000 women giving birth yearly without adequate (or any) prenatal care, that has 30 to 40 percent of its children who have never seen a dentist is a nation that ought not be debating whether it should "set limits." *It has set limits!* What we should be debating is the ethics of the choices that we have, in fact, already made.

The earlier we admit that we cannot give all of the health care which might be considered "beneficial" to all our citizens is the moment that we start healing our health-care system and making better choices. Somebody, at some point, has to ask the simple question: "How do you buy the most health for our society?"

Rationing of medicine is not a future possibility, it is a present reality. Call it an error of *omission* rather than *commission*, but let us be morally honest and admit that as a nation our present policy denies health care to millions of people.

However unfortunate the current status is, it will inevitably get worse. An increasing number of thoughtful health-care experts argue that further and more specific rationing is inevitable. The ingredients that produce that inevitability are an aging population, an increase in the prevalence of chronic disease, and the emergence of an array of expensive medical technologies to cope with those developments. Aaron and Schwartz in *The Painful Prescription* made the case for the inevitability of health-care rationing.[3] The Oregon Health Decisions people found last year:

> We cannot live under the idea that we can give everybody all the
> health-care that they need. Rationing of health-care is inevitable
> because society cannot nor will not pay for all of the services
> modern medicine can provide. People in this state must search their
> hearts and their pocketbooks and decide what level of health-care
> can be guaranteed to the poor, the unemployed, the elderly and
> others who depend on publicly funded health services.[4]

Despite efforts at cost reductions of all types, there is no
significant evidence, so far, that any significant savings will be made
by any existing health cost containment strategies. Health
expenditures rose more rapidly after 1980 than earlier. The trend
continued, with no abatement, through 1988. To say that improving
efficiency is an adequate solution to these problems is, to quote the
wise words of Daniel Callahan, "wishful thinking with little
historical or present basis."[5] Even if some savings can be made,
which is surely possible, new technologies are constantly being
introduced that drive the health costs higher and higher.

Given those painful realities, I suggest that we openly discuss
how we can devise policies that will give the most health to the
most Americans. I believe if we already "ration" medicine, we
should be asking how we *rationally ration* health care, rather than
irrationally ration it as we are now doing. The choices will be
painful, particularly politically painful. But perhaps we will discover
that we can invoke the same words for setting health-care priorities
that Mark Twain used to describe Wagner's music: "It's not as bad
as it sounds."

The Eighth Commandment: "Thou Shalt Not Worship Graven Images of High Technology"

In the words of Shakespeare, "We all owe God a Death."[6] One
way to meet the painful gaps left by our present health-care system
is to reallocate some of the money now spent on the terminally ill.
Few people will defend the present system. Every day in American
hospitals, people are brought back from death so they can face death
again tomorrow, after considerable additional resources are spent on
them. We have developed a range of Faustian technologies which
are part miracle, part manacle. Many times they only prolong dying.
It is now a frequent story in America that families, experiencing the
death of a loved one, consider the health-care system their enemy.
We have gone from longevity to "prolongevity."

The prolongation of life as a value often runs head on into another value--the relief of suffering. We refuse to acknowledge the conflict and, to the extent that we do, we blindly spend massive resources prolonging lives that have no happy outcome.

A doctor can and must ask, "What is good for the patient?" But public policy cannot be made by asking what is marginally beneficial for each individual patient. What is ethically proper for one patient may cumulatively be impossible public policy. Someone must weigh the total social priorities. The sum total of myriad individual ethical decisions can be unethical public policy.

We must recognize what is going on today in hospitals. They are not treating great numbers of people in every community who do not have the resources to get good health care; at the same time they are using technologies that cost more and more dollars to keep sicker and sicker people alive for a few more days. By our moral and legal ambivalence we are misallocating billions of dollars desperately needed elsewhere. While some needlessly live, often in great pain, others needlessly die, often in great need. We are not controlling our technologies, they are controlling us.

But, by itself, limiting medical technology for the dying also is not going to solve our painful dilemma. While there is clearly excess in the treatment of the terminally ill, the savings are modest and will not solve our problem. It is difficult to predict death in advance. Much of this money is well spent and necessary. Those who claim that this alone will solve the dilemma both over-promise on these savings and underestimate the difficulty in ethically saving much money in this area.

The Ninth Commandment: "Thou Shalt Not Let Young Children Suffer Because of Health Care Given to the Elderly"

In the rationing of medicine, age should be a criterion. We already ration for age; that is to say, we ration *for the benefit* of the aged. Our current system gives much more generous benefits to the aged than it does to any other group in America. We are subsidizing through a number of programs, all the elderly, whether needy or not. We have, for what appeared to be good, sufficient, and compassionate reasons, given generous benefits to the elderly.

The second step which we must also inevitably take is to means-test some entitlements to the elderly. This is not politically easy, but as a matter of distributive justice it is more than possible to reduce or eliminate the benefits we now pay the wealthy elderly in favor of programs for the impoverished young.

We must do even more. We must ask, "Should age itself ever be a consideration in limiting the delivery of health care?" No one *wants* to say yes to this question; but I suggest that we will *have to say* yes. The obligation of the government toward the elderly cannot be unlimited. No level of government can be expected to cover, without restraint, the exploding health-care costs of the elderly. Government must make rational and compassionate allocations to all its citizens and it must increasingly weigh the benefits and burdens between generations. It is marvelous idealism to say all U.S. citizens should have a "right to health care," but at this point in history that is merely rhetoric.

The delivery of expensive medical miracles to the explosive, growing number of elderly is creating an unsustainable economic and social burden. We are allocating our governmental benefits to those who lobby us the hardest and comprise the biggest voting block, but we are not making rational allocations. Our present policies, in light of those realities, will prevent adequate health care for other generations, especially younger generations. It is already having a distorting effect.

The longer I was in government, the more I realized that we are moving into an era where we shall have to make hard choices. There is a public policy teeter-totter; when we push one side up, alas, another side goes down. It is sad but true that we now have a system that allows the elderly to consume far more medical resources than we give to children.

Inevitably, we shall have to recognize age as a valid ethical consideration in the delivery of medical care. Is it not only fair, but desirable, to have a different level of care for a 10-year-old than for someone who is 100? Should not public policy recognize that some people have far more statistical years ahead of them than others?

The aged are not a static group. It is a status that we all pass through. We all age daily. In a marvelously egalitarian way, time takes its toll on all of us. The elderly are the same people--at a different stage of their lives--whom we worry about when we deny prenatal care to pregnant women.

I care a great deal about myself, but I care also for my children. I want to be valued as a senior citizen but I do not want to impose unnecessarily on my children and spend massive resources for a few more months of pain-racked existence. I fear death in the forgotten corner of a nursing home, caught in the twilight zone between life and death, with technology giving me not a longer life but a longer death. I do not want the same standard of medical care that should be given to someone who is 20. I have lived my life--experienced joy and sorrow.

All cultures distinguish between death after a normal life-span and death which is premature. Death due to age is universally accepted and understood. Death before a normal life-span is usually invested with elements of tragedy, as it is in our society.

We shrug and call pneumonia an "old man's friend" and yet rage with Lear at the death of the young. We understand with an atavistic wisdom that we cannot live forever and that death in old age is natural and inevitable. At some point, to fight against death is not only useless, but unseemly.

Yet there is reason to pause. The ghost of the British system hangs over this debate, a system that seems cruel to our eyes because it rations certain scarce resources on the basis of age. I do not argue for such a system.

We have other ethical options between massive oppressive technology imposing a slow painful death on us, and an arbitrary rationing using age as the criterion. I do not argue that age should be *the* criterion, but *a* criterion.

I find it hard to believe that the health-care system should consider a person's blood pressure, whether or not they smoke, how much alcohol they drink, and what their cholesterol count is, but not consider their age. I believe age should not be the only consideration. But it should be a consideration along with many others in the allocation of medical resources. That does not give anyone license to abandon the elderly, or to treat them as superfluous.

I certainly consider age when it comes to the way in which I treat myself. Why shouldn't the health-care system? I no longer climb trees or play Rugby. I do not lower myself in my own self-esteem when I realize that I have an older body. I treat it with more care. I recognize that my time is limited. I spend more time smelling the flowers.

Conclusion

We must recognize that age is a valid and ethical consideration in the delivery of health care. We must do so not to abandon the elderly, but to put their needs in perspective with other health care demands of our society.

Earlier I mentioned "Ten Commandments," but I am not going to state the tenth one. I am hoping instead that readers will add their own Tenth Commandment. I do this as an invitation to all who care about solving the difficult problems I have addressed in this essay.

I conclude with the old Middle East proverb which says that "The beginning of wisdom comes when a person plants a tree, the shade under which he knows he will never sit." I reflect deeply on that proverb. The ultimate question of an aging society is "How can we do justice to all sectors of the society, including the elderly, but not *only* the elderly?" Today we find resources that are desperately needed elsewhere going inefficiently or wastefully to the elderly.

Notes and References

1. Peter Peterson and Neil Howe, *On Borrowed Time*, (San Francisco: Institute for Contemporary Studies, 1988), p. 11.

2. Ibid., p. 89.

3. H. Aaron and W. Schwartz, *The Painful Prescription: Rationing Hospital Care* (Washington, D.C.: The Brookings Institution, 1984).

4. John Kitzhaber, "Uncompensated Care: The Threat and the Challenge," *The Western Journal of Medicine*, Vol. 148 (June 1988), p. 711.

5. Daniel Callahan, *What Kind of Life? The Limits of Medical Progress* (New York: Simon & Schuster, 1990) p. 11.

6. William Shakespeare, *Henry IV*, Part 2, Act 3, Scene 2, line 253.

PART TWO

Philosphical Foundations

3

A Philosophy of Finitude:
Ethics and the Humanities
in the Allocation of Resources

Edmund D. Pellegrino

Introduction

In recent years, there has been increasing support for social policy that factors "finitude" into allocation decisions, particularly those affecting aged persons. On this view, it is argued that the inevitable finiteness of human life impels us to set certain limits on health care. The pursuit of the illusion of earthly immortality, it is held, is responsible for the wasteful use of health-care resources. Were we willing to accept our finitude, it is maintained, we would desist from requesting such care, accept our end when it comes, and refuse to provide public funds for those who seek immortality through medical technology.

In this essay, I shall examine three aspects of finitude as it applies to social policy: (1) the meanings of the concept of "finitude"; (2) how it is being used to set limits on health care; and (3) how the humanities enrich our understandings of finitude. I will end with some personal, philosophical, and religious reflections.

I shall delimit my discussion in three ways. First, I shall attempt no sophisticated philosophy of finitude, but only a propaedeutic sketch. Second, I shall not cover specific ethical issues since others have this assignment. Finally, I shall not seek "lessons" from the humanities. The humanities teach best when they are least didactic.

Ordinarily, discussions of the ethics of allocation of health-care resources are based in discussions of justice. The usual questions are: What are the moral claims of the aged for access to health care? How can limited resources best be distributed between generations and between different kinds of health-care? Who shall carry the social or fiscal burden? How do we deal with the growing phenomenon of ageism? What concept of justice is most appropriate? These and related questions make up a significant portion of the topics to be covered later in this symposium.

Arguments for rationing based in "finitude" have entered the debate only lately, and more implicitly than explicitly. You will have difficulty finding the term "finitude" as such in the databases relevant to biomedical ethics.[1] But the idea of finitude is a very old one; reflections on mortality, aging, and dying and how to confront them have occupied thinkers in the most primitive as well as the most advanced civilizations.[2]

In the ordinary dictionary sense, finitude is simply synonymous with finiteness. Applied to the human condition, finitude states the immutable fact of human limitations in time and space. Aging, dying and death are limitations on human existence. Per se, the term "finitude" has no ethical force. It takes on ethical dimensions when we go beyond its dictionary meaning, to use the fact of finitude as justification for a social policy that would set limits on health-care.

A "philosophy" of finitude may be construed in several ways: (1) formally, as a systematic and critical reflection on the deepest meanings of human limits, (2) informally, as a perspective for confronting our mortality in a reasonable and rational way, both as individuals and as a society, and (3) pragmatically, as a *de facto* justification for setting limits. Let us examine these three conceptions and their relative suitability as a basis for resource allocation in the care of the elderly.

The Formal Philosophical View

In 1975 Tristram Engelhardt brought the formal sense of finitude into bioethical discourse when he proposed what he called his "Counsels of Finitude."[3] Drawing on the philosophies of Hegel and Hartshorne, Engelhardt tentatively proposed that finitude could be a rubric for setting priorities in health care. The "counsels" he suggested were: accepting the naturalness of death and seeing painful and premature death, not death itself, as the principal enemy of medicine. If physicians educated patients in how to live with and accept their mortality, they would be less prone to seek expensive life-prolonging or futile treatments.[4]

Engelhardt drew heavily on Hegel's discussion in the "Philosophy of Nature" on the naturalness of death, on the rejection of immortality, and on the necessity of individual death in serving the higher purposes of the community and the species.[5] In Hegel's view, society's progress depends on the death of individuals. "The fact of the matter is that humanity is immortal only through cognitive knowledge, for only in the activity of thinking is the soul pure and free rather then mortal and animal-like."[6] Only in the values of the community can individual finitude be transcended "and it is through the conscious recognition of the inevitability and need of death that men are led to transform the natural bonds of desire and instinct into ethical institutions. Thus, death, as the negative of natural life, is the link between the natural and the ethical level of the rational individual's existence."[7]

An equally influential concept of finitude is Heidegger's, which Engelhardt finds somewhat less persuasive. Heidegger's perception is more personal and subjective than Hegel's.[8] It places emphasis on the individual and not the social meaning of death. It consists in our constant awareness of non-being in the presence of being " . . . man's coming to grips with his own limitations, his living in the presence of his death."[9] This awareness induces "dread," a uniquely human phenomenon, which is the boundary condition of human existence. Yet this realization of death may give the courage to do what must be done before the end. Heidegger's concept has yet to be examined in any detail in relationship to the allocation of health resources. Were it to be examined, the resultant policy might differ materially from the Hegelian conclusions.

Both Hegel's and Heidegger's notions of finitude start with the obvious fact of our mortality but each places it in a complex ontological context. The leap from these abstract formulations to public policy is long and perilous.[10] Given the way Hegel's philosophy has been used to advance the absoluteness of the state, and Heidegger's own dangerous flirtation with German National Socialism, both of these philosophers should be approached with caution as a basis for any social policy.[11]

On a personal level, neither Hegel's nor Heidegger's conception of finitude is likely to be a consolation to many aged or dying people. Hartshorne's concept of "contributionism" of "transcending self-interest as our final concern," is more attractive. "If, and only if, we can regard our entire lives as contributions to the good of those who will survive us and only if we can find part of our present satisfaction in the thought of such contributions to the future of life beyond ourselves, can we find death positively acceptable."[12] Hartshorne sees our finitude defined by the fact that there must be some end to novelty in our lives, that at some time we will exhaust the variety of our satisfactions. Kass, in a different way, expresses something of the same thought in his treatment of finitude as a virtue.[13] Both Hartshorne and Kass bring us closer to the second conception of a philosophy of finitude: the informal development of a philosophical perspective; a way that reasonable and rational persons might view the fact of mortality with equanimity.

Finitude As a Philosophical Attitude

Every important philosopher of every school and in every era has wrestled with a rational and reasonable way to confront the dilemma of our aging and dying. This is consistent with one of the aims of ancient philosophy which is to teach how one should live[14]-- especially in old age: "Never can philosophy be sufficiently praised; the man who harkens to its precepts is enabled to pass every season of life free from worry."[15]   To learn to live is also to learn how to die. Socrates' own death is a vivid and eloquent discourse on old age and dying. This theme was particularly strong among the Middle and Later Stoics such as Seneca, Epictetus, Cicero, and Marcus Aurelius. The Stoics accepted aging and death as built into the natural order, as facts we cannot alter but which the philosophical person can approach with calm resignation. By taking this view, the wise person accepts death and old age and extracts from them their particular virtues while being resigned to their inevitability.

This philosophical way of confronting aging and dying still provides comfort and strength for many. It is the perspective which implicitly inspires most writers on the ethics of allocation when they allude to "limits." It is this perspective which many ethicists hope elderly people will adopt voluntarily so that they will "let go" at the right time, and forego expensive treatments, and vacate social roles they have outlived. On this view, the empirical fact of finitude becomes an ethical imperative in both a personal and societal "philosophy." Callahan uses this idea implicitly when he speaks of restructuring our personal and social values concerning how long we ought to live and what choices our society should make in the allocation of our resources. He and others imply a duty of the aged to move from a misguided perception of longevity and endless medical rescue to acceptance of some arbitrary "cut off" age.[16]

The Pragmatic Use of Finitude

The least formal conception of a "philosophy" of finitude is the most prevalent today.   Policy-makers and their technical advisors usually dispense with philosophical justifications.   They move directly to the raw fact of finitude.   Their concerns are with aging as a utilitarian problem of resource allocation in the face of infinitely expanding demands and present and future scarcity.   They may allude, in passing, to the ethics of intergenerational justice, acceptance of aging, or setting limits to public responsibility.   But their argument--their "philosophy" in the very loosest conception of that term--is that if we do not ration health care to the aged, we will compromise almost every other social good--education, housing, jobs, security, and the environment.

This is really an argument for exigency as the ordering principle. Whatever ethical objections may be raised must yield to the demands of survival.   Whatever our views of finitude, it is argued, they must give place to the realities of fiscal and resource management.   Moreover, if the elderly do not accept voluntarily that rationing is in their best interests, then "society" must intervene, through the political process, to impose rationing, to set an age for cutting off public support, and to limit research or treatment of the diseases that afflict the aged.

This pragmatic conception of finitude, though it may eschew or even deny being a philosophy, cannot avoid being one.   Like the formal and informal philosophical approaches, it presupposes a perspective on aging and its meaning, and it uses the fact of finitude as the starting point of its line of reasoning.   Arguments of this kind are not what they appear to be on the surface--merely logical analyses of competing facts, ethical principles, values, or economic and political theories.   They are expressions of deeper philosophies of the nature, purpose, and meaning of human life and the human condition.   They also express a social vision, a conception of the kind of society we are or ought to be.

Some Reflections on the Pragmatic Approach

The pragmatic conception of a philosophy of finitude is the one most frequently encountered in public and private discussion and the one most dominant in legislative responses to the "problem" of aging. For this reason, some reflection on the line of argument it generates is appropriate to this discussion.

First of all, this approach treats aging primarily as a problem to be solved, not as a universal and fundamental personal human experience. It objectifies aging and looks to economics, politics, and the social sciences for solutions. It measures the value of aged persons by ratios of cost to benefit, effectiveness, and social utility. It is too often unidimensional. If age is primarily an economic problem, then the questions are: How much money do we spend on it? And, what do we get in social utility for our money? At what age do we cut off certain kinds of care? If aging is primarily a biological problem, the question is whether we should try to uncover its causes, slow its progress, enabling people to die "healthy" and thus "squaring off the curve" of the life-span. If aging is primarily a social problem, then what social institutions do we need to deal with it? Aging is, of course, all of these things, but it is not totally synonymous with any of them.

The pragmatic argument from finitude begs some of the most important ethical questions because it makes assumptions about the kind of life we want to live. It assumes a society which forecloses any sacrifices of its open-ended materialism to help the more vulnerable of its members. It is not the well-to-do retirees, but the frail, poor, and abandoned aged who will be the major victims of any rationing system. To speak to them of "finitude" and "limits" is a bit ludicrous, given that social and economic finitude is already their daily lot.

Using the bare fact of finitude as the *leitmotif* of an ethics of rationing also assumes that the young are willing, for an immediate fiscal benefit, to foreclose care for themselves when they become elderly. It presumes also that the potential social benefits of research in Alzheimer's disease, arteriosclerosis, arthritis, and other disorders at "the ragged edges" as Callahan has termed them, should be forsaken because they usually afflict older people. Are middle-aged people who are already in sight of these diseases willing to give up the benefits of future cures in the interests of finitude? Should they do so? What about the enormous economic benefit of technological break-throughs? These questions are too lightly dismissed. Most of the cost of chronic illness goes into nursing or home care which is labor-intensive. How logical economically is a philosophy of limits which opts for the expenses of caring for but not curing the more devastating chronic diseases?

A philosophy of finitude construed simply as setting limits makes further assumptions, i.e., that there is, indeed, an economic crisis in which health care is already compromising other social goods like education, environment, and housing. Are those deficiencies in other social goods due to lack of resources or to a lack of will or motivation to redistribute available discretionary resources? Can we look at the pattern and amount of our discretionary expenditures--alcohol, drugs, tobacco, gambling, recreation, etc.--and argue that there is an ethical justification for setting the kind of limits some are proposing? Can the medical profession speak of rationing when we tolerate disorderly and unnecessary work-ups, use high technology when low technology is equally or more effective, when we indulge patients' demands for dubious or ineffective medications and treatments of all sorts? Can administrators speak of limits in the face of the large operating overheads they expend in order to compete, advertise, and "dominate" in the marketplace?[17]

These questions are not meant to argue for blank-check medicine for any age group. They are not meant to defend prolonged or painful dying, or marginally beneficial, futile, or frivolous treatments. But use of the concept of finitude, as *de facto* justification for setting limits, sustains a social vision that many would find ethically impoverished. This might well not be what the public would choose if it really had to confront the issues.

Moreover, the present line of argument starts from the assumption that we must not change the kind of society we are, that utilitarianism, pragmatism, and individualism are untouchable values. I believe Callahan has rightly asked, What kind of life do we want to live? His question is couched in terms of finitude, thus: how are we to best accommodate the limits imposed upon us by our mortality and our finite resources?[18] To do so, he feels we must move from an individualistic to a more communitarian ethic in health policy and to a realization by the elderly themselves of their disproportionate needs for health care.

This is closer to the root of the problem than most of the tinkering with health plans and insurance schemes which occupy policy-makers. To define what kind of life we want, we must first ask what kind of persons we want to be or, concomitantly, what kind of society we want to have. What is our vision of a humane and caring society? Callahan strives to answer this question by striking a balance between the extremes of no limits (which is irrational) on the one hand and involuntary euthanasia of the aged (which is morally unacceptable) on the other.

Perhaps a more critical question is: How much are we willing to sacrifice of our present self-indulgent lifestyle of limitless consumption to become a better society, one which is more caring, more humane, more concerned--not just for the aged, but for all who are vulnerable? To answer this question, we must refocus our social vision through the lens of a proper philosophy of finitude. Finitude is an experience in which all humans share--the individual with, and in, the community.

Eventually, we must all encounter the facts of our own mortality and the decline in function and powers that precedes it. We need a philosophy of finitude based in the human phenomenon of aging, one not energized by setting limits as the preordained primary goal. We also need a philosophy that teaches how, as individuals and a society, we can confront, live with, adapt to, and assist each other to live the experience of finitude with dignity, compassion, and in a morally respectable way. The elderly and the young, in my view, both have an obligation to make some sacrifice of self-interest in each other's interests.

Callahan's proposals also include assumptions about the functions of medicine. He suggests that prevention, and "adequate care" should replace more technological approaches. The difficult question of how one defines adequate levels of care and the consequences of abandoning the search for cures of certain diseases is obvious. It is not likely that most people would accept the consequences of medicine so defined. It leaves open, too, the clinician's question: What shall I do with this patient, *now* in distress, and in need of a treatment which I know will be effective and beneficial? Does a social policy of limits excuse the physician from her traditional commitment to do what is in the best interests of her patient? What is the role of the profession when social policy imposes ethically dubious roles on physicians and other health-care providers? Can medicine, or society, be in possession of knowledge that can offer a radical cure, or alleviate suffering, and not use it?

The development of a morally defensible philosophy of finitude, and its application to the complicated problems of an aging society, allows for no panacea. It cannot be the product of any one discipline. Our current preoccupations with the biology, economics and sociology of aging clearly do not suffice; nor will the application of principles of justice, beneficence, or autonomy, however sophisticated. To be sure, these are critical sources for the empirical and ethical dialogue propaedeutic to any new vision of society and aging. But aging is not a discipline-specific problem. There is need for an account which draws on a deeper and more positive conception of finitude than is customary in the current debate.

Finally, the present line of argument for rationing health care is uniformly couched in negative terms. Society is to set limits through public policy. The elderly must be prevented from taking unfair advantage of the young. They must desist from requests for expensive treatment after a certain age. No really positive reasons are given which might call on the altruism and rationality of the aged. Appeals to finitude as a stimulus and opportunity to efface self-interest, so others may have greater access to society's resources, are notably absent. If there is to be a new social vision, the young must recognize the plight of the aging, and the aging must recognize the needs of the young. A satisfactory philosophy of finitude must be based in a mutuality of obligations rather than setting limits on one group.

Finitude and the Humanities

Are there sources for understanding finitude outside philosophy and the social sciences? Can the humanities play a part in generating this richer, more authentic, and more humane perception of finitude? I shall take the humanities in the classical sense to encompass history, philosophy, literature, and languages. This is not to deny the values of the fine arts or the humanistic end of the spectrum of the social sciences. Myth and stories and the whole apparatus of the narrative school in ethics and sociology have much to contribute as well.[19] For simplicity, and want of time, I shall limit myself to one humanistic discipline, namely literature.

First, let me establish that we should not expect "lessons" from any of the humanities. Writers and poets invariably fail as preachers. When they preach, they fail as artists--witness most novels of social significance. Good writers rarely prescribe solutions for society's practical problems. Even if they wanted to, they have neither the experience, nor the expertise, to do so. Their utopias are imaginary exercises, literary thought experiments, not actual blueprints for a perfect society. Literature is not a catalogue of "lessons" to be learned or a handbook for living. Nor are the technical skills of the humanist helpful in the resolution of potential problems.[20] The more literature becomes a technical specialty, the less it is able to teach us. To expect didactic lessons from literature, then, is to destroy its power to delight and to subvert its power to teach.

But, in its own special way, literature does have moral purpose. It can be, as Collingwood put it, "the cutting edge of philosophy."[21] Good literature is "applied" in the sense that it is relevant to our lived experience. It is also never really morally neutral. That is why the great texts, classical or modern, have been so influential and so intensely studied as moral guides--positive as well as negative. "I have claimed that true art is essentially and primarily moral--that is life-giving. Moral in its process of creation and moral in what it says."[22] It "tests values and raises trustworthy feelings about the better and the worse of human action."[23] The humanities teach with a special voice, but it is not the voice of the classroom.

Literature teaches by evoking vicarious experiences of life's most fundamental and universal encounters. Reading Shakespeare's *King Lear* or Sophocles' *Oedipus* "teaches" us about finitude and the frailties of aging in a way no gerontologist can.

Literature enables us to feel and see in stories, plays, and poems how humans play out the challenges of aging, finitude, and dying and what those experiences mean to identifiable characters. We are offered individualized, particular instantiations of finitude which takes it out of the realm of the abstract. We are shown the different ways in which various characters confront death and old age. Consequences can be played out without our having to live through each variation ourselves. We can see where each choice leads us. All the challenges of living too long, of dying too soon, of despair, of frailty--all the innumerable permutations of the phenomenology of finitude--are exhibited in the world's literature.

Literature immerses us in the experience of finitude while we are still outside it. We can, therefore, criticize, identify with, or reject the way in which the characters in a story confront it. A story forces us to reflect and to grow in our perceptions of our own finitude even if we are young. The normative and ethical, the good and bad, the whole of the human condition are open to scrutiny from a distance.

Literature teaches ethics not by precept, ethical argument or dogmatic assertion--all of which would destroy its specific power to teach morals. Rather, it shows us right and wrong, good and evil, consequences, acts, virtues and intuitions in the lives of characters and the concrete situations of their lives.[24] It teaches more by evocation than by invocation.

Literary Perspectives on Finitude

For philosophers, finitude is a concept to be analyzed, clarified, and set into some ontological frame of reference. For creative writers, it is a subject for imaginative penetration of a universal human experience--one that is felt and experienced in a unique way by individual persons. Because of this difference, we do not encounter the term "finitude" in literature, but its surrogates, those life experiences that force human beings to face their finiteness--the experiences of aging, dying, death, and the yearning for immortality.

Those experiences are ever-present subjects for reflection in all of the world's serious literature. It would be vain to try to represent or categorize the multitudinous variations on these themes played out in verse and prose, in music and the visual arts. For example, on one theme alone, aging, and in one limited area of medicine and literature, one annotated bibliography provides over 200 references.[25] The index to any of the standard books of quotations (Oxford, Bartlett, Mencken, etc.) gives evidence of the number, and variety, of literary allusions to such key words as age, death, dying, mortality, and immortality.

These literary allusions abound in richness and depth of insight. But they contrast widely in the ways they construe finitude and its surrogates. They offer no clear conception upon which a social vision or philosophy can be securely grounded. Still, they serve an important purpose. They alert us to the multitonal chorus to which philosophers and social planners must listen if their policies are to be humane and just. How we take these literary depictions very much determines how we might allocate our resources.

Let us take just two finitude surrogates--aging and mortality-- and examine how they are treated in literature. These two are particularly relevant to our theme of ethics and health care for the elderly. We are being urged to ensure that aged persons recognize their finitude and voluntarily relinquish their claims to health care after a certain age; or if they fail to do so, society will do so for them. A corollary argument is that expensive technology should not be used by very seriously ill persons, since that would amount to a denial of finitude in the pursuit of earthly immortality.

Aging: Blessing or Burden, Gift or Drain on Society

For some authors, aging is a dread, a disgrace to human dignity, and a sad end to the toils and joys of human life:

For when youth passes with its giddy train
Troubles on troubles follow, toils on toils . . .
Joyless, companionless and slow
Of woes the crowning woe. --Sophocles[26]

With his advancement in years many troubles beset him . . .
--Horace [27]

What is this deplorable lust for life that holds us bondage to such uncertainties and dangers? --Lucretius[28]

O Harsh Old Age, how hateful is thy reign. --Euripides[29]

Others are more optimistic. For them, age is a time for fulfillment, for relief from cares and opening to new kinds of delectation. Cicero, for example, sees virtues where others see deficiencies. For him, exclusion from power, loss of strength, loss of sensual pleasure, and fear of death are compensated by greater chances for intellectual and spiritual growth and freedom from the bondage of the body with death.[30] Luigi Cornaro, in his "Treatise on a Sober Life," called old age "the most beautiful period in Life"[31] --extolling very much the same attractions as Cicero. So, too, did Browning's Rabbi Ben Ezra--"Grow old along with me. The best is yet to be."[32] Among contemporary writers, we find the graceful yet realistic acceptance of both the infirmities and satisfactions of aging in the works of May Sarton,[33] John La Farge,[34] and Malcolm Cowley.[35]

Equally ambivalent are the attitudes about what the aged can contribute to society. Some see the elderly as sources of wisdom, sagacity, and the bearers of the tradition; others satirize their weakness, follies, and fallibilities.

In Proverbs and Leviticus, we find praise for the old: "You shall rise in the presence of grey hairs, give honor to the aged and fear your God" (Leviticus 19:32); or "Grey hair is a crown of glory . . . ." (Proverbs 16:31). Cicero insists that it was the faculties of "reflection, reason, judgment" possessed by older men that were of the greatest service to the state.[36]

Cicero spoke for a slower-paced world than ours. However, in a time of rapid change, as Aldous Huxley reminds us, the vaunted sagacity of the aged may be illusory:

> Experience of the past is inadequate in the face of a rapidly and radically altered context of modern living. This tends to erode the sense of obligation to the elderly and disvalues their "wisdom," which can so easily be outstripped by the pace of events.[37]

Today a dominant theme is denial of finitude. The advertising media show us old people of astonishing youthfulness, beaming happily from the tennis courts of the retirement community being advertised. This is the modern resurrection of the longevity and immortality legends which sustain the hope for the total defeat of human finitude. Every culture has longevity legends from the literature of the Greeks to the legends of Indian, Chinese, Japanese, Persian, and Celtic cultures.[38]

The modern version of the immortality myth lies in faith in the thaumatury of molecular biology to enable us to live long and "die healthy." This is the modern version of Descartes' dream that "we can be free of an infinitude of maladies both of mind and body and even possibly the infirmities of old age, if we had sufficient knowledge of the causes and all the remedies which nature has provided us."[39]

But, even before the wonders of technology, humans found it difficult to accept the ineradicability of their finitude. To be sure, the prophets reminded men and women forcefully of their mortality: "Your fathers, where are they? And the prophets, do they live forever?" (Zechariah 1:5); "All flesh shall perish together and shall return again into dust." (Job 34:15) Nonetheless, it has always been hard to think of our own finitude:

All men think all men mortal but themselves. --Edward Young[40]

There is no man so decrepit that as long as he sees Methuselah ahead of him, he does not think he has another twenty years left in his body. --Montaigne[41]

No one is so old as to think he cannot live another year. --Cicero[42]

It is reasonable to ask people, especially the aged, to take finitude into account in their demands and claims on society. But clearly, human psychology being what it is, the illusion of immortality, or at least the hope of "one more year," will be difficult to set aside.

On the other hand, literature warns us that the longevity we yearn for may resemble hell more than heaven. As witnesses, we have the Greek myth of the young man Tithonus, who was granted immortality, but not eternal youth,[43] and Jonathan Swift's miserable Struldbrugs who were likewise afflicted. They "had not only the infirmities and follies of older men but many which rose from the dreadful prospect of never dying."[44] They yearned for death as aging reduced them to shrivelled semblances of themselves. Swift prophesied that these "immortals" would become "proprietors of the whole nation and engross the civil power . . . which must end in the ruin of the public"[45] with devastating social consequences. Fortunately, it appears that there is a biologic upper limit to longevity despite our hopes and our technology.[46]

Age and the "Fixed" Period

We find in literature, too, a devaluation of age which suggests that those who have outlived their usefulness should move on, as Jonathan Swift suggested, as a matter of conscience: "three-score I think pretty high; 'twas time in conscience he should die."[47] Napoleon would have agreed: "There ought not be any generals over sixty years of age on active service."[48] Osler put the upper age of utility even lower.[49] This viewpoint is gaining ground today as the young complain of the effects on their lives of supporting an aging population. This overt ageism may infuriate some older people and spur them to resistance. But it will depress others severely, especially the chronically ill, making them susceptible to suicide or a request for euthanasia.

Old Age and Virtue

Plato's dialogue with the old man Cephalus in the *Republic* offers another fascinating insight--that our personal reactions to finitude are closely related to our characters and the way we have lived. "But of these things and of those that concern relatives, there is one certain cause: not old age Socrates, but the character of the human beings. If they are balanced and good-tempered, even old age is only moderately troublesome. If they are not, then both age, Socrates, and youth alike turn out to be hard for that sort." [50]

These ambiguous and contradictory conceptions of aging and finitude have had their impact on social policy. Since the time of primitive man, social attitudes have vacillated between high respect and honor for the aged to their devaluation as burdens. In primitive societies, they were offered their choice of suicide or being killed. Sumner, in his *Folkways*, attributes the differences in a society's attitudes to aging on whether a society's resources were scarce or plentiful.[51] Benevolence has always been hard to sustain when it means sacrifice. It seems clear that the perception of scarce resources is driving our social vision of aging today. We hope the consequence will not be a choice between euthanasia or suicide as it was in primitive societies.

The Life-Cycle

Perhaps the most frequent and most graphic image of aging is the image of the life-cycle which flourished in the Renaissance.

Ancient writers like Hesiod, Aristotle, and Avicenna had introduced this notion of natural stages of life and suggested the ways we might adapt to each. The most graphic example, of course, is Shakespeare's.[52] The life-cycle idea carried with it a philosophy of finitude still influential with the literate public today. Like the other literary images, it can offer either hope or despair.[53]

The themes we find in the great writers are mirrored in the descriptions of elderly persons themselves--sometimes in equally eloquent language. Shura Saul has provided vignettes about aging submitted by young and old people. They reveal the same profusion and confusion of themes we find in literature--courage and fear, tranquility and turmoil, acceptance and rejection of the infirmities of age, respect and disdain. Each response is personal and experiential and therefore unique in its own way.[54] Particularly revealing are the vignettes of the old, themselves, those who, as Mauriac said, are in the "antechamber of eternity."[55]

Ethics and a Philosophy of Finitude:
The Possibilities

What are we to make of these multitudinous, contradictory, contrary, variable and often intermingled themes of finitude the humanities present to us? It would be difficult, indeed, to fashion from them a coherent philosophy of finitude. Today we can extend life as we never could before, and the number of people living beyond the Biblical allotment is unprecedented. We have made aging a problem to be solved, without yet plumbing the depths of the mystery of the experience of finitude. Do the cacophonous voices of literature make a viable connection between finitude and ethics impossible? Should we give up the effort, yield to expediency, and leave the ethics of aging to the marketplace, politics, economics, or management science where ageism can not only flourish but be legitimated? If we wish to avoid these extremes, we must somehow enrich our policy perspectives by insights from the humanities. But as we have seen, literature could support a variety of social visions. The humanities have much to teach us about finitude but no consistent story we can all appropriate.

I do not think philosophy alone as a discipline can elaborate a sound ethics of finitude. There are serious deficiencies in extant ethical theories when it comes to providing a rationale for obligations to the aged.[56] In the case of Kantian deontology, benevolence to the aged would be one of the imperfect duties and therefore not mandatory. Utilitarianism faces the familiar difficulties of a valid moral calculus. Carried to its logical extrapolation, utilitarianism runs the risk of giving social sanction to euthanasia.

Some progress might be made if we take the path of virtue ethics as William May and others have done, emphasizing both the obligations and duties of the aged. May, thus, returns to one of the oldest aims of philosophy, i.e., how to live a morally good and spiritually sound life in the face of our finitude.[57] This is the way of Marcus Aurelius, Seneca, and the Stoics.

But virtue ethics is no panacea either. It has great value in enabling individuals to cope with their finitude in a calm and "philosophical" way. It helps develop social policy if the "virtuous" aged will see their duty clearly and "let go." This is problematic, however, in a democratic, pluralistic society in which individualism and freedom are the most cherished social values and the capabilities of medical science tempt even the virtuous to illusions of immortality.

The proposals now being debated for an ethically defensible basis for health-care allocation are contradictory. They reflect widely divergent social visions and differences in their conceptions of finitude. A few examples will suffice to make this point: Churchill puts his emphasis on a needs-based right to care;[58] Dougherty on a change in marketplace values which will assure a right to health-care;[59] Wikler examines an interesting strategy which binds the young person to allocate resources prospectively over the life-span;[60] and Daniels justifies a complete life span approach.[61]

Jecker criticizes both Daniels' and Callahan's methods of limit setting.[62] Others have proposed a Quality Adjusted Lifeyears (QALYS) criterion for the allocation of resources based on the number of quality life years a patient is likely to survive after a given treatment. Grimes shows how this method of macro-allocation neglects the needs of individuals and favors the young.[63] Schneider rejects the whole idea of age-specific rationing and urges instead increased research in the diseases of aging like Parkinson's and Alzheimer's diseases. In this way the costs of extended care can be reduced since the years of disability would be compressed.[64]

While no generally acceptable resolution seems likely, an adequate philosophy of finitude should, at a minimum, be based on some common conception of finitude that goes beyond simply setting limits. This is an extremely difficult task in a pluralistic society, yet it cannot be escaped.

Moreover, the "problem approach" must yield to a broader, more humane, more communitarian approach--one in which policy and economics are driven by ethics and not the other way around.

Given the individualistic, libertarian, cost-conscious trends of contemporary society, there is little hope that these two desiderata can be met adequately. Perhaps, as in the past, the common good sense and good will of the American people can be resuscitated. This probably will not come about by reasoned argumentation, but by a confrontation with the brutal consequences of a policy based primarily in economics or a libertarian philosophy.

The Place of Religious Commitment

Secularism's dominance notwithstanding, many Americans still draw on the values of the Judaic and the Christian traditions in their view of aging. I wish to offer a brief reflection on an aspect of those traditions. By this, I mean no offense to those who do not share these beliefs, nor do I suggest that they are less humane, or less compassionate in their perceptions of finitude. But those who hold to the Jewish and Christian traditions are bound together by a life perspective which converts aging from a problem to a moral responsibility. In place of cost-effect-benefit analysis, Christianity calls for some measure of effacement of self-interest and sacrifice. The aged are not just a social problem. They are our brothers and sisters. Sacrifice for the good of the vulnerable is a Christian duty, not a burden to be eliminated as it is in some philosophies of finitude we have mentioned. Nor is elimination of the problem by euthanasia acceptable.

Ultimately finitude is a challenge in the spiritual realm, a point that gets little hearing in a secular society. I agree with Kass that the yearning for long life and immortality masks a yearning for the perfection and fulfillment of our human nature.[65] This cannot be attained by endless prolongation of a life, even one of endless health, pleasure, or productivity. As Hartshorne points out, there is a limit to the novelty of our pleasures and satisfaction in living.[66] The deeper longing is for union with the True and the Good, and that means with God. Finitude is a burden because it confronts us with the possibility of non-being, more specifically with the complete absence of any possibility of attaining that fullness of being which only union with the transcendental can satisfy.

Philosophical definitions of finitude will never be entirely satisfactory either for individuals or for a social vision. The ancient separation of religion and philosophy is methodologically appropriate, but philosophy needs religion if it is to yield meaning. And religion needs philosophy if these meanings are to satisfy the mind. Philosophy needs to be illuminated by the greatest works of literature of all--the literature of the great religions.

In the Christian tradition, this illumination comes from the Bible. Here, finitude is still shrouded in mystery, but we can deal with the mystery because we believe aging, and death are the antechambers of fulfillment of our spiritual destiny as created beings. Finitude becomes an experience we face positively with the help of faith and charity. If we live by the spirit of The Sermon on the Mount, we will see our obligations to the elderly as obligations of charity, like our obligations to all the vulnerable, weak, and oppressed.

The Gospels teach the aged that they do have an obligation to accept aging and dying when they are inevitable. The aged are called to make sacrifices for the good of the community and future generations, and to see in aging an opportunity for something more than selfish indulgence and detachment from life's problems. The Gospels teach a social vision that is communitarian not individualistic, that recognizes the need to make sacrifices for the care of the more vulnerable among us. They teach that rationing is a last resort. There is much we can, and should, give up before we discriminate against a large segment of humanity. Finitude for the Christian can never simply be a problem to be solved--a matter of biology, economics, sociology or philosophy.

Christian acceptance of finitude could never justify active euthanasia or assisted suicide.[67] For Christians, finitude is built into our lives by God. Our lives are gifts of God over which we are stewards, but not absolute masters. Acceptance of finitude entails accepting death when it comes. It rejects the pursuit of earthly immortality by artificial prolongation of the dying process. To take advantage of effective and beneficial medical treatment on the one hand, and to reject what is ineffective or superflous on the other, are charitable acts. To cut off life abruptly at our choice of time or by our own hands, or to ask for it at the hands of others, is to deny the reality of the Passion and Atonement in our lives. It is to belie Jesus' own admonition that we must take up our cross and follow Him.

Conclusion

Philosophy and literature remind us that public policy is about people and not units of production and consumption. Together with the visual arts (which I have for lack of time not discussed),[68] they remind us of universally recurrent themes which must be factored into any resource allocation policy. These factors are essential to any creditable ethics of aging. At the very least, these insights will modulate the extreme positions to which economics, politics and biology can so easily lead. At their best, they will revitalize and rehumanize our struggle with the realities of scarcity and need as well as our finitude.

My hope is that personal, existential, experiential, and phenomenological insights into our ineradicable finitude will force us to think through what kind of society we are, want to be, or ought to be. Perhaps our shared experience of finitude will make us more, rather than less, caring for the aged, the elderly, the young, and the sick. I hope so.

Notes and References

1. A search through the database of the National Reference Center for Bioethics Literature located at Georgetown University turned up only one "finitude" reference--Engelhardt's paper quoted below.

2. Paul Radin, *Primitive Man as Philosopher* (New York: Dover, 1957). Some of the insights of "primitive" societies are as perceptive as any recorded in the literature of "advanced" civilization. See especially chaps. 8 and 9.

3. H. T. Engelhardt, "The Counsels of Finitude," *The Hastings Center Report,* Vol. 5 (1975), pp. 29-36.

4. H. T. Engelhardt, "The Lesson of Finitude," *Western Journal of Medicine,* Vol. 14 (Aug 1986), pp. 187-188.

5. G. W. F. Hegel, *Hegel's Philosophy of Nature,* edited and translated with an introduction and explanatory notes by M. J. Petry (New York: Allen and Unwin, 1970). Engelhardt uses two rather brief citations, p. 179 and pp. 209-210 in this work of Hegel.

6. G. W. F. Hegel, Lectures 445-446, *Vorlesungen,* Vol. 5, p. 229, as cited in Terry Pinkard, "The Successor to Metaphysics: Absolute Idea and Absolute Spirit," *The Monist,* in preparation.

7. G. W. F. Hegel, *System of Ethical Life* (1802/3) and *First Philosophy of Spirit* (Part III of the System of Speculative Philosophy 1803/4), edited and translated by H. S. Harris and T. M. Knox (New York: State University of New York Press, 1979), p. 44.

8. Martin Heidegger, *Being and Time,* translated by John Macquarrie and Edward Robinson (New York: Harper and Row, 1962). See also John Sall, "World, Finitude, and Temporality in the Philosophy of Martin Heidegger," *Philosophy Today,* Vol. 9 (1965), pp. 44-46.

9. C. R. Bukala, "Heidegger Plus: A Dialectic of Living-Dying-Living," *Philosophy Today,* Vol. 27 (1983): 158; and Charles E. Scott, "Heidegger's Attempt to Communicate a Mystery," *Philosophy Today,* Vol. 10 (1966), p. 35.

10. Paul Edwards, "Heidegger and Death: A Deflationary Critique," *The Monist*, April 1976, pp. 161-183.

11. Bernard Williams, *Ethics and the Limits of Philosophy* (Cambridge: Harvard University Press, 1985), p. 40. See also George Santayana, *The German Mind, Philosophical Diagnosis* (New York: Thomas Crowell, 1968), p. 97.

12. Charles Hartshorne, "The Acceptance of Death" in *Philosophical Aspects of Thanatology*, edited by F. M. Hetzler and A. H. Kutscher (New York: Arno Press, 1978), p. 84. See also Charles Hartshorne, *The Logic of Perfection* (LaSalle, Ill: Open Court, 1962), p. 245ff.

13. Leon R. Kass, *Toward a More Natural Science* (New York: Free Press, 1985), pp. 299-317.

14. Plato, *The Republic*, translated with notes and commentaries by Allan Bloom (New York: Basic Books, 1968).

15. "On Old Age," *The Basic Works of Cicero*, edited with an introduction and notes by Moses Hadas (Modern Library: New York, 1951), p. 127.

16. Daniel Callahan, *What Kind of Life?   The Limits of Medical Progress* (New York: Simon & Schuster, 1990). See also Daniel Callahan, "Adequate Health Care," *Daedalus*, Vol. 115 (Winter 1986), pp. 261-266.

17. Edmund D. Pellegrino, "Rationing Health Care: The Ethics of Gatekeeping," *Journal of Contemporary Health Law and Policy*, Vol. 2 (1986), pp. 23-45. See also Steffie Woohlandler and David U. Himmelstein, "Current Concepts: Initial Treatment of Patients With Extensive Trauma," *The New England Journal of Medicine*, Vol. 324 (May 2, 1991), pp. 1253-1263.

18. Daniel Callahan, *Setting Limits: Medical Goals in an Aging Society* (New York: Simon & Schuster, 1987).

19. Judith Wilson Ross, "Personal Choice and Public Rationing," this volume.

20. Robert N. Bellah, "The Humanities and Social Vision," in *Applying the Humanities*, edited by Daniel Callahan, Arthur L. Caplan and Bruce Jennings (New York: Plenum, 1985), p. 112. See also Kathryn Montgomery, "Hunter Literature and Medicine," in *Applying the Humanities*, pp. 289-304.

21. W. Collingwood quoted in John Gardner's *On Moral Fiction* (New York: Basic Books, 1978), p. 10.

22. Gardner, *On Moral Fiction*, p. 15

23. Ibid., p. 19.

24. Sally A. Gadow, "Humanities, Teaching, and Aging," in *Vitalizing Long-Term Care*, edited by S. Spicker and S. R. Ingman (New York: Springer, 1989), pp. 119-137.

25. Gerald J. Gruman, *A History of Ideas about the Prolongation of Life* (New York: Arno Press, 1977). See also Gerald J. Gruman, ed., *Roots of Modern Gerontology and Geriatrics: Fredrick D. Zeman's "Medical History of*

Old Age" and *Selected Studies by Other Writers* (New York: Arno Press, 1979).

26. Sophocles, *Oedipus at Colonus,* translated by F. Storr, Loeb Classics, Vol. 1, p. 263.

27. Horace, "Ars Poetica," *Complete Works of Horace,* translated in meters of the original by Charles E. Passage (New York: Frederick Ungar, 1983), p. 363.

28. Lucretius, *De Natura Rerum,* pp. 1076.

29. Euripides, *The Supplicant Women,* pp.1108.

30. Cicero, "On Age" in *The Basic Works of Cicero,* edited with an introduction and notes by Moses Hadas (New York: Modern Library, 1951), p. 132.

31. Luigi Cornaro, *The Art of Living Long* (London: Health for All Publishing Co., 1951).

32. Robert Browning, *The Poems of Robert Browning, Selected and edited by C. Day Lewis* (New York: Heritage, 1971), p. 244.

33. May Sarton, *At Seventy: A Journal* (New York: W. W. Norton, 1984).

34. John La Farge, *On Turning Seventy* (New York: The America Press, 1962).

35. Malcolm Cowley, *The View from 80* (New York: Penguin, 1980).

36. Cicero, *The Basic Works of Cicero,* edited with an introduction and notes by Moses Hadas (New York: Modern Library, 1951), p. 134.

37. Aldous Huxley, *Texts and Pretexts: An Anthology with Commentaries* (New York: W.W. Norton, 1960), p. 146.

38. Gerald J. Gruman, *A History of Ideas About the Prolongation of Life* (New York: Arno Press, 1977). This is a valuable and compendious review with many references upon which I have drawn freely.

39. Rene Descartes, *Discourse on Method, Part VI,* in *Great Books of the Western World,* edited by Robert M. Hutchins, Vol. 31 (Chicago: Encyclopaedia Britannica, 1980), pp. 96-103.

40. Edward Young, *Young's Night Thoughts* (Edinburgh: W. P. Nimmo, 1868).

41. Michel de Montaigne, *Essays I,* in *Complete Works: Essays, Travel Journal, Letters,* translated by Donald Frame, Vol. 20 (Stanford: Stanford University Press, 1957).

42. Cicero, *De Senectute,* Vol. 24.

43. Edith Hamilton, *Myths* (New York: Mentor Press, 1953), pp. 289-290.

44. Jonathan Swift, *Gulliver's Travels* (New York: Modern Library, 1931), pp. 241-242.

45. Ibid.

46. S. Jay Olshansky, Bruce A. Carnes, and Christine Cassel, "In Search of Methuselah: Estimating the Upper Limits of Human Longevity," *Science,* Vol. 250 (Nov. 2, 1990), pp. 634-640.

47. Jonathan Swift, "A Satirical Eulogy on the Death of a Late Famous Gentleman," in *Satires and Personal Writings* (New York: Oxford University Press, 1932).

48. Napoleon, *The St. Helena Journal*, Dec. 11, 1816.

49. William Osler, "The Fixed Period," in *Aequanimitas and Other Addresses* (Philadelphia: Blakistor, 1943), pp. 373-394.

50. Plato, *The Republic* (328a-328b), translated with notes and commentaries by Allan Bloom (New York: Basic Books, 1968).

51. William Shakespeare, *Folkways* (New York: Ginn, 1906).

52. William Shakespeare, *As You Like It*, Act II, Scene VII, Line 139.

53. E. D. Pellegrino, *"Aging, Ethics and the Life Cycle: Some Contemporary Reflections on a Renaissance Concept, Center for Renaissance and Baroque Studies,"* University of Maryland, College Park, Conference on Aging and the Life Cycle in the Renaissance, 1988, in press.

54. Shura Saul, *Aging: An Album of People Growing Old* (New York: John Wiley, 1974).

55. Francois Mauriac, *Cain, Where is Your Brother?* (New York: Cowsid McCann, 1962), p. 21.

56. Donald Marquis, "Ethics and the Elderly, Some Problems" in *Aging and the Elderly*, edited by S. Spicker, K. Woodward, and D. van Tassel (Atlantic Heights, N.J.: Humanities Press, 1986), pp. 341-358.

57. William F. May, "The Virtues and Vices of the Elderly" in *What Does it Mean to Grow Old?* edited by Thomas R. Cole and Sally A. Gadow (Durham: Duke University Press, 1986), pp. 44-61.

58. Larry R. Churchill, *Rationing Health Care in America* (Notre Dame, I.N.: University of Notre Dame Press, 1987).

59. Charles J. Dougherty, *American Health Care: Realities, Rights, and Reforms* (New York: Oxford University Press, 1988).

60. Daniel Wikler, "Ought the Young Make Decisions for Their Aged Selves?" *Journal of Medicine and Philosophy*, Vol. 13 (Feb. 1988), pp. 57-71.

61. Norman Daniels, "The Biomedical Model and Just Health Care: Reply to Jecker," *Journal of Medicine and Philosophy*, Vol. 14 (Dec. 1989), pp. 677-680.

62. Nancy S. Jecker, "Towards a Theory of Age-Group Justice," *Journal of Medicine and Philosophy*, Vol. 14, No. 6 (December, 1989), pp. 655-676.

63. David S. Grimes, "Rationing Health Care," *Lancet*, Vol. 85 (Mar 14, 1987), pp. 615-616.

64. Edward Schneider, *"Options to Control the Rising Health Care Costs of Aging Americans,"* Journal of the American Medical Association, Vol. 261 No. 6, (Feb. 10, 1989), pp. 907-908.

65. Leon Kass, *Toward a More Natural Science* (New York: Free Press, 1985).

66. Charles Hartshorne, "The Acceptance of Death" in *Philosophical Aspects of Thanatology*, edited by F. M. Hetzler and A. H. Kutscher (New

York: Arno Press, 1978), pp. 83-87.

67. E. D. Pellegrino, "Doctors Must Not Kill," *Journal of Clinical Ethics,* Vol. 3, No. 2 (Summer 1992), pp. 95-102.

68. See Geri Berg and Sally Gadow, "Toward More Human Meanings of Aging: Ideals and Images from Philosophy and Art," in *Aging and the Elderly,* edited by S. Spicker, K. Woodward and D. van Tassel (Atlantic Heights, N.J.: Humanities Press, 1988), pp. 83-94.

4

Ethical Options
in the Care of the Elderly

J. Wesley Robb

Introduction

It is difficult to address the issue of health care in terms of a single population of persons in our society. The health and well-being of one group of persons cannot be separated from the society of which that group is a part, whether it be persons with AIDS, cancer, heart disease, or whatever illness one might want to suggest. The same principles of justice, beneficence, and autonomy--the cardinal virtues of caring for the sick--apply. The reality of the interrelationship of the social fabric is relevant to a discussion of health care for the elderly.

However, special comment is warranted when the numbers of a group reflect a significant proportion of the population or those with special health-care needs require the utilization of a disproportionate amount of the available health-care resources. A consideration of the health care of the elderly thus justifies our attention.

Population projections indicate that the number of Americans 65 years of age and older will increase from 25.7 million in 1980 to 35 million by the year 2000 and 67.1 million by 2050. By the middle of the twenty-first century it is predicted that 21.7 percent of the population will be 65 or older.[1] New developments in medical technology, with doubtless more to come, and an increasing number of pharmaceutical agents that will prolong life as well as the widespread concern about diet, exercise, and personal well-being are indicative of some of the reasons for an increasing number of people who live beyond fourscore years.

When health care, whether for an older person or not, involves chronic illness and results in a marginal quality of life, prudent choices must be made in the light of an ethical framework. We need to ascertain the most compelling ethical option. The increasing amount of literature in the field of gerontology, as well as the concern of Congress for the care of the elderly, indicates the complexity of the problem and demonstrates the interrelationship between the economic aspects of our health-care delivery system and other social needs that deserve our attention. There is no simple answer, particularly in a democracy where individual freedom is cherished in relationship to the needs of others and the welfare of the community as a whole.

It is not the purpose of this essay to outline a system of health care that will fulfill the demands of the ethical principles I am advocating, but rather it is my intent to provide criteria for making ethical judgments that will be useful in evaluating health-care delivery programs for the elderly.

What Is an Ethical Option?

Ethics, as a discipline within philosophy, is concerned with evaluating and establishing the *criteria* for normative judgments of value (good and bad) and judgments of responsibility and duty (right and wrong). Therefore, any consideration of an option for moral choice must be grounded in an adequate normative framework of meaning that provides a rationale for the decision that is being made.

In practical, everyday experience, it is doubtful that we consistently apply the same normative standard in our moral choices and the ethical reasons by which we justify them. In one situation we may act out of a sense of high moral purpose, in another out of bald self-interest or sheer pragmatism, and in another out of special concern for what the law dictates. It is much easier to provide a theoretical framework for what our choices *should* be than what our choices actually are in relationship to the pressures and realities of life situations. This is the fundamental difference between ethics as a theoretical discipline and applied ethics that moves within the context of actual life situations. Therefore, when we ask the question about what our ethical options are for the health care of the elderly, we are confronted with deciding among competing interests and demands. In other words, what are the normative principles that should guide our choices and what is possible given the fiscal, political and other social realities that limit the realization of what would be the most desirable from an ethical point of view? We do not live in a Leibnizian best of all possible worlds. This is the challenge when we apply ethical reflection to concrete problems.

Within the western philosophical and religious tradition that has helped shape the democratic principles upon which this nation was founded, there are at least three principles that have been central. When translated into the language of health care they are: justice, beneficence, and autonomy. These ethical norms are central within the medical community as the *sine qua non* for medical practice. Let us examine each of these ethical norms as they apply to the distribution of our health-care resources and especially as they relate to the care of the elderly.

Justice

The achievement of justice has been the central moral mandate within our judicial system. Yet even a cursory look at our legal system indicates that we fall far short of realizing that goal. Special privilege and power undermine our attempt to achieve justice for all of our citizens. I need not cite the litany of recent events in our social and political history that underscore this fact. If the full realization of social justice is a hope that remains distant, how can we expect the principle of justice to have any meaning as we consider our health-care delivery system?

While the Constitution provides for the protection of human rights and equal protection under the law, these provisions have not been interpreted by the federal courts as being applicable to health care and other primary social needs. As the result, the provision of health care varies from state to state. While Medicare and Medicaid attempt to meet the health-care needs of the elderly, they are grossly inadequate to provide the quality and extent of care that is needed. The inadequacies of these programs exist within a society where over 30 million Americans have *no* protection for health care, either public or private. Concerns about health care for the elderly must be placed within the larger framework of concern for the health of all of our citizens, as well as for their other primary social needs-- food, housing, employment, education and a myriad of other basic necessities. The question about which has priority is a social, political and legislative question that must be undergirded by a concern for social justice.

Surveys indicate that most of our citizens assume that everyone is entitled to adequate health care. Both sides of the aisle in Congress agree, yet we have no national health-care policy; rather we tinker with the system piece by piece.

These comments raise the more fundamental question: How shall we understand justice? In its clearest and simplest form, justice as equity means that we treat similar cases in similar ways. Frankena's formulation of Kant's principle of universalizability is helpful. "If one judges that X is right or good, then one is committed to judging that anything exactly like X, *or like X in relevant respects,* is right or good."[2] Likewise the application of John Rawls' principle of equality of fair opportunity is informative in our understanding of the application of the principle of justice to health care. Although Rawls does not include the need for health care within the purview of distributive justice, I agree with Allen Buchanan when he suggests that the principle of fair opportunity is applicable.[3] Norman Daniels also appeals to Rawls' fair opportunity principle as a basis for his attempt to establish a criterion for a just distribution of health-care resources upon an individual's "normal opportunity range."[4] I recognize that there are many problems in adapting Rawls' system to the issue of justice in the distribution of our health-care resources since his principle of fair opportunity refers to "abilities and skills" and the responsibility of society to provide opportunities for their development. However, as Gerald R. Winslow points out, Rawls saves himself from betraying the principle of justice as equity by his application of the "difference principle" which "works to the benefit of the least advantaged and thus tends to equalize opportunities in the long run."[5] Thus, justice as fairness when applied to health care for the elderly, especially the frail and disabled who are particularly vulnerable and "least advantaged," becomes a moral mandate in a just society.

Serious consideration of these principles in the development of policies for the distribution of health-care resources would preclude, in my view, discrimination based upon such arbitrary factors as age. It goes without saying that age brings with it certain limitations of function and the decline of the general health of the individual. If we apply Kant's principle of universalizability to the problem of aging, however, we would provide the same resources for a person of 70 as we would an individual of 55, providing their conditions are alike "in similar respects."

It might be argued that no two situations are identical; therefore, each situation must be judged on its own merits without reference to others whose health-care needs and prognoses are similar. Take, for example, two patients who need a heart transplant; one is 70 and has terminal cancer with, according to the best medical judgment, a year to live while the other patient is 55, has no terminal disease, and would probably live to old age. They are not alike "in similar respects." Hence, the principle of universalizability would not be violated if the younger person received the heart. The difference between them that matters is their physical condition, *not* age. Let us further suppose that they both only had a year to live and there was only one heart available for transplant. Does the application of the principle of equity mean that we would toss a coin in order to decide? Such a decision to resort to chance would, in my view, betray our responsibility to make as prudent a judgment as possible in the light of other factors. It should be understood that the principle of justice must be applied as consistently as possible within the context of a given situation. This is the kind of dilemma we face when we apply ethical theory to concrete situations. However, we should avoid, as far as is humanly possible, a triage situation in which we make age the primary, determining factor. Mark Siegler is very clear on this point when he says,

> "Discrimination in health-care for the aged is not justified because it threatens to undermine the traditions of clinical medicine, which are based upon medical needs and preferences; and because it threatens to undermine the traditions of our society, which are based upon moral virtues of charity and compassion."[6]

If age is a factor in the allocation of health-care resources, it must be evaluated in relationship to the general health of the individual and not viewed as an arbitrary line of demarcation. I have in mind the arbitrary role that age sometimes plays in health-care decisions in Britain. During a 1984 sabbatical there I interviewed a leading epidemiologist. I asked him, "Since I am 64 years of age, would you suggest I go home in the event I have a kidney problem?" And he replied, "By all means." In all likelihood, anyone over 70 years of age will not receive dialysis and, although there is no written policy setting an age limit, this is a widely understood standard. The decision is based upon the appropriateness of care in relationship to the availability of limited resources. As a result, many elderly patients fall through the cracks--people who otherwise could live a productive and satisfying life.

Daniel Callahan, one of the more strident voices, insists that our allocation of health-care resources be "aged-based" rather than "need-based." Age becomes a determining factor when an individual has reached, what he calls, a "natural life-span." His views are discussed in many of the other essays in this volume. I would agree that in those clear cases of terminal illness, prudent judgment should be used regarding the decision to prolong life when it would be of little benefit to the patient, particularly where there is great pain and the poor quality of life is too heavy a burden to bear. I also have little difficulty with Callahan's contention that we have become slaves to technology that plagues our society (what I call technological messianism). Such untempered faith in technology clouds our rational capacities for judicious decisions. This fact, combined with the common notion that death is the great enemy to be defeated at all cost, distorts our ability to make responsible judgments when further medical assistance is not efficacious.

Having said all of this, however, I have difficulty applying Callahan's standard of a "natural life-span" to the chronically ill. Take, for example, the victim of a stroke who needs long-term care in a nursing facility, whose quality of life is very poor, and who, in all probability, will never return to "good health." Let us assume the patient has not indicated a desire that life is so burdensome he does not want to live. The patient contracts pneumonia. Do we conclude that he has reached his "natural life-span" and should not be given antibiotics? It is clear that this patient is using a disproportionate amount of our limited medical resources. Should this be the determining factor in our decision?

Callahan wants to avoid such a conclusion, but does he? When the cost of care is placed within the context of an aged-based criterion, the conclusion that antibiotics are inappropriate for the patient I have described might easily be reached. In his discussion of the chronically ill, he states:

> There are a large and growing number of elderly who are not imminently dying but who are feeble and declining, often chronically ill, for whom curative medicine has little to offer. This kind of medicine may still be able to do something for failing organs. . . . but it cannot offer the patient as a person any hope of being restored to good health. A different treatment plan should be in order. That person's history has come to an end. . . .[7]

The fact that he applauds the British practice of uniformly denying certain types of health-care assistance based upon age, would indicate that Callahan makes age more of a determinative factor than is warranted. We all view aging and the illnesses that accompany it from different perspectives of what would constitute a "natural life-span." My concern is that the criterion for determining a "natural life-span" would be done in some arbitrary way that would violate the integrity of the individual. As I shall point out later, autonomy has limits, but it should be safeguarded as much as possible.

I applaud Callahan for biting the bullet on the delicate issue of health care for the elderly. But I think he cuts too fine in proposing what is, in effect, a rationing of health care for the elderly based upon his somewhat ambiguous criterion of a "natural life-span." I do not believe that his proposal meets the standards that justice requires because there is little assurance that such a poorly defined concept of "natural life-span" would be uniformly understood in its application unless he were willing to take a statistical, actuarial approach. This, I believe, he would reject because it would lack any element of human compassion.

Callahan, as well as Richard D. Lamm and Norman Daniels, favor rationing as a responsible approach to the distribution of health-care resources. They would argue that, in fact, a form of rationing is in place with diagnosis-related groups (DRGs) and other limitations imposed by Medicare, and private health-care providers. It has been suggested that rather than applying some external standard, such as the Oregon experiment that restricts care for Medicaid recipients, the answer is in making our health-care system more efficient and affordable by applying more prudent judgments on a case-by-case basis. Callahan believes that this is a pious hope and that it cannot significantly reduce health-care costs. From his point of view, the present system is basically flawed and the only way to reduce costs and allay fiscal crisis is to take a stringent rationing approach.

I would contend that there is a difference between judicious clinical decisions and rationing. The decision about appropriate care should be made in consultation with the patient and the family. It is true that by tradition most physicians have seen themselves as their patients' advocates and have regarded costs as secondary, if not irrelevant to their primary function. The almost unlimited use of diagnostic techniques, and the virtually unchecked practice of prescribing pharmaceutical agents have led us to the intolerable burden of the high cost of health care. Little emphasis is placed upon these matters in the education of physicians. As a result, we have a major educational task to inform medical students, physicians, and the lay public that prudent and judicious management of health-care is mandatory. I agree with Arnold S. Relman when he says,

> We need not become the helpless economic victim of technology unless we lack the will to evaluate it critically and employ it only when medically indicated. All the evidence suggests that there are vast savings to be made through the elimination of unnecessary services and facilities.[8]

In a convincing essay, Norma G. Levinsky argues that age as a criterion for rationing care is arbitrary and counter-productive. The criteria, she believes, should be based upon "the probability that the patient will benefit rather than his or her age."[9] I heartily agree. As I have suggested elsewhere, there are alternatives to formal rationing methods. Among these are cost-containment, assessment of medical practice and the use of medical technology, health education and preventive medicine, availability of alternative health-care plans, and rational physician supply and demand.

Beneficence

The ethical mandate that we be beneficent, that is charitable and kind, is one of the primary moral characteristics of a civilized society. The concern for being beneficent to our elderly population is widespread throughout our country and, within recent years, special focus has been made on provisions that would enhance the quality of care in nursing homes and provide more adequate supplemental care in the home.

There is little question that if we apply the standard of beneficence to the care of our elderly, we will have to put more of our fiscal resources into improving the care now offered and extend the provisions of Medicare to include long-term care. Other western nations, notably Britain and Germany, have done remarkably better in providing both home care and long-term nursing-home care than we have done. In the case of Germany, the state has joined forces with religious communities to provide beneficent care for the elderly. While there are many weaknesses in the British system of health care, their emphasis has been on home nursing assistance in contrast with expensive critical care in a hospital. The goal is to sustain functional independence as far as possible. Too many of our nursing home facilities are warehouses that provide little opportunities for rehabilitation or functional independence. Medicaid coverage is inadequate, staff turnover is high because of low pay and the physical facilities are inadequate. This is far from any minimal standard of beneficence.

United States Congressman Henry A. Waxman, chairman of the Energy and Commerce Committee's Health Subcommittee, has led the charge for better protection of the health care for our elderly. He has consistently opposed cuts in the Medicare and Medicaid programs and wants the provisions of these agencies to include more adequate home assistance and a higher quality of care within nursing homes.[10] Beneficent community concern for the elderly is being expressed through the establishment of adult day-care centers with a great deal of volunteer assistance. Successful centers are providing day-care in a number of states. These centers are supported, for the most part, by local agencies and private donations. They give a respite to the home-care giver and often add a quality of care the home provider cannot give through emotional support and social contact with others. Both the caregiver and the patient benefit from this program. In deciding what beneficent care means, especially in those cases involving chronic long-term illnesses, we are not dependent on hunches for our decisions. Anne R. Somers suggests that one of the guiding principles for a national long-term care policy should include

> a health data base . . . for each enrollee through an initial, and periodically reviewed, computerized health-risk assessment. This record, together with multidisciplinary functional assessment at the time of application for benefits, should help in determining eligibility, therapy, and placement.[11]

The increasingly sophisticated techniques in determining the probable outcome for a wide variety of illnesses make her suggestion plausible. The Joint Commission on the Accreditation of Hospitals favors "quality assessment based on severity-adjusted outcomes" in monitoring hospitals. Also, the federal government, through the Health Care Financing Administration and the recently established Agency for Health Care Policy and Research, has begun a program that will serve to evaluate medical interventions and other forms of therapy that will assist in the assessment of patient outcomes. This is called "outcomes management."[12] Such information will not provide us with complete answers for evaluating appropriate care, but will serve to inform our intuitions and caring instincts. These means must be carefully used in order to preserve the patient's autonomy and meaningful interaction between the physician, the patient, and the family.   All of these trends and proposals are salutary as we endeavor to be more humane and caring for the elderly and fulfill the demands that beneficence requires.

Autonomy

For most of us, respect for the autonomy of the individual is high on the agenda of moral mandates.   Autonomy connotes the right of self-determination, freedom of movement and action, and the determination of our own destiny.   Our choices define who we are and preserve our sense of selfhood and identity.   As often expressed by existentialists, "We are our choices."   This cherished freedom, however, stands in relationship to others and to the society of which we are a part.   This fact is particularly crucial as we consider autonomy and the elderly.

As we advance in age and become frail and more dependent, many factors limit our choices.   Among these may be fiscal, familial, and institutional constraints.   The vulnerability of the elderly demands that, from an ethical perspective, we give special and thoughtful attention to their right of self-determination, assuring that the individual is adequately informed about matters of health and the options that are available for care.   Bart J. Collopy raises a very important question: "Should the self-determination of the elderly or the decisions and standards of caregivers have priority?"[13] This question is at the heart of the ethical issue and applies to home care, institutional care, or any other relationship the individual might have to any group or individual upon which that person is dependent.[14]

Most of the literature regarding patient autonomy relates to crisis situations that involve acute care.   An increasing amount of attention is now being given to the problem of the patient's autonomy in long-term care in a nursing facility, while little consideration has been given to home care.   A recent *Hastings Center Report* is helpful in this regard.   This study attempts to outline a model for home care that will accommodate autonomy and strike a balance between autonomy and beneficence.   The authors suggest that within the home care setting, depending upon the sensitivity of the home-care providers, consideration for the right of self-determination may be either enhanced or diminished. "Emboldened autonomy," they point out, "though clearly problematic, is not the rule in home care.   For many frail elderly, long-term care at home leads in quite a different direction--toward progressive erosion of autonomy."[15]   How can the accommodation between autonomy and the erosion of autonomy be ameliorated?   The authors believe there is a "middle ground where clients develop mutually accommodating and reciprocal relationships with caregivers."[16] This suggestion of "accommodation" might be applied to the problem of autonomy within institutional settings as well, though the formal structure of institutions might make it more difficult to achieve.

Conclusion

Rationing of health care for the elderly is discriminatory; it violates the principle of justice, and it threatens the right of self-determination.   Given the fact of the limitation of our health-care resources, can we avoid discrimination against the elderly?   I think this is possible, though admittedly difficult.

First, we must educate everyone involved in the provision of health care, as well as the lay public, that prudent judgment in the use of our health-care resources is mandatory.   Second, we should seriously take an inventory of how we allocate all of our national resources in terms of meeting primary human needs including the provision for adequate health-care for all of our citizens.   Third, we must make clear that a moral right is not equivalent to what one might desire or want.   As this applies to health care for the elderly, the right of self-determination must be seen within the framework of what seems to be medically indicated for the preservation of a quality of life that includes the capacity for a sense of self-identity. It is doubtful that when patients request that "everything be done" they understand what that entails.   It has been my observation that, when self-determination for health care is granted, patients generally choose without a full understanding of the prognosis and the quality of life that might be anticipated.   Fully informing the patient about these matters is often a psychological and personal problem for the health-care providers more than it is for the patient and the family.   It also involves a commitment of time on the part of the health-care team of which the physician is the key.   Fourth, and perhaps the most important, all persons should be aware of the legal provisions in the form of advanced directives that can express their right to choose the care they believe to be appropriate.   We should hope that the new federal legislation calling on hospitals to seek information regarding patients' preferences for life-sustaining measures will lead to better communication with better informed patients.

Such approaches might serve as alternatives to the establishment of arbitrary and externally imposed standards for care that would violate the principle of autonomy so basic in a free society. The issues are complex and there is no one solution and no single ethical option. However, I believe that whatever option for care of the elderly we might choose, the preservation of the principles of justice, beneficence, and autonomy should be paramount. In a nation as affluent as our own, the primary needs of all of our citizens can and should be met. All we lack is the will and social vision to do so. If one wants to argue from a utilitarian ethical stance, such provisions for the primary social needs of our people are in the interest of us all, even in our own self-interest. However, it is hoped that our moral concern for social justice would be more lofty and worthy.

Notes and References

1. S. .F. Spicker, S. R. Ingman, and I. A. Lawson, editors, *Ethical Dimensions of Geriatric Care* (Boston: D. Reidel, 1987), p. xiv.

2. W. Frankena, *Ethics,* second edition (Englewood Cliffs, N.J.: Prentice Hall, 1973), p. 25 (italics added).

3. A. Buchanan, "Justice: A Philosophical Review," in *Justice and Health Care,* edited by E E. Shelp (Boston: D. Reidel, 1981), p. 20.

4. Norman Daniels, "Equal Opportunity, Justice, and Health Care for the Elderly: A Prudential Account," in *Ethical Dimensions of Geriatric Care,* edited by S. F. Spicker, S. R. Ingman, and I. A. Lawson (Boston: D. Reidel, 1987), p. 206.

5. G. R. Winslow, *Triage and Justice* (Berkeley: University of California, 1982), p. 118.

6. M. Siegler, "Should Age Be a Criterion in Health Care?" *The Hastings Center Report,* Vol. 14, Oct. 1984, p. 27.

7. Daniel Callahan, *Setting Limits: Medical Goals in an Aging Society* (New York: Simon & Schuster, 1987), p. 170.

8. A. Relman, "Is Rationing Inevitable?" *The New England Journal of Medicine,* Vol. 322 (June 21, 1990), p. 1810.

9. N. G. Levinsky, "Age as a Criterion for Rationing Health Care," *The New England Journal of Medicine,* Vol. 322 (June 21, 1990), p. 1813.

10. B. Yarwood, "Congressman Waxman on Priorities of the U.S. Congress," *Provider,* Vol. 15 (June 1989), p. 24. See also H. A. Waxman, "Consensus Call for Nursing Home Reform," *Provider,* Vol. 12 (Nov. 1986), p. 15.

11. A. R. Somers, "Insurance for Long-Term Care," *The New England Journal of Medicine*, Vol. 317 (July 2, 1987), p. 28.

12. M. Epstein, "The Outcomes Movement--Will It Get Us Where We Want to Go?" *The New England Journal of Medicine*, Vol. 323 (July 26, 1990), pp. 266-270.

13. B. J. Collopy, "Autonomy in Long-Term Care: Some Crucial Distinctions," *The Gerontologist*, Vol. 28, Supplement (June 1988), p. 10.

14. Institute of Medicine, *The Elderly and Functional Dependence* (Washington, D.C.: National Academy of Sciences, 1977).

15. B. Collopy, N. Dubler, and C. Zuckerman, "The Ethics of Home Care: Autonomy and Accommodation," *The Hastings Center Report*, Vol. 20 (Supplement), March/April 1990, pp. 8-9.

16. Ibid.

5

Natural Life-Span and Natural Law Ethics

Anthony Battaglia

Introduction

The idea that we should learn to accept the natural limits of our lives--a natural life-span--reintroduces into ethical discussion a normative concept of nature. It provides us with the opportunity to look again at the place of nature in ethics. Surprisingly, perhaps, we find useful resemblances between the natural-law tradition and the idea of a natural life-span that illumine both.

In Daniel Callahan's version of a natural life-span, the needs of others and the limits of society's resources make it the wise and good thing for us to rethink our attitude toward medicine and death and, thus, to accept tolerable limits to our lives.[1] Although not cast in the mold we have come to expect of natural law ethics, this suggestion nevertheless represents a modern usage of a natural law argument. Callahan is not saying that we must allow biology to dictate our morality. Nature enters his argument, instead, in an appeal to our moral nature, our confidence that we can count on one another to respond to the facts of our physical situation with intelligence and generosity. In raising the issue of our attitudes toward our own death, of the obligations of communities toward the individual and of the naturalness of death, he illumines the way in which moral agreement is reached on matters with no clear precedent. Specifically, he forces us to ask whether we ought to learn to be content with a natural life-span or whether we ought to expect society as a whole to provide us with the means for a longer life at public expense. The question is a vital one and can best be understood as a unique modern example of natural law ethics.

Since both *nature* and *natural law* are moot concepts today, I begin not directly with the natural law tradition, but with some of the difficulties the terms *nature* and *natural law* bring with them. After examining these, I go on to show how generalizations from the natural law tradition and modern understandings of both human knowledge and political philosophy can lend both direction and urgency to the discussion of the limits of human life and the acceptance of a natural life-span.

Not Quite Natural

The word *nature* is not only contested territory, it is a forest so thick with the overgrowth of generations that we could innocently stroll into it and never be seen again. We could spend a great deal of time contrasting nature with culture. We could contrast nature with the supernatural. We could contrast human nature with the natural, physical world. We could contrast benevolent Mother Nature with violent "nature red in tooth and claw." In natural law theory, the normative force of nature derives from a contrast between the way things really are--and according to which we ought to behave--and their surface appearances. Later I shall return to the version of this sense of natural, modified by the insistence that what we consider natural is arrived at by a group's judgment, our best wisdom on the topic.

In order to avoid some of the difficulties of the word *natural*-- especially difficulties which arise from too great an insistence that we already know what is natural to human beings--I want to begin with a recent discussion of nature in a commonsense, non-moral context. The clearest way to open a path here seems to be to rely upon the "end of nature" to clarify the limitations of the term. The phrase is the title of a recent book by naturalist Bill McKibben.[2]

McKibben's title reflects his consciousness that we have lost something precious--perhaps precious beyond measure--as a result of the technological changes we have wrought on the earth. To some extent we have done what we set out to do and learned to control nature. To a greater extent we have changed nature unintentionally, without realizing what we were doing. But the result, he thinks, is that nature is at an end. By nature, he means neither "the whirling fuzziness of electrons and quarks and neutrinos," nor "the vast and strange worlds and fields and fluxes that scientists can find with their telescopes." For McKibben, nature means the world of our everyday awe. "The nature that matters is the temperature, and the rain, and the leaves turning color on the maples, and the raccoons around the garbage can."[3] Where previous generations have looked up at the sky and wondered at the beauty of a sunset, the knowledgeable among us these days look at the same sky and gauge how bad the smog is tonight. The impact of the end of nature will be enormous, not least upon religion. "We can no longer imagine that we are a part of something larger than ourselves--that is what all this boils down to."[4]

Instead, *we* make the world. We "affect its every operation (except a few--the alteration of day and night, the spin and wobble and path of the planet, the most elementary geologic and tectonic processes) . . . . And there is nobody above us. God, who may or may not be acting in many other ways," has let us have our way with this aspect of creation.

> When he asks, as he does in Job, "Who shut in the sea with doors . . . and prescribed bounds for it?" and "Who can tilt the waterskins of the heavens?" we can now answer that it is us. Our actions will determine the level of the sea, and change the course and destination of every drop of precipitation.[5]

The biblical references are appropriate and important. McKibben is "a reasonably orthodox Methodist,"[6] and the temper of his book is often that of a life-saddened prophet, unheeded and too late. He thinks our victory over nature is to be compared with King Midas' pursuit of wealth: We have what we wanted, but it brings us not comfort but distress.

His argument is that one of the things it means to live in our time is that we cannot make appeals to the natural world outside of human beings without acknowledging that our responsibility now extends into nature itself. The drought that afflicts us has been affected by our population migrations and our ecological insults to air and water. We can take less comfort from bowing to such a nature, with human handprints all over it, than we could in facing the nature which was beyond our influence. In the old nature we could see blind chance or God's loving providence. Its majesty was beyond our tampering. Nature was *other.* It is so no more.

Whatever the larger, ecological import of his argument, McKibben is right with regard to a natural life-span. Reintroducing the word *natural* here flies in the face of our recognition that the hour of our death becomes more and more a matter of culture, not nature. Pneumonia, chicken pox and other childhood diseases, complicated bone fractures--even heart attacks and strokes--are no longer the killers and maimers they once were. In any random gathering of a score of adults we are likely to find people who would have died in earlier times of injuries and diseases which today are survived routinely and without permanent mark. Some of these former killers have disappeared, or all but disappeared, from our awareness. We can expect that human medicine will keep more and more such menaces at bay. Technology and good nutrition will keep more of us alive long beyond our years of self-support and therefore help create a problem for us and for the future generations who will be asked to support us. Moreover--and this is the other side of our changed relationship to nature--the diseases of which we are now dying may themselves be the by-product of our unnatural interference with nature.

Thus, the end of nature means that the terrible inexorability of death, to which all must bow, is less sovereign and less other. We seem to be able to make deals with it and to postpone its arrival more than other generations could. To introduce the word *natural* into such a discussion is to search for a kind of innocence, a wholeness in our relation to our own death, that may be gone forever. It no longer seems inevitable that we "go when our time comes." Our time to die seems more and more subject to a different, less inexorable kind of fate. It singles us out, like bad luck: a severe accident, or one out of reach of the paramedics, or an illness beyond the ever-extending reach of modern medicine, or beyond our pocket-book. Death looks more and more the result of factors such as these than of the human condition itself.

Talk of a natural life-span, or of natural law, had better take into account such changes in our relationship to nature. The whole force of these developments has been to make death seem more and more of an avoidable accident. If death must come, we have learned to think that it will be only after we have fought it to the very end, and we will feel defeat at our inability to beat death back one more time. Talk of a natural life-span, of accepting death, of a tolerable death, all seem peculiar. We are about to conquer death, as we have conquered nature, are we not? It is no surprise that many people find the discussion of a natural life-span incomprehensible or threatening.

To add discourse about natural law ethics to this discussion seems only to add to the confusion. If we are only now seeing that nature (in McKibben's sense) is coming to an end, a related perception has been worrying the moral tradition of natural law reasoning for some time. It is the suspicion that we cannot disentangle ourselves from the world enough to distinguish between what we humans have made (culture, related to the Latin *cultus* = grown) and what the world is without us (nature, related to the Latin *natus* = born). Our idea of nature is bound to be a cultural construct; and culture itself seems to be natural to us!

Stanley Fish makes this point in his recent book, *Doing What Comes Naturally.* For Fish, the actions which "come naturally" are the ones we do because they are "the unreflective actions that follow from being embedded in a context of practice. This kind of action . . . is anything but natural in the sense of proceeding independently of historical and social formations."[7] They seem natural to us because they come easily, but they come easily because we have been led to take them for granted by the consensus of our community. We are led to internalize the patterns of our social world, and "once those formations are in place (and they always are), what you think to do will not be calculated in relation to a higher law or an overarching theory but will issue from you as naturally as breathing."[8] It looks and feels like nature, but it is really culture.

Fish's point has been around a while, but it is still fresh enough. The contrast between our naive sense of the givenness of the world and our schooled awareness of its madeness continues to be one of the intellectual challenges of our times. But though it has been noticed before, it is not introduced often enough into discussions of natural law.[9]

If I have lingered over the difficulties that surround the word nature, it is because only by acknowledging them can we get past them. Daniel Callahan is not unaware of developments like these, and his suggestion about a natural life-span can be taken to presuppose them. It is because of his sophistication that his argument is interesting as a use of natural-law reasoning. He wants us to begin creating a new set of moral practices, one more in keeping with the realities of human life. These realities include life-enhancing ones like the ties that bind us in communities of meaning, love, and need with our fellows, as well as life-limiting ones such as scarce material resources and the inevitability of death. To say that this is a natural law argument is to use the term in a peculiar sense--one which needs to be defended. In order to make sense of this claim, we need to look first at the idea of a natural life-span and then place Callahan's proposal in the context of natural law ethics.

More Than "More of the Same"

Arguments about the place of death in human life were not unknown in contemporary medical ethics before Callahan's recent work. Leon Kass, for example, discusses many of the relevant issues in a 1983 essay.[10] Kass combs the Greek and Hebrew classics, especially Homer and Plato, to uncover the attitude toward dying that we can learn from the ancients. They teach us, he concludes, that what we yearn for is not merely more of the same physical life; "no amount of 'more of the same' will satisfy our deepest aspirations."[11] Thus, Odysseus declines the possibility of immortality when Calypso offers it; he responds to the offer in a moving passage that Kass paraphrases: "[t]o suffer, to endure, to trouble oneself for the sake of home, family and genuine friendship, is truly to live."[12] Such a choice is already a mark of Odysseus's excellence and is the basis of the noble and just deeds which are a further display of that excellence. And what can be said of Homer's hero can be said also of *The Symposium*, of *Genesis*-and of Descartes too, and Bacon.[13] Occasionally explicit and everywhere implicit in Kass's analysis is the difficulty of making these points for mortals less heroic than Odysseus, in a time where the polyphony of cultural voices seems to leave us with neither Plato's ardor for "the good" nor the Bible's flinty sense that we have lost the original harmony of creation. But it is a difficulty to which Kass does not direct any special attention.

Callahan's approach to this matter is far more urgent. The attitude toward death for which we admire Odysseus can no longer be considered beyond the capabilities of ordinary people. Grim necessity deprives us of the detachment which allows us to contemplate Odysseus abstractly or to think that such a choice is only for heroes. Rather, medicine has lulled us into thinking that Calypso's offer is being made again--and that we can all accept it without a thought of its consequences. Reality is otherwise. Not at the height of our powers, like Odysseus, but nonetheless really, we must learn to choose our humanness and accept our mortality. Surely, life cannot be infinitely extended and, anyway, the costs for doing what we now do to extend it are great enough to give us pause. Already in our aging society we are spending a large share of the gross national product on the elderly without even reaching to all the members of the society. Callahan has accepted the challenge that he sees reality forcing upon us and has set himself the thankless task of leading a national discussion on death and dying. In *Setting Limits* his aim is to "establish the plausibility of thinking that if death must come at all, death in old age after a full and--on the whole--complete life is as acceptable as death is ever likely to be for human beings."[14] In terminology he uses elsewhere, a "tolerable death"[15] is one which comes at the end of a "natural life-span"[16]--a suggestion that has consequences for medicine and our attitudes toward death at every level.

Callahan's proposal is a subtle one that attends to the complexities of a highly emotional issue. Any brief statement of his proposal runs a risk of omitting a detail that someone might consider essential. Nevertheless, let me try. His suggestion is that the long process of creating a new cultural consensus about aging and death needs to be begun. As a starting point, he suggests that we learn to think of a full life as one that has fulfilled an inner dynamic: "(a) when one's life possibilities have on the whole been accomplished; (b) one's moral obligations to those for whom one has had responsibility have been discharged; and (c) one's death will not seem to others an offense to sense or sensibility, or tempt others to despair and rage at the finitude of human existence."[17] Such a natural life-span should be thought of as a biographical and not a biological fulfillment; nevertheless we can think of it as coinciding roughly with our reaching our late seventies or early eighties,[18] although there will be exceptions. Beyond this point, medical attention should be limited. The shorthand summary of these limitations is: Relieve suffering rather than resist death.[19] Callahan wants us to focus on the larger issues involved in thinking about and accepting death, and it is to these issues that we will soon turn.

Still, we should note that his argument is more modest than it is sometimes taken to be. By democratic means, he thinks, we ought to move gradually to a social policy which will recognize that our public money ought to be spent on better public goals than extending the lives of those whose age and health indicate that they have completed their biographical lives.[20]

It is this proposal that will be considered in the remainder of this essay. How ought we to think of this use of *natural* from the perspective of natural law ethics?

Natural Law Today

The tradition of natural law ethics is considerably broader than the best known of its contemporary applications--its use to condemn the unnaturalness of contraception--implies. Because this is so, I will explain in this section what I mean by that tradition.

Natural law ethics is, first of all, the idea that morality is natural to human beings. The normative cluster of concepts by which we identify what it means to be a human being includes a capacity for morality, a capacity that is realized, more or less, in healthy, adult humans.

Secondly, in terms of the methodology of ethics, natural law is the idea that the content of morality can be known to us *naturally*. This methodological conclusion follows from the naturalness of morality itself. Human reflection, especially the traditions we call theology and philosophy, is an essential component of ethics, as it is of human life; but it is only one component of the learning-through-living that is the root of the naturalness of morality.

Thirdly, regarding the content of morality, to say that morality is natural to us is to say that human morality is based on reality or on our common humanness. This common humanness need not be thought of as "human nature" arrived at as a result of metaphysical reflection; it can be much more empirical. We can draw conclusions about our common humanness by observation; in pursuing the goals which seem to be necessary for human flourishing, we all act according to our common humanness. Reflection upon ourselves as human beings leads us to an idea of the nature from which our best actions flow and to which they best conform. Discourse about natural law is a result of reflection on such human behavior and of the conviction that we can learn from observing the broad similarities among moral systems. These similarities are important enough to form the core around which wise choices must be made.

In pursuit of a common life and out of a shared sense of what promotes their well-being, human beings construct cultures containing social and moral institutions. Recognition of the importance of this culture building is one of the distinctive features of our times. It ought not to be thought of as separate from human "nature;" the need for and capacity for culture is as certain a part of human nature as anything we know. Learning about cultural diversity has posed a great challenge to natural law theories, but human moral systems have considerable unanimity on certain matters. Certain vague but important generalizations about morality, which can be taken to be its constants, can be stated as both form and content, as a bare outline of morality and about how to make moral and legal decisions.

Such new ideas as cultural diversity, pluralism, and historicity, pose a challenge for ethical thinking in general, and even more to theories of natural law. In this situation of pluralism, what concrete results can be expected from a natural law theory? When the topic to be approached is as new and as broad as the natural life-span, several possibilities might be pursued. One possibility would be to argue by analogy from a strand of the past to an aspect of the natural life-span idea and thus develop a normative conclusion. We might begin with some aspect of human rights, or perhaps some traditions' conclusions about acceptance of the inevitability of death, and work from there to a position that might be identified with natural law. But, here, I am choosing a different path and stressing instead the process by which moral practices and rules are derived.

The promise of natural law is that we can learn from our human past enough to provide us with an orientation and a framework on which to build toward a new institutionalization. In this case, for example, natural law reflection leads us to expect a generosity in human beings that balances our desire for survival with other, more complex, desires and needs.[21] Thus natural law provides us with a sense of what can be expected of human beings and an orientation toward how to turn this vague sense into a useful moral rule or institution. An appeal to natural law is an appeal to the best wisdom of human beings over the generations. It is an appeal to human reason. Human reason being the precious but vulnerable tool it is, such an appeal has great strengths. It does not, however, promise us a truth as stable as nature itself so often seems.

Where philosophical differences divide natural law theorists is in how to understand the gap between the generalities on which we can all agree and the much more detailed specifics which will characterize a particular society. Sooner or later, all natural law theorists have to come to grips with cultural diversity, but they do so at different points in their argument and in different ways. The gap cannot be leapt over by *a priori* reasoning. In the past, the creative choices behind such diversity were sometimes attributed to individual geniuses known and unknown: the wise. Today, a more culturally-attuned version of such a claim would emphasize more the broad consensual basis needed for culture-building. That is, to get from the generalities of natural law to specific moral institutions we must go through the slow, incremental process of creating a consensus and the cultural institutions which embody such consensus.

The best such understanding of natural law, it seems to me, contains a commitment to a widespread, democratic testing of morality in the experiences of ordinary people in situations where they are able to respond freely and make choices without domination or oppression. I believe that the better instincts of

Jefferson and Franklin were right not only with regard to government but also to morality--it derives its power from consent.

The work of the German philosopher/political scientist, Jürgen Habermas, with its emphasis on free communication, leads to a methodology similar to the one I am suggesting.[22] A decade or so ago, Habermas seemed to assume that the outcome of such free communication would be a single moral language, normative for all, a kind of empirical morality quite similar in its universality to some more traditional versions of the natural law. In terms of the philosophy out of which I am working, such an option seems to be a religious ideal rather than a provable conclusion from experience: the hope that all humans will be one in a single, universal, liberated community. But Habermas's democratic insistence on free communication need not be tied to such an eschatological hope; it can be taken as the human ideal most worth striving for.

A few points about alternative theories should be made explicitly, for the sake of completeness. No claim is being made here for an easy transfer from the scientific laws of nature to moral natural laws. Biological nature is still somewhat inescapable (in spite of the end of nature) but its rule need not be taken as our morality. In this respect the expression, "natural life-span," contains an ambiguity. This ambiguity is expressed by saying that what is being named is a biographical, not a biological fact. The claim for a natural life-span, as I understand it, is that experience tells us that the limits of life must be accepted and we can predict that such acceptance will come at a certain time in our lives. The claim is that we can be guided by the experience of past generations, not that we can read our destiny from our biology.[23]

Without pursuing further the details of natural-law theories, it should be clear that what distinguishes such theories, and what makes them useful tools for ethical reflection, is that they appeal to our ability to learn (from our knowledge of ourselves) how we ought to act. In appealing to natural law, one is appealing to the common experience of human beings. Unlike some other theorists of natural law, I find the most useful methodology is a broadly empirical and historical one. Ethics is a broadly humanistic enterprise, and though deductive reason has its place in that enterprise, it is not enough. We learn about human beings in many ways. The knowledge that comes to us through history and literature is as important as philosophy and theology; such humanistic knowledge is at least as useful as the knowledge we gain from the more empirical methods of the social sciences, sociobiology, and so forth. Studying our common experience in such a way leads to results that are rather more vague than our moral intuitions demand, but they may be the most universal moral advice we have. In any case, such results have the advantage of being a place from which to start.

A Useful Example

Emphasis on learning from the past does not get us very far in answering questions about a natural life-span. The issues we face about "a tolerable death" provide us with no easy precedents to read. The reason a natural life-span has become an issue is the possibility of extending life through new medical techniques. There is little past to learn from. Not so very long ago, living out a biblical life-span was rare enough to be worthy of respect and honor. Living longer, into the hundreds, was worthy of quite special notice. Although Kass rightly reads the classics to find a message or attitude from which we can benefit, the present issue--whether we ought to learn to be content with a life biographically fulfilled even though more biological life could theoretically be possible--is a new one. In this respect, as so many others, we are learning to live at the end of what has, up till now, seemed to be inevitable and natural.

Some people will turn away from the questions of limiting our quest for more life with a sense of pride that we have come so far and are facing completely new challenges. Others will deny that our situation is all that new. For still others the question becomes focused on which analogy from the past is the most illuminating: Should we be thinking in analogies to suicide, or to heroic self-sacrifice? Or to the Holocaust? Should we be worried about the possibilities of the massacre of the aged? Should we focus on questions of rights? (I am particularly mindful of the last of these, but will not pursue it here.) An emphasis on free and open communication should be enough to guarantee that analogies to mass death are groundless.

But I am presently asking more limited questions. Can death be tolerable? What makes death tolerable? Does it make sense to ask people to learn to accept their limits and their death? Can persons be asked to allow the society around them to turn needed resources toward those who have not yet lived out the potentialities of their biographies? Is this a hopelessly optimistic wish? A related issue lies just under the surface, and cannot be avoided. It emerges in the questions at the end of the previous paragraph and is the issue of justice. Under what conditions will people consider it just that they be allowed to die?

An example drawn from the recent practice of the Roman Catholic church in North America illumines these issues. Natural law is often associated with the Catholic moral theology, but, as I have already said, the version of natural law to be found there is often quite different from the one I am presenting. The best known use of natural law in Catholic practice is in the context of sexual ethics and draws on quite different philosophic roots than this paper. Nevertheless, on practical questions, a certain consistency shows through in spite of these differences. In March 1990, Archbishop Roger Mahony wrote to priests and nuns, over sixty-five years old, recommending that they take seriously an accompanying request to serve as human subjects testing a potentially dangerous AIDS vaccine.[24] The letter was couched in relatively non-directive language and did not put any pressure on its recipients. He did not say that he wanted them to take part, but only that they take the possibility seriously.

A copy of the letter to the nuns was given to me by a woman who did not know of the parallel letter to priests. She was enraged that women were being asked by patriarchal authority to risk their lives and interpreted it as another act against women by an unfeeling or exploitive male institution. Such responses were not uncommon, even among those who knew the entire context of this action, and I have continued to hear of ambiguities in the process. Still, the majority of the professional ethicists whose comments I have seen had favorable things to say about the request. Many of them had comments to make about the archbishop's action that are not relevant to our present concerns--issues around experimentation and consent. Our immediate interest, however, is in the idea that persons approaching the end of their active careers might consider actions which put their lives at risk. The archbishop's letter called older priests and nuns to consider taking a risk whose results might lie five or so years in the future. Many elements of this case are not analogous to the ordinary experience of non-celibate, non-clerical people. Still, the example bears witness to the idea that death is not an absolute evil and that the acceptance of death is to be thought of as a natural part of life.

Although Archbishop Mahony's actions were initiated and developed in the context of institutionalized religion, and have some of the elements of heroism associated with priests and nuns, the general orientation of his suggestion is rooted in a broader, less ecclesiastical tradition. On this understanding of human beings and of our possible attitudes toward death, natural law theorists of all persuasions will agree. The most canonical version of the natural law tradition--I am thinking here of Thomas Aquinas--recognizes that humans seek a variety of goods, among them physical survival and a life without pain, but also a life spent in harmony with others, exercising fully our intellects and our capacity to love and to live in community.[25] St. Thomas optimistically thinks that these goods interrelate harmoniously with each other. Some modern readers, too, might opt for a version of the moral life which sees all of these interweaving with each other in harmony. However, it is one of the empirical sources of modern pluralism that, for many, these goals are not so easily reconciled and that the relations we humans see among our various goals will always be subject to criticism and, therefore, unstable. Morality will always have to be figured out anew for each generation, for each new community, for each individual. Nevertheless, the underlying generalization about the place of love and community in human life that St. Thomas derives from the natural law tradition continues to be reaffirmed throughout that tradition.

Two Conditions to Be Met

Thus, certain conclusions are warranted. Life is a good to be pursued, indeed to be treasured. But it is not the only such human purpose. The natural law tradition includes a number of others. In the Christian tradition, the force that is as strong as death is usually summarized simply as love--the love of God, the love of humans for one another. It is an image that can also be found in Greek thought--think of Odysseus--and indeed it can be found almost everywhere.

A similar orientation informs the argument of Daniel Callahan. Although we may seek survival, it is not our only good. Instead, we wish to live our lives well, given the conditions of our humanness. The proposal behind the notion of living a natural life-span is that we can realize at some point that our lives are behind us and that the resources which we need to prolong our lives are necessarily taken from others whose lives are still ahead of them. When the people to be deprived by our efforts at life-extension are our loved ones--our spouses and children, for example--it seems fair to conclude that self-sacrifice will make sense to many of us. But what if it is society--anonymous society--who asks us to make this choice?

The choice becomes harder to make when the ones who benefit from one's death are farther removed from one's love--neighbors, fellow citizens, all humanity. Even in the case of accepting death to provide for one's loved ones--especially in the case of accepting death for the common good--it seems likely that two conditions must be met: Our choice must emerge from a context of broad public support, and its institutions must be seen as just.

The first is that the action taken seem reasonable and honorable in a widely-accepted and clearly-articulated sense.   A high cultural and religious value must be placed on it and it must be rewarded as an honorable choice by the members of one's society whose opinions count in helping us maintain our sense that we have lived our life well.   This emphasis on cultural and religious value needs to be emphasized.   The anthropology behind this suggestion rests on the conclusion that we are not the self-sustaining individuals described in the most extreme versions of modern individualism, but are members of communities just as much as we are separate selves. From the beginning we depend on other people and cannot live without their love and their physical support.   The ties that bind us to society can be loosened as we become physically able to provide for ourselves, but they can rarely, if ever, be entirely cut.   It is at least arguable that the self-esteem and independence that sustain us are always mediated to us through the language and culture we share with others.   The suggestion has been powerfully made recently that our culture has been misled by "inadequate social science, impoverished philosophy, and vacuous theology"[26] to underestimate the cultural matrix on which we depend.

Callahan's proposal that we learn to live within the limits of a natural life-span is not least a part of the natural law tradition in its recognition of the importance of culture and community.   One reason his suggestion has been so often misunderstood may be our own context in an oxymoronic "culture of individualism."   To say that culture can enable us to face death well is to say that, at the limits of human life, culture is indistinguishable from religion.   But not all cultures can perform this enabling function equally well.   To say that people are naturally inclined toward the things that promote human community, is not the same as saying that they will be equally well nourished by just any community, even with no sense of participation whatsoever.   Without a strong sense of communal participation, can people be willing to enter into death sooner than they need to?

Facing death is more of a challenge now, after the end of nature. Dying makes even less sense when it seems to come as a result of human choices that might have been made differently than it does when it comes with the inexorability of fate. Depriving death of its naturalness makes it much, much harder to face. If, nevertheless, we draw the lesson from the past that we can face death with equanimity under certain conditions, those conditions become even more important. The first such condition is that the dying are able to recognize that they live on as a part of those they leave behind--a participation that is easiest seen in the case of family and other loved ones. Death seems easiest to bear, and even to choose, when it serves a purpose and protects the welfare of those we love. Given Callahan's other conditions (an appropriately ripe old age, etc.) clinging to life in a way that impoverishes one's loved ones will seem to many people to be the wrong choice. The farther we get from such familiarity, the more difficult the choice of natural life-span becomes. It will require all the efforts of culture and religion to stretch those bonds outward so that we feel a part of those we leave behind in our community, our country, our common humanity, and the like. And all such efforts will be thwarted unless a second condition is fulfilled. The choice of a natural life-span must take place in a context in which the requirements of justice are met.

Whatever differences arise in facing death must be seen to be equitable ones. In this context, the economic reasons for limiting medical care take on greater importance. They become the closest counterpart we have to fate, and they take the place of nature. Unlike the nature of old, however, economics is capable of manipulation and deception. The processes by which the economic factors are allocated--discussion, politics, power--become important and will seem just to people only under certain conditions. The most important of these seems to me to be a sense that the rules that have been arrived at are fair and that they will be administered fairly. Procedures are among the things that natural law seems to be clearest about.

To make these points about justice--about the mediation of culture and the weakness of our American cultural bonds in a culture of pluralism--is to recognize the challenge they pose. Creation of cultural institutions to support a revised sense of our mortality will not happen automatically or effortlessly. Necessity constrains our choice, and human creativity is needed to institutionalize it well. We would choose to live on if there were no good reason not to. All other things being equal, a diminished life is better than no life at all. But the scarcity of the world's resources means that other things are not equal. Our continued living when our biographical life is really behind us may be a happy stroke of luck or a result of our own healthful living and should be rejoiced in. But it looks different when extending our lives medically means that other's lives are going to be reduced because ours are extended. Caught between our desire for life and our desire to live our lives well, necessity forces us to recognize that death can be the lesser of two evils. In order to do so, we will have to learn to create a cultural consensus in which death can be accepted for the common good.

"A good society," says Callahan, "is one that finds ways to avoid requiring too much heroism."[27] The natural law tradition suggests that it is possible to find such ways of making sense of accepting death even in a world in which medicine has replaced nature. It suggests that humans want more than *merely* more of the same life, and that we can even learn to forego some of that merely extended life if we are given good enough reasons and social support to do so. The process of creating that social support is the uncharted waters of this argument. Callahan's suggestion that the process will be a generation-long one that is only now beginning,[28] should not be overlooked. Shaping a culture has always happened unintentionally in the past. To say that we should set out to do so consciously for the first time is to be a part of a new human adventure, one for which the past offers nothing but clues. Moreover, the facing of death is an area in which people often seem susceptible to great manipulation. People can be willing to die for "God and Country" in a way that can offend moral sensibility. A sense of justice may be natural to us humans, but the specification of what counts as justice is more culturally shaped than we often think. It is here that the insistence on democratic processes and uncoerced communication becomes a necessary insistence, even if we can go no farther. We have run as close to specifics as we ought to go.

The pressure of necessity will lead us, sooner or later, to face the limits of what we can expect society to do to extend our lives. A social consensus will eventually be reached on these matters. Whatever it will be, as just as it can be, will depend a great deal on the process by which it is arrived. Instead of proposing a specific arrangement in these matters, I have emphasized here the processes and possibilities that a natural law theory seems to suggest. Instead of drawing conclusions about the future shape of a natural life-span, I am pushing the normative process down into the democratic process, where a moral consensus on these matters will have to be reached. Once it is available we will be able to appeal to it in making moral judgments. But even now we are at the point at which our moral obligation and our creativity begin. Whatever our judgments at this point, they need to be articulated and heard. If we are to leap from abstractions about human nature, if we think that there is more to natural law than merely a form of rationalism, we will need to help create this new consensus. We will need to be participants in the ongoing discussion of the meaning of life and the meaning of death in which our culture (or our subsection of it) grapples with the questions of what is a reasonable, or natural, life-span.[29]

Notes and References

1. Daniel Callahan, *Setting Limits: Medical Goals in an Aging Society* (New York: Simon & Schuster, 1987).

2. Bill McKibben, *The End of Nature* (New York: Random House, 1989).

3. Ibid., p. 83.

4. Ibid.

5. Ibid., p. 84.

6. Ibid., p. 71.

7. Stanley Fish, *Doing What Comes Naturally, p. IX* (Durham: Duke University Press, 1989).

8. Ibid.

9. See Anthony Battaglia, *Toward a Reformation of Natural Law* (New York: Seabury Press, 1981).

10. Leon Kass, *Toward a More Natural Science: Biology and Human Affairs* (New York: Free Press, 1985), pp. 299-317.

11. Ibid., p. 314.

12. Ibid., p. 311.

13. Ibid., p. 317.

14. Callahan, *Setting Limits*, p. 69.

15. Ibid., p. 66.

16. Ibid., p. 65.

17. Ibid., p. 66.

18. Ibid., p. 171.

19. Ibid., pp. 171-173.

20. Ibid., pp. 222-224.

21. There have been theories of natural law that have had a more dour understanding of human nature, but they have been few and I pass over them here.

22. Jürgen Habermas, *The Theory of Communicative Action*, Vol. 1, translated by Thomas McCarthy (Boston: Beacon Press, 1984), pp. 1-5.

23. The version of natural law that is responsible for the condemnation of contraception has been aptly called "Catholic Moral Rationalism" by Jesuit

John Langan ("Catholic Moral Rationalism and the Philosophical Bases of Moral Theology," *Theological Studies*, Vol. 50 (March 1989), pp. 25-43. Although in decline, some contemporary ethicists, like Germain Grisez and Jesuit John Finnis, still propose similar positions. See Germain Grisez, *The Way of the Lord Jesus*, Vol. 1 of *Christian Moral Principles* (Chicago: Franciscan Herald Press, 1983); and John Finnis, *Natural Law and Natural Rights* (Oxford: Clarendon Press, 1980). Their positions deserve more attention (and criticism) than I will be giving them here. Interested readers may want to look at evaluations such as those of Russell Hittinger and Lloyd L. Weinreb in Russell Hittinger, *A Critique of the New Natural Law Theory* (Notre Dame: University of Notre Dame Press, 1987); and Lloyd L. Weinreb, *Natural Law and Justice* (Cambridge: Harvard University Press, 1987). In a paper of this length it would be impossible to critique their positions and do justice to our topic. However, they might approve the spirit, though probably not the letter, of much that follows.

24.   Bill Kenklin, "Mahony's Call for Religious to Try AIDS Vaccine Sparks Anger, Praise," *National Catholic Reporter*, March 23, 1990, p. 4.

25.   Thomas Aquinas, *Law and Political Theory*, Vol. 28 of *Summa Theologia*, translated by Thomas Gilby, O.P. (London: Eyre and Spottiswoode, 1963).

26.   Robert N. Bellah, Richard Madsen, William M. Sullivan, Ann Swidler, and Steven M. Tipton, *Habits of the Heart: Individualism and Commitment in American Life* (Berkeley: University of California Press, 1985), p. 84.

27.   Callahan, *Setting Limits*, p. 106.

28.   Ibid., p. 10.

29.   An earlier version of this paper was read by Judith W. Kay. Her comments helped me improve it.

PART THREE

Clinical Perspectives

6

Surrogate Decisions
for Nursing Home Residents

Jeanie Kayser-Jones

Introduction

In recent years much has been written about the escalating cost of health-care and the need to decrease health-care costs. Some believe we are spending too much on the care of the elderly at the expense of children, while others argue that the health-care needs of older people are not being met adequately by our existing institutions.

Nursing homes are one example of our failure to provide adequate care for the elderly. While concerns about the increasing cost of health care are justified, I am fearful that the cost of care may take priority over what is humane and just when health-care decisions are being made for the elderly. This is especially worrisome in nursing homes where a large proportion of patients, due to mental impairment, cannot participate in the decision-making process.

In the past, most ethicists have focused on the use of life-sustaining technologies such as mechanical ventilation, renal dialysis, cardiopulmonary resuscitation, and nutritional support and hydration in acute care settings. An exception is a recent publication, *Everyday Ethics: Resolving Dilemmas in Nursing Home Life.*[1] This book emphasizes ethical issues that occur in the day-to-day life of nursing home residents such as the assignment of roommates, the use of restraints, and telephone privileges.

The treatment of acute illness in nursing homes is an ethical issue of great magnitude that has not been adequately explored despite the fact that about 20 percent of people over the age of 60 will spend some time in a nursing home.[2] Most nursing home residents have three or four chronic conditions such as arthritis, congestive heart failure, and osteoporosis. Frequently, they suffer from an acute illness such as urinary tract infections, upper respiratory infections, and myocardial infarctions. Whereas in the acute hospital there is concern that technology is over-utilized to treat acute illnesses, in the nursing home much less technology is available, and acute illnesses may be treated less aggressively.

In nursing homes, decisions to treat or withhold diagnostic and therapeutic intervention occur daily in an environment that is not conducive to careful decision-making. Support services such as X-ray, laboratory, and pharmacy departments are usually not available. Physicians visit infrequently, and in many nursing homes there is an insufficient number of adequately trained staff.[3] Moreover, many nursing home residents, due to mental impairment, are unable to participate in decisions about their health-care, and ethics committees are usually not available. When critical decisions are being made, residents often must depend upon a family member, friend, or guardian to speak for them.

When patients lack the ability to make a treatment decision, a surrogate decision-maker, someone to make decisions on their behalf, should be designated. Usually, this is a close family member. Several documents have focused on issues such as the importance of identifying a surrogate, the substantive principles of surrogate decision-making, and the qualities of a surrogate decision-maker. Guidelines have been developed,[4] but their implementation is sometimes problematic. The case study presented here (part of a five-year project that investigated the sociocultural factors that influenced the evaluation and treatment of acute illness in nursing homes) will illustrate the problems that can occur in surrogate decision-making. Further, it will pose ethical questions for consideration.

Papers that discuss ethical issues are often theoretical or hypothetical. They tend to focus on the increasing numbers of the elderly, the escalating cost of health care, and on concepts such as autonomy, scarcity of resources, and intergenerational equity. When discussing ethical issues, I believe it is important to use an actual case study that presents the human perspective because the decisions that are being made affect real people--our grandparents, our parents, and perhaps one day ourselves.

The Case Study

Mrs. Johnson (a pseudonym) was an 85-year-old woman who had been in the nursing home for two years. She was one of eight children; one sister and two brothers were still living. She also had a niece who visited regularly. Mrs. Johnson was ambulatory, could feed herself, and she enjoyed company. According to her niece, her memory had been fair until the past six months when she began to develop serious memory problems.

Mrs. Johnson was admitted to the nursing home with a diagnosis of Alzheimer's disease, congestive heart failure, atrial fibrillation, and hypertension. Two years earlier she had had a stroke. On a Friday, the nurses noticed that Mrs. Johnson had left-sided paralysis, and that she could no longer speak. The doctor was called; he examined Mrs. Johnson and said she had had another stroke. The physician called her sister and told her, "the situation is hopeless." The doctor presented the option of tube feeding, saying it could be done but it would be painful. He then asked the sister what she wanted him to do. The sister said that years ago, Mrs. Johnson had indicated that she did not want any tubes used to prolong her life. The doctor and the patient's sister, therefore, agreed on no heroics, and the doctor wrote an order for "supportive care only, no code."

The nurses observed that, although Mrs. Johnson could not speak, she turned her head from side to side when she heard voices. They attempted to give her liquids and soft foods, but she choked when they tried to feed her. From time to time, Mrs. Johnson rattled the side rails with her unparalyzed right hand. Her sister reported that the two of them had devised a system whereby Mrs. Johnson communicated with her by blinking her eyes, and the nurse aides noted that when they bathed Mrs. Johnson, she was able to assist them in turning, from side to side.

Four days after the stroke, my research assistant spoke with Mrs. Johnson's physician, asking if he planned to transfer her to an acute care hospital. He replied, "No, she is going to stay here; she is going to stay here and die." Six days after the stroke, the nurses noted that Mrs. Johnson was still able to blink her eyes when asked to do so. On the eighth day after the stroke, the doctor wrote an order to discontinue all oral medications. He also wrote in the progress notes:

Unable to take in oral liquids since cerebral vascular accident (CVA). Patient is non-verbal. Eyes deviated to the right. Left flaccid paralysis, Cheyne-Stokes respiration. Skin turgor good. Patient appears comfortable. Patient has had a large CVA and significant recovery at this time appears remote. Knowing the patient's depressed state prior to her stroke, I don't feel she would want measures that would prolong her life in this condition. She appears comfortable. Don't believe intravenous fluids would increase her comfort.

When I learned of this woman's condition (six days after the stroke), I immediately went to see her. I arrived at the nursing home in the evening and asked the charge nurse about the patient's condition. "She's not feeling well," she replied, "she's going downhill." I went to see Mrs. Johnson. She was receiving oxygen but little in the way of nursing care. Her mouth was dry and crusted. There was a dry glycerin and lemon swab on the bedside stand. Her paralyzed left hand and arm had fallen down between the bed and the siderail. Apparently, it had been in that position for a long time; her hand and lower arm were extremely edematous. I lifted her arm, positioned it on the pillow, and called her name. Her eyes moved in the direction of my voice. I walked to the opposite side of the bed and again called her name; she turned her head toward the sound of my voice.

I then went to the nursing station and asked the charge nurse how the decision had been made to withhold treatment from this patient. The nurse said that according to the doctor, Mrs. Johnson had had a massive stroke, and he thought that even if he did something for her, she would just be a total-care patient. Therefore, there was no point in treating her. He had explained this to Mrs. Johnson's sister on the telephone. The nurse said, "She still responds to voices, and with her right arm she shakes the siderail. She is very strong; she is not comatose." I asked if the patient was going to be tube-fed. The nurse said, "I don't know; it depends on the doctor. She hasn't had anything for one week and her heart is still beating so strongly."

Mrs. Johnson died nine days after the acute stroke. After her death, I called her sister and asked if I could talk with her. She was leaving on a vacation and said she did not have time to meet with me. I then called the niece, explained the research project to her, and asked if I could meet with her. When I told her about the purpose of my visit she said, "You have come to the right person because I can tell you a lot about how such decisions are made."

She explained that although Mrs. Johnson's sister was her legal guardian, the two of them had never had a close relationship. After

Mrs. Johnson's first stroke, her sister decided that she should be placed in a board and care home. The sister sold all of Mrs. Johnson's personal belongings and closed her apartment. Until a month before she died, Mrs. Johnson begged to be taken back to her home for a brief visit. But her sister never took her out of the nursing home, and she never told Mrs. Johnson that she had sold her belongings. The niece said the sister had not gone to Mrs. Johnson's wake or funeral. "There was absolutely no affection between those two sisters. She could turn the tears on and appear as if she really cared, but deep down she really did not care."

It appeared that the niece was very fond of her aunt, and I wanted to know how she felt about Mrs. Johnson's care during the last days of her life. "There is some controversy as to whether or not to give fluids to patients like your aunt," I remarked. She quickly replied, "I was wild about that!" She explained that Mrs. Johnson's sister and the doctor made the decision to withhold fluids without asking for her opinion. The niece said that she told her aunt that she thought Mrs. Johnson should be getting fluids, but the aunt replied that the two sisters had discussed the matter, and that Mrs. Johnson had always said she did not want to be kept alive with machines. "I'm not talking about machines," the niece replied, "I'm talking about liquids."

The niece then inquired of the nurses, "Is this a normal procedure, not to give people fluids? I did not want her to die of thirst," she said. "I did not want her to starve to death." The nurses replied, "It doesn't make any difference." Still concerned, the niece called the doctor and asked about giving fluids to her aunt. He insisted that the sister did not want anything done to sustain life. The niece emphasized that she was not talking about machines. "I too would not want to be kept alive on machines," she said. "But I wasn't talking about machines; I was talking about fluids." The niece told the doctor, "I don't want my aunt to die of thirst," and he replied, "We don't know if she is suffering or not, but she is probably not aware of that." The niece continued, "I wanted to ask him, 'How do you know? Do you know what it is like to die of thirst?'"

"It was a terrible, terrible thing for them not to give her some fluids. The first few days she was clearly suffering." The niece noted that on one occasion when she visited Mrs. Johnson she grabbed hold of her hand and worked until she removed a ring from her finger. "She looked at me as if she were pleading with me to do something. I know she was thirsty." "How do you know she was thirsty?" I inquired. "My aunt was receiving oxygen, and there

was a bottle of water attached to the oxygen tank, and the water
was bubbling. She looked at the oxygen water bottle, and then she
looked at me--she kept looking at the water. I know she was
thirsty."
The niece explained that Mrs. Johnson had married into a
wealthy family. Her husband wanted to make sure that she was
well cared for, and he left her a substantial amount of money. Mrs.
Johnson's sister was the executor of her estate. "I tell all of my
friends, don't leave your money to the same person who is the
executor of your estate, and don't have that same person be your
legal guardian because they know what you have, and there could
be a conflict of interest." The niece was convinced that the sister
knew that it was costing a lot to keep Mrs. Johnson in the nursing
home, and she did not want the estate to be depleted by the cost of
nursing-home care.
Again, she repeated, "It was a terrible thing not to give her
fluids. It was the most cruel thing I have ever seen; I have never
seen anything so awful in my whole life. There should be a doctor
who oversees all the other doctors. There should be a board of
doctors to see that people get fluids and do not die of dehydration.
Maybe if she had been given fluids she would have come out of the
stroke. My aunt was starved to death."

Ethical Concerns in Surrogate Decision-Making

There are many ethical questions surrounding Mrs. Johnson's
care. These questions will be presented, and specific details of the
case will be discussed within the theoretical framework of surrogate
decision-making. Examples of the questions that arise include:

- Did Mrs. Johnson receive reasonable care from her physician and
  nurses?
- Did her age and mental status affect the decision-making process?
- Was there a conflict of interest on the part of her sister who was
  her legal guardian and acted as a surrogate decision-maker?
- Is the legal guardian always the best person to make decisions for
  incompetent patients, or should others also be consulted?
- If the legal guardian is not an advocate for the patient, who should
  take responsibility for patient advocacy?
- Do health-care professionals have an ethical responsibility to ensure
  that morally valid surrogate decisions are made?

Thomasma and Pellegrino have stated the following conditions for morally valid surrogate decision-making:

1. The surrogate should provide convincing evidence that he knows the patient's values. Simply being a member of the family is insufficient.
2. There should be no obvious conflict of interest on the part of the surrogate such as personal interest in acquiring an estate or a desire to be rid of the expense and burden of caring for a chronically ill patient.
3. Health-care professionals must be aware of the possible existence of psychological and emotional conflict on the part of surrogates. Undertreatment or non-treatment may be consciously or unconsciously urged as a way of "getting even" for past problems.
4. Finally, the decision must be in the best interest of the patient.[5]

In light of these conditions, I shall now turn to specific details of this situation and reflect on some ethical issues inherent in the case. First, when the doctor examined Mrs. Johnson and concluded that she had had a stroke he told her sister, "The situation is hopeless." Was the situation really hopeless? Or did the doctor use this language to convince the sister that treatment would be to no avail? When information is not presented honestly and objectively, families cannot make an informed decision, and they are therefore denied autonomy.[6]

A recent discussion of the Nancy Cruzan case stated:

> The well established standard for good medical decision-making is patient-centered, promoting the individual's well-being according to his or her own values and preferences, and involves the participation of the individual, the physician, and frequently the individual's family members.[7]

Surely, this decision was not patient-centered, and it did not promote Mrs. Johnson's well-being. Nor is it likely that such decisions can be made quickly by telephone as was done in this case.

Secondly, the doctor gave the sister two pieces of information: (1) that the situation was hopeless, and (2) that tube feeding would be painful. Given this information, they agreed on no heroics. The discussion of the Cruzan case, mentioned above, stated: "Caregiving professionals and institutions should make available to patients a full range of options for treatment, including the option of supportive care for dying patients."[8] Clearly, in this case, a full range of treatment options was not presented to the sister. Furthermore, there is no scientific evidence that tube feeding is painful. During the course of our research, some patients told us that feeding tubes were not painful. We must also ask if giving fluids in this case would be considered heroic care. Did the nursing staff have any responsibility to discuss this situation with the physician and family? Based on their observations of Mrs. Johnson, did they think the case was hopeless?

Third, in the progress notes the doctor said, "Knowing the patient's depressed state prior to her stroke, I don't feel she would want measures that would prolong her life in this condition." Depression is very common following a stroke. Yet the depression was not treated after Mrs. Johnson's first stroke, and it was then used as a rationale for not treating her when the second stroke occurred. Apparently, the physician used the patient's depression as an excuse for not treating her, a clear violation of the principle that decisions should be in the patient's best interest.

Fourth, when the nurses tried to feed Mrs. Johnson, she choked on the food. They knew she could not swallow, and they also knew that she responded by blinking her eyes. Furthermore, she rattled the bedrails and, when being bathed, she assisted her caregivers in turning from side to side. Yet they did not discuss her condition with the physician, and they did not ask if he wanted fluids given in some other way. The nurses had information that perhaps the doctor did not have. Whereas doctors make infrequent visits to nursing homes, the nurses are there 24 hours a day. The nurses could have taken the lead in bringing together the family, the physician, and the nursing staff to discuss Mrs. Johnson's care.

Fifth, when the physician did not prescribe medical treatment, the nurses were negligent in providing basic care. Mrs. Johnson's mouth was dry and crusted, and her arm was extremely edematous after hanging in a dependent position between the bed and the bedside rail. When a decision is made not to treat a patient medically, this does not relieve the nursing staff of its obligation to provide basic nursing care. The physician left an order for "supportive care." How do doctors and nurses define supportive care? A physician, who was interviewed during the course of our study, expressed concern that, if doctors do not treat an acutely-ill patient, then the nursing staff may ask, "Why should we provide nursing care?" In some cases we found that, when patients were not treated medically, basic nursing care was not given.[9] In many cases, nursing care constitutes the main and often the only reason patients are residing in nursing homes. There is, therefore, no ethical justification for not providing nursing care.

Sixth, according to the nurses, the doctor said that even if he did something for Mrs. Johnson she would just be a "total care patient." Thus, there was, no point in treating her. The question arises, is complete dependency an adequate reason for not treating a patient? If so, then there are many people in our society who would not be entitled to medical care. Did the nurses have an ethical obligation to challenge the physician on this decision? Was it acceptable for them to acquiesce? When we asked about the possibility of providing fluids and nutrition *via* a nasogastric feeding tube, a nurse said, "I don't know, it depends on the doctor; he knows what is best." Ethically, it was irresponsible for the nurses to not participate in the decision, especially when they had important information about Mrs. Johnson's condition.

Seventh, did the doctor and the nursing staff know about the unfriendly relationship between the two sisters? When a family member is acting as a surrogate decision-maker, health-care professionals are not absolved of the moral responsibility to be alert to possible conflicts of interests on the part of the surrogate. Professionals ought to ask relatives who are visiting the patient if there are others who should be consulted; if so, it is important to listen to the concerns of other family members.[10] The niece clearly expressed her interest in and concern for the patient when she asked the nurses and the doctor about giving intravenous fluids to her aunt, but her concerns were ignored.

Eighth, what responsibility do nurses and physicians have to family members who care about the patient but who may have no voice in the decision-making process? When a family member's concerns are ignored, they may be left with feelings of guilt or anger if they believe a relative was not properly cared for during the last days of life. When the niece approached the nurses and asked about giving intravenous fluids to her aunt, they replied that giving fluids would not make any difference. The niece was not convinced. She then called and asked the doctor if her aunt should be receiving fluids. He replied, "We don't know if she is suffering, but she is probably not aware." The niece, however, felt that Mrs. Johnson was suffering. She believed that her aunt tried to communicate her need for water by repeatedly looking at the water bottle that was attached to the oxygen tank. "My aunt was starved to death," she insisted. How did she cope with this thought and the feelings such a thought would evoke after Mrs. Johnson died? When doctors and nurses are not honest, trust is destroyed, and families will retain neither respect nor confidence. When there is disagreement among family members, health-care professionals are obliged to investigate why disagreement exists and whether conflicts of interest are present.[11]

Conclusion

Physicians, because of their position in society, have an enormous amount of power. They have an ethical responsibility to use that power to do good and not harm. They also have an ethical responsibility not only to diagnose but to explain the diagnosis and treatment options to patients and their families in objective, understandable language. Nurses also have a considerable amount of power because they are on the scene and may have information that the doctor does not have. They, too, have a responsibility to use that power to do good.

Clearly, Mrs. Johnson deserved more than she received from her doctor, the nurses, and her sister. In addition to not treating the acute stroke, there was no evidence of compassion for her as a human being and no sensitivity to her needs as she lay dying for nine days. With all of our sophisticated knowledge, surely we can do better than this.

Today, one often hears the comment that people are living too long. Some see the elderly as a drain on our national resources, and sometimes they are seen as depleting assets that are vital to the youth of our nation. Rather than asking if people are living too long, perhaps we should ask: Do we as a society have the will and the humanity to care for those who must depend upon us in the frailty of old age?

In 1952, Aneurin Bevan, the minister of health in the United Kingdom from 1945 to 1951, wrote, "No society can legitimately call itself civilized if a sick person is denied medical aid because of lack of means."[12] Nearly forty years later, we must ask: Can we as a society legitimately call ourselves civilized if we do not provide sensitive, humane care to the elderly during the last days of their lives.

Notes and References

1. Rosalie A. Kane and Arthur L. Caplan, *Everyday Ethics: Resolving Dilemmas in Nursing Home Life* (New York: Springer, 1990).

2. Ibid.

3. J. S. Kayser-Jones, C. L. Wiener, and J. C. Barbaccia, "Factors Contributing to the Hospitalization of Nursing Home Residents" *The Gerontologist*, Vol. 29, No. 4 (1989), pp. 502-510.

4. President's Commission for the Study of Ethical Problems in Medicine and Biomedical and Behavioral Research, *Deciding to Forego Life-Sustaining Treatment* (Washington, D.C.: U.S. Government Printing Office, 1983); and The Hastings Center, *Guidelines on the Termination of Life-Sustaining Treatment and the Care of the Dying* (Briarcliff Manor, N.Y.: The Hastings Center, 1987). See also U.S. Congress, Office of Technology Assessment, *Life Sustaining Technologies and the Elderly*, OTA-BA-306 (Washington, D.C.: U.S. Government Printing Office, 1987).

5. D. C. Thomasma and E. D. Pellegrino, "The Role of the Family and Physicians in Decisions for Incompetent Patients," *Theoretical Medicine*, Vol. 8 (1987), pp. 283-292.

6. Jeanie Kayser-Jones, "The Use of Nasogastric Feeding Tubes in Nursing Homes: Patient, Family, and Health Care Provider Perspectives," *The Gerontologist*, Vol. 30, No. 4 (1990), pp. 469-479.

7. J. J. Glover, A. Mastroianni, K. R. Anderson, and J. Lynn, "Abridged Brief as *Amicus Curiae* of the American Geriatrics Society in Support of the Petitioner, Nancy Beth Cruzan, by Her Parents and Co-Guardians Lester L. and Joyce Cruzan," *Journal of the American Geriatrics Society*, Vol. 38, No. 5 (May 1990), pp. 570-576.

8. Ibid.

9. J. S. Kayser-Jones, A. Davis, C. L. Wiener, and S. Higgins, "An Ethical Analysis of an Elder's Treatment," *Nursing Outlook*, Vol. 37, No. 6 (Nov/Dec 1989), pp. 267-270.

10. Dallas M. High, "Caring for Decisionally Incapacitated Elderly," *Theoretical Medicine*, Vol. 10, No. 1 (1989), pp. 83-96.

11. Ibid.

12. Aneurin Bevan, *In Place of Fear* (New York: Monthly Review Press, 1964)., p. 100.

7

The Appropriateness
of Life-Sustaining Care
for Older People

Donald J. Murphy

Introduction

Life-sustaining care for older people will undoubtedly be one of
the most scrutinized areas of health care in the next couple of
decades.   Limiting life-sustaining interventions for old people is
already a leading proposal for health-care rationing.[1]

Determining appropriate use of life-sustaining interventions is a
high priority for others besides ethicists, economists, and third party
payers. At the risk of stating the obvious, it is extremely important
for clinicians and patients. Yet one must ask, if appropriate use of
life-sustaining therapy is so important for clinicians and patients,
why do we sense that much life-sustaining therapy is used
inappropriately, particularly for older patients?

The explanation may lie in our failure to account consistently for
the multiple factors associated with life-sustaining care.   These
factors include: (1) effectiveness, (2) patient preferences, (3) cost, (4)
availability, (5) provider preferences, (6) family preferences, (7)
symbolism, (8) spirituality, and (9) culture.

This essay will explore the first three factors as they relate to
three types of life-sustaining care for the elderly: cardiopulmonary
resuscitation (CPR), hemodialysis, and enteral feedings.   Effectiveness
and patient preferences can be combined to determine medical
appropriateness. Cost-effectiveness analysis can be used to determine
economic appropriateness.

This analysis suggests that: (1) CPR is both medically and economically inappropriate for certain groups of older people; (2) hemodialysis is medically and economically appropriate for older people; and (3) depending on the definition of effectiveness, enteral feedings are medically, but not economically, inappropriate for older patients with persistent vegetative state (PVS).

CPR

Effectiveness

The outcome of CPR depends on whether CPR is initiated in or out of the hospital. Although it is not yet clear that age alone has a significant effect on the outcomes of CPR, it is clear that old people have a small chance of surviving to leave the hospital after CPR. If CPR is initiated in the hospital, the older patient has a 0-17 percent chance of surviving to leave the hospital,[2] depending on the prior health of the patient and the exact setting of the cardiac arrest. If CPR is initiated out-of-hospital, the older patient has a 0-10 percent chance of surviving to leave the hospital.[3] In some cities with state-of-the art paramedic services, the survival to discharge rate is as high as 10 percent for older people. In the majority of cities and rural communities in the U.S., the survival to discharge rate for out-of-hospital CPR is probably less than 5 percent, particularly for older patients who have multiple chronic problems.[4]

Preferences

Patients' preferences for CPR are not as clear as their outcomes. The literature suggests that at least a majority of older people opt to forego CPR when given the choice.[5] A recent study by Everhart and Pearlman indicates that patients with better understanding of CPR are less likely to opt for CPR.[6] For example, 87 percent of the 30 veterans in intensive care units favored "resuscitation" given their current health prior to an arrest. However, only 43 percent favored "resuscitation and mechanical ventilation" in the same setting. The reality is that resuscitation without mechanical ventilation is very unusual. Unless the patient is choking on food or has a particular type of arrhythmia that is monitored in an intensive care unit, CPR almost always involves intubation and mechanical ventilation.

The following hypothesis is one that future research can and should test: *The vast majority (more than 90 percent) of older people will opt to forego CPR when they fully understand the implications of CPR.*

Most older people, like the rest of the population, have exaggerated expectations of CPR. They believe CPR has a great chance of restoring them to their current state of health. Much of this misperception results from the media. For example, a majority of older people learn about CPR from television.[7] Shows such as "911" and "St. Elsewhere" have typically portrayed successful, and often quite easy, resuscitation attempts. Lay people come to believe that CPR works more often than not.

Clinical experience indicates that once older people understand CPR, the overwhelming majority prefer to forego CPR.[8] This is especially true considering that researchers have just begun to explore patients' preferences for CPR. The domains that have yet to be adequately included in utility studies include: (1) probability of outcome, (2) alternatives to CPR, and (3) marginal cost-effectiveness.

First, the hypothesis suggests that as older patients' understanding of the outcomes of CPR (mortality, morbidity, and length of survival) increases, the value these patients place on CPR decreases. Support for this hypothesis is obtained by simply asking health-care professionals if they would want CPR if they were old. The vast majority of health-care professionals would opt to forego CPR.[9]

Second, the hypothesis suggests that relatively healthy older people would forego CPR if they had a better understanding of the alternative, sudden death. Sudden death is an enemy we in the medical profession wish to conquer.[10] On the other hand, many older patients, though quite content with life and hoping to live for another 10 years, find sudden death an attractive way to die. It is quick, painless, and is not preceded by weeks or months of suffering.

Third, the hypothesis suggests that many older people favor a judicious use of limited health-care resources and that they themselves would discourage use of life-sustaining therapies that are only marginally beneficial. It is unlikely that many older people understand the marginal cost-effectiveness of CPR. It is possible that their preferences for CPR would be significantly influenced by this information. In summary, the additional understanding of CPR would tend to diminish an older person's preference for CPR.

When the discrepancy between effectiveness of and preference for a therapy is so great, we should conclude that the therapy is inappropriate. In other words, it is not medically indicated or it is futile.[11] CPR for many chronically ill older people is not medically indicated.[12]

Cost

The marginal cost-effectiveness[13] of CPR for chronically ill older people can be determined by the following equation:

Cost of CPR - Cost of no CPR / Probability of surviving with CPR
- Probability of surviving without CPR

If we choose one percent as the probability of surviving to discharge for out-of-hospital CPR, the resulting marginal cost benefit ratio would range from $225,000 to over $2 million per survivor, depending on the average length of hospital stay used in the calculation. In other words, society would be paying a minimum of a quarter of a million dollars, and perhaps as high as $2 million, in order for a chronically ill elder to return home (or to a nursing home) after CPR.

A more commonly used figure is the cost-per-year-of-life saved. Without better data on the long-term outcomes of CPR for chronically ill older people, we could not calculate this figure. However, if we assume that the average life expectancy of a chronically ill older person who has survived CPR is six months, the cost-per-year-of-life saved would range from $500,000 to $4 million (marginal cost divided by average life expectancy in years). Six months may actually be an overestimate, in which case the cost-per-year-of-life saved would be even higher.

At some point, we must admit that saving a life is not worth the expense to society. The "cost" of that life will of course depend on many factors, including age and health of the patient. Society may decide that $2 million is not too great a marginal cost to save the life of a child with leukemia. On the other hand, society may decide that 1/2 million dollars is too great a marginal cost to save the life of a chronically ill elder whose life expectancy is limited anyway. One hypothesis that deserves exploration is that older people themselves would judge the marginal cost benefit ratio of CPR inordinately high and thus consider it economically inappropriate.

In summary, CPR for chronically ill older people is both medically and economically inappropriate. The presumption that prevails in society today is that all older people are entitled to CPR and that CPR will be withheld only from those with Do-Not-Resuscitate orders.[14]   Based on this model of appropriate life-sustaining care, this presumption should change.   If the hypotheses outlined above are supported by further research on effectiveness, preferences, and cost, we should plan to develop new DNR policies that more effectively limit the use of inappropriate CPR.[15]

Hemodialysis

Effectiveness

Although hemodialysis may not improve the outcomes of some patients who are critically ill,[16] it clearly is effective for older patients who have chronic renal failure.[17]   The one-year survival rate is 77.4 percent for patients 65 to 74 years old, and 68.9 percent for patients 75 years and older.[18]   Unlike CPR, chronic hemodialysis accomplishes its goal in virtually all older people.

Preferences

Most studies indicate that patients on chronic hemodialysis rate their quality of life less than people without this burden.[19]   Some patients prefer death to continued hemodialysis.   In the study by Neu and Kjellstrand, one-half of the patients were competent when a decision was made to withdraw dialysis.[20] We may never know how demented patients view their quality of life on dialysis, but the prevailing impression is that most of these patients would not prefer long-term dialysis.[21]

On the other hand, many patients prefer long-term dialysis because they consider their quality of life very satisfactory, particularly patients on home dialysis.[22]   New treatments such as erythropoietin, which improves the anemia associated with chronic renal failure, show great promise for improving quality of life even more.[23]

The evidence suggests that most patients would rather receive dialysis than be treated palliatively, at least in the early stages.   The preference for dialysis, therefore, is much greater than it is for CPR.

Cost

The cost per life-year of patients treated with in-hospital dialysis has been estimated to be $10,000 in 1985 U.S. dollars,[24] $25,000 in 1977 U.S. dollars,[25] and $48,700 in 1980 Canadian dollars.[26] The cost for chronic ambulatory peritoneal dialysis is approximately 65 percent of the cost of hospital dialysis.[27] These figures would of course be higher if expressed in 1990 dollars. They would be significantly higher if the analyses focused only on older patients with significant comorbidities; that is, patients whose life expectancy is relatively short regardless of their kidney disease. For example, in 1978 patients with end-stage renal disease (ESRD) in Colorado used an average of $44,400 worth of charges in their last year.[28]

The cost-per-life-year of dialysis for patients with a low probability of surviving one year would indeed be high, perhaps high enough that society would consider therapy for these patients economically inappropriate. For most older patients with ESRD, the cost per life-year (perhaps as high as $50,000 in 1990 dollars) would probably not be considered economically inappropriate at this point in time.

As budgetary constraints grow, however, society may have to adjust the economic appropriateness threshold. Annual expenditures in Medicare's ESRD program had reached almost $2 billion for 92,770 beneficiaries in 1984.[29] This cost was grossly underestimated when Congress established the ESRD program in 1972. If the cost-effectiveness of Medicare's ESRD program is compared with other treatments for the same or other patient populations, it may be found wanting. We will then need to reconsider Great Britain's approach to the older patient with ESRD.[30]

Enteral Feedings

Effectiveness

The effectiveness of enteral feedings is similar to that of dialysis. Stated simply, it invariably works. With few exceptions, enteral feedings provide adequate nutrition. Despite complications, it is effective in maintaining physiologic functions.[31]

If we assume that one of the essential goals of medicine is either to restore the health or to maintain the health (as impaired as it may be) of a sentient person, then enteral feedings are frequently ineffective. Older patients in a persistent vegetative state--whether from stroke, advanced dementia, or head trauma--have lost their sentience. Enteral feedings effectively maintain their biologic life but cannot restore that which allows them to interact as humans. From this perspective, enteral feedings are futile.[32]

Preferences

Measurements of preferences for enteral feedings are similar to those for CPR. People can express what they may or may not desire in a hypothetical scenario, but we have no measurements of what patients who are receiving enteral feedings actually think about this therapy (in contrast to dialysis where we have some sense of how patients feel about the therapy). When considering hypothetical scenarios, one half of nursing home residents favor the use of enteral feedings as a life-sustaining measure[33] and 28-40 percent of patients in intensive care units favor this option.[34] These numbers would likely be much lower if the scenario was one of persistent vegetative state. If, as Schneiderman has suggested, persistent vegetative state is like a form of banishment,[35] it is hard to imagine that more than 1 percent of the population would want this form of life-sustaining care. Recent ethical and legal perspectives suggest that a significant proportion of older people would opt to forego enteral feedings if they truly understood the ramifications of long-term enteral feedings.[36]

Based on effectiveness and preferences, enteral feedings are medically appropriate for older patients who are sentient. Nevertheless, many of these patients may wish to forego this therapy. For patients with persistent vegetative state, enteral feedings are medically inappropriate.

Cost

Cost-effectiveness studies have not been done for enteral feedings in long-term care. However, the cost-per-life-year can be estimated as the cost of long-term care ($20,000 to $50,000) plus the additional cost of the nutritional supplement. One must consider that these figures actually represent the charges, not the true economic costs of providing care to these particular patients. The true costs would be higher than the charges. The total cost-per-life-year would be similar to that for chronic dialysis (e.g., $50,000 to $100,000). In some cases, it may be higher. For example, the estimated cost of caring for Nancy Cruzan for one year was $140,000.[37]

Currently this cost-per-life-year is not high enough to judge the therapy economically inappropriate. But considering the many other unmet health-care needs, not to mention other unmet social needs in our society,[38] we may need to lower the threshold for economic appropriateness in the coming decades.

Conclusion

Over the next decade life-sustaining care for older people will be more scrutinized by patients, providers, and payers. Although many factors determine the appropriateness of this care, three factors are primary: effectiveness, patient preferences, and cost. Study of these factors, particularly of patient preferences, is in its infancy. Nevertheless, analysis of these factors suggest that CPR and long-term enteral feedings are inappropriate for most older people, whereas hemodialysis is appropriate for most older people.

Society needs more research on these three primary factors in order to guide health-care policy. However, society may not be able to complete all the desired studies before it must make some difficult decisions about the appropriateness of life-sustaining care for older people.

Notes and References

1. M. B. Kapp, "Health Care Tradeoffs Based on Age: Ethically Confronting the 'R' Word," *The Pharos*, Summer 1989, pp. 2-7; R. D. Lamm, "Critical Decisions in Medical Care: Birth to Death," *Southern Medical Journal* Vol. 82 (July 1989), pp. 822-824; H. T. Englehardt, Jr. and M. A. Rie, "Intensive Care Units, Scarce Resources, and Conflicting Principles of Justice," *Journal of the American Medical Association*, Vol. 255 (March 7, 1986), pp. 1159-1164; Norman Daniels, *Am I My Parents' Keeper?* (New York: Oxford University Press, 1988); Daniel Callahan, *Setting Limits: Medical Goals in an Aging Society* (New York: Simon & Schuster, 1987).

2. S. E. Bedell, T. L. Delbanco, E. F. Cook, and F. H. Epstein, "Survival After Cardiopulmonary Resuscitation in the Hospital," *The New England Journal of Medicine*, Vol. 309 (Sept. 8, 1983), pp. 569-576; G. E. Taffet, T. A. Teasdale, and R J. Luchi, "In-hospital Cardiopulmonary Resuscitation," *Journal of the American Medical Association*, Vol. 260 (Oct. 14,1988), pp. 2069-2072; I. Fusgen and J. D. Summa, "How Much Sense Is There in an Attempt to

Resuscitate an Aged Person," *Gerontology*, Vol. 24 (1978), pp. 37-45; R. C. Peatfield, R. W. Sillett, D. Taylor, and M. W. McNicol, "Survival After Cardiac Arrest in Hospital," *Lancet*, Vol. 1 (June 11, 977), pp. 1223-1225; R. S. Gulati, G. L. Bhan, and M. A. Horan, "Cardiopulmonary Resuscitation of Old People," *Lancet*, Vol. 2 (July 30, 1983), pp. 267-269.

3. J. W. Bachman, G. S. McDonald, and P. C. O'Brien, "A Study of Out-of-Hospital Cardiac Arrests in Northeastern Minnesota," *Journal of the American Medical Association*, Vol. 256 (July 25, 1986), pp. 477-483; D. D. Tresch, R. K. Thakur, R. G. Hoffmann, et al., "Should the Elderly be Resuscitated Following Out-of-Hospital Cardiac Arrest," *American Journal of Medicine*, Vol. 86 (Feb., 1989), pp. 145-150; W. T. Longstreth, L. A. Cobb, C. E. Fahrenbruch, and M. K. Copass, "Does Age Affect Outcomes of Out-of-Hospital Cardiopulmonary Resuscitation?" *Journal of the American Medical Association*, Vol. 264 (Oct. 24/31, 1990), pp. 2109-2110; D. J. Murphy, A. M. Murray, B. E. Robinson, and E. W. Campion, "Outcomes of Cardiopulmonary Resuscitation in the Elderly," *Annals of Internal Medicine*, Vol. 111 (Aug. 1, 1989), pp. 199-205; G. E. Applebaum, J. E. King, and T. E. Finucane, "The Outcome of CPR Initiated in Nursing Homes," *Journal of the American Geriatric Society*, Vol. 38, Oct. 1990, pp. 197-200.

4. Applebaum et. al., "The Outcome of CPR Initiated in Nursing Homes."

5. M. A. Everhart and R. A. Pearlman. "Stability of Patient Preferences Regarding Life-Sustaining Treatments," *Chest*, Vol. 97 (Jan. 1990, pp. 159-164; D. J. Murphy, "Do-Not-Resuscitate Orders: Time for Reappraisal in Long-term Care Institutions," *Journal of the American Medical Association*, Vol. 260 (Oct. 14, 1988), pp. 2098-2101; S. E. Bedell, and T. L. Delbanco. "Choices About Cardiopulmonary Resuscitation in the Hospital: When Do Physicians Talk with Patients?" *The New England Journal of Medicine*, Vol. 310 (April 26, 1984), pp. 1089-1093; N. G. Smedira, B. H. Evans, L. S. Grais, et al., "Withholding and Withdrawal of Life Support from the Critically Ill," *The New England Journal of Medicine*, Vol. 322 (Feb. 1, 1990), pp. 309-315; C. J. Stolman, J. J. Gregory, D. Dunn, and J. L. Levine, "Evaluation of Patient, Physician, Nurse, and Family Attitudes Toward Do Not Resuscitate Orders," *Archives of Internal Medicine*, Vol. 150, (March 1990), pp. 653-658; T. J. Starr, R. A. Pearlman, and R. F. Uhlmann, "Quality of Life and Resuscitation Decisions in Elderly Patients," *Journal of General Internal Medicine*, Vol. 1 (Nov/Dec. 1986), pp. 373-379; R. F. Uhlmann, R. A. Pearlman, and K. C. Cain, "Physicians' and Spouses' Predictions of Elderly Patients' Resuscitation Preferences," *Journal of Gerontology*, Vol. 43 (Sept. 1988), pp. M115-M121.

6. M. A. Everhart and R. A. Pearlman, "Stability of Patient Preferences Regarding Life-Sustaining Treatments," *Chest*, Vol. 97 (Jan 1980), pp. 159-164

7. D. O. Miller, M. Gorbien, and D. W. Jahnigen, "Cardiopulmonary Resuscitation: How Useful? Attitudes and Knowledge of an Elderly Population," *Journal of the American Geriatric Society*, Vol. 38 (August 1990), pp. A-

38 (Abstract).

8. Murphy, "Do-Not-Resuscitate Orders."

9. L. L. Brunetti, S. D. Carperos, R. E. Westlund, "Physicians' Attitudes Towards Living Wills and Cardiopulmonary Resuscitation," *Journal of General Internal Medicine*, Vol. 6 (1990), pp. 323-329.

10. S. E. Epstein, A. A. Quyyumi, and R. O. Bonow, "Sudden Cardiac Death Without Warning: Possible Mechanisms and Implications for Screening Asymptomatic Populations," *The New England Journal of Medicine*, Vol. 321 (1989), pp. 320-324; P. J. Podrid, "Silent Ischemia, Ventricular Arrhythmia and Sudden Cardiac Death," *Journal of the American College of Cardiology*, Vol. 16 (1990), pp. 55-56.

11. D. J. Murphy and D. B. Matchar, "Life-sustaining Therapy: A Model for Appropriate Use," *Journal of the American Medical Association*, Vol. 264 (Oct. 24/31, 1990), pp. 2109-2110; L. J. Schneiderman, N. S. Jecker, and A. R. Jonsen, "Medical Futility: Its Meaning and Ethical Implications," *Annals of Internal Medicine*, Vol. 112 (June 15, 1990), pp. 949-954; S. H. Miles, "Informed Demand for 'Non-beneficial' Medical Treatment," *The New England Journal of Medicine*, Vol. 325 (Aug. 15, 1991), pp. 512-515.

12. D. H. Solomon, "The US and the UK: An Ocean Apart?" *Journal of the American Geriatric Society*, Vol. 38 (March 1990), 259-260; R. Baker, "Beyond Do-Not-Resuscitate Orders," in *Rationing of Medical Care for the Critically Ill*, edited by M. A. Strosberg, I. A. Fein, and J. D. Carroll (Washington, D.C.: The Brookings Institute, 1989), pp. 52-63; R. Buckman, and I. Senn, "Eligibility for CPR: Is Every Death a Cardiac Arrest?" *Canadian Medical Association Journal*, Vol. 140 (1989), pp. 1068-1069; J. Hammond and C. G. Ward, "Decision Not to Treat: 'Do Not Resuscitate' Order for the Burn Patient in the Acute Setting," *Critical Care Medicine*, Vol. 17 (Feb. 1989), pp. 136-138; P. J. Podrid, "Resuscitation in the Elderly: A Blessing or a Curse?" *Annals of Internal Medicine*, Vol. 111 (Aug. 1, 1989), pp. 193-195; T. Tomlinson and H. Brody, "Ethics and Communication in Do-Not-Resuscitate Orders," *The New England Journal of Medicine*, Vol. 318 (Jan. 7, 1988), pp. 43-46; L. J. Blackhall, "Must We Always Use CPR?" *The New England Journal of Medicine*, Vol. 317 (Nov. 12, 1987), pp. 1281-1285; A. S. Brett and L. B. McCullough, "When Patients Request Specific Interventions: Defining the Limits of the Physician's Obligation," *The New England Journal of Medicine*, Vol. 315 (Nov. 20, 1986), pp. 1347-1351; L. Volicer, Y. Rheaume, J. Brown, et al., "Hospice Approach to the Treatment of Patients with Advanced Dementia of the Alzheimer Type," *Journal of the American Medical Association*, Vol. 256 (Oct. 24/31, 1986), pp. 2210-2213; G. J. Annas, "CPR: When the Beat Should Stop," *The Hastings Center Report*, Vol. 12 (Aug. 1982), pp. 27-29; R. A. Carson and M. Siegler, "Does 'Doing Everything' Include CPR?" *The Hastings Center Report*, Vol. 12 (Oct. 1982), pp. 27-29.

13. D. J. Murphy and D. B. Matchar, "Life-sustaining Therapy: A Model

for Appropriate Use;" A. S. Detsky and I. G. Naglie, "A Clinician's Guide to Cost-effectiveness Analysis," *Annals of Internal Medicine*, Vol. 113 (May 1990), pp. 147-154.

14.   K. Gleeson and S. Wise, "The Do-Not-Resuscitate Order: Still Too Little Too Late," *Archives of Internal Medicine*, Vol. 150 (1990), pp. 1057-1060.

15.   G. L. Snider, "The Do-Not Resuscitate Order: Ethical and Legal Imperative or Medical Decision?" *American Review of Respiratory Disease*, Vol. 143 (1991), pp. 665-674.

16.   E. R. Maher, K. N. Robinson, J. E. Scoble, et al., "Prognosis of Critically-ill Patients With Acute Renal Failure: APACHE II Score and Other Predictive Factors," *Quarterly Journal of Medicine*, Vol. 72 (March 14, 1989), pp. 857-866; J. E. Dobkin, R. E. Cutler, "Use of APACHE II Classification to Evaluate Outcome of Patients Receiving Hemodialysis in an Intensive Care Unit" *The Western Journal of Medicine*, Vol. 149 (Nov. 1988), pp. 547-550.

17.   A. T. Roy, L. E. Johnson, D. B. N. Lee, N. Brautbar, and J. E. Morley, "Renal Failure in Older People: UCLA Grand Rounds," *Journal of the American Geriatric Society*, Vol. 38 (March 1990), pp. 239-253.

18.   U.S. Congress, Office of Technology, *Assessment, Life-Sustaining Technologies and the Elderly*, OTA-BA-306 (Washington, D.C.: U.S. Government Printing Office, 1987).

19.   R. W. Evans, D. L. Manninen, L. P. Garrison, Jr., et al., "The Quality of Life of Patients With End-Stage Renal Disease," *The New England Journal of Medicine*, Vol. 312 (Feb. 28, 1985), pp. 553-559; D. G. Husebye, L. Westlie, T. J. Styrvoky, and C. M. Kjellstrand, "Psychological, Social, and Somatic Prognostic Indicators in Old Patients Undergoing Long-term Dialysis," *Archives of Internal Medicine*, Vol. 147 (Nov. 1987), pp. 1921-1924; B. Oldenburg, G. J. Macdonald, and R. J. Perkins, "Prediction of Quality of Life in a Cohort of End-Stage Renal Disease Patients" *Journal of Clinical Epidemiology*, Vol. 41 (June 1988), pp. 555-564.

20.   S. Neu and C. M. Kjellstrand, "Stopping Long-Term Dialysis: An Empirical Study of Withdrawal of Life-Supporting Treatment," *The New England Journal of Medicine*, Vol. 314 (Jan. 2, 1986), pp. 14-20.

21.   M. Kaye and J. W. Lella, "Discontinuation of Dialysis Therapy in the Demented Patient," American *Journal of Nephrology*, Vol. 6 (1986), pp. 75-79.

22.   R. W. Evans, D. L. Manninen, L. P. Garrison, Jr., et al., "The Quality of Life of Patients With End-Stage Renal Disease," in U.S. Congress, Office of Technology Assessment, *Life-Sustaining Technologies and the Elderly*.

23.   Canadian Erythropoietin Study Group, "Association Between Recombinant Human Erythropoietin and Quality of Life and Exercise Capacity of Patients Receiving Hemodyalysis," *British Medical Journal*, Vol. 300 (1990), pp. 573-578; R. W. Evans, B. Rader, D. L. Manninen, and Cooperative Multicenter EPO Clinical Trial Group, "The Quality of Life of

Hemodialysis Recipients Treated with Recombinant Human Erythropioetin," *Journal of the American Medical Association*, Vol. 263 (Feb. 9, 1990), pp. 825-830.

24. R. Sesso, J. M. Eisenberg, C. Stabile, S. Draibe, H. Ajzen, and O. Ramos, "Cost-effectiveness Analysis of the Treatment of End-Stage Renal Disease in Brazil," *International Journal of Health Services*, Vol. 6 (1990), pp. 107-114.

25. S. D. Roberts, D. R. Maxwell, and T. L. Gross, "Cost-Effective Care of End-Stage Renal Disease: A Billion Dollar Question," *Annals of Internal Medicine*, Vol. 92 (Feb. 1980), pp. 243-248; P. V. Stange and A. T. Sumner, "Predicting Treatment Costs and Life Expectancy for End-Stage Renal Disease," *The New England Journal of Medicine*, Vol. 298 (Feb. 16, 1978), pp. 372-378.

26. D. N. Churchill, B. C. Lemon, and G. W. Torrance, "A Cost-effectiveness Analysis of Continuous Ambulatory Peritoneal Dialysis and Hospital Hemodialysis," *Medical Decision Making*, Vol. 4 (1984), pp. 489-500.

27. S. D. Roberts, D. R. Maxwell, and T. L. Gross, "Cost-Effective Care of End-Stage Renal Disease;" P. V. Stange, A. T. Sumner, "Predicting Treatment Costs and Life Expectancy for End-Stage Renal Disease;" D. N. Churchill, B. C. Lemon, and G. W. Torrance, "A Cost-effectiveness Analysis of Continuous Ambulatory Peritoneal Dialysis of Hospital Hemodialysis."

28. N. McCall, "Utilization and Costs of Medicare Services by Beneficiaries in Their Last Year of Life," *Medical Care*, Vol. 22 (1984), pp. 329-342.

29. U.S. Congress Office of Technology Assessment, *Life-Sustaining Technologies and the Elderly*.

30. C. Potter and J. Porter, "American Perceptions of the British National Health Service: Five Myths," *Journal of Health, Politics, Policy and Law*, Vol. 14 (Summer 1989), pp. 341-365.

31. B. Lo and L. Dornbrand, "Understanding the Benefits and Burdens of Tube Feedings," *Archives of Internal Medicine*, Vol. 149 (Sept. 1989), pp. 1925-1926; T. E. Quill, "Utilization of Nasogastric Feeding Tubes in a Group of Chronically Ill, Elderly Patients in a Community Hospital," *Archives of Internal Medicine*, Vol. 149 (Sept. 1989), pp. 1937-1941; J. O. Ciocon, F. A. Silverstone, L. M. Graver, and C. J. Foley, "Tube Feedings in Elderly Patients: Indications, Benefits, and Complications," *Archives of Internal Medicine*, Vol. 148 (Feb. 1988), pp. 429-433; D. G. Smith, and R. S. Wigton, "Modeling Decisions to Use Tube Feeding in Seriously Ill Patients," *Archives of Internal Medicine*, Vol. 147 (July 1987), pp. 1242-1245.

32. Schneiderman, Jecker, and Jonsen, "Medical Futility."

33. J. Kayser-Jones, "The Use of Nasogastric Feeding Tubes in Nursing Homes: Patient, Family and Health Care Provider Perspectives," *The Gerontologist*, Vol. 30 (August 1990), pp. 469-479.

34. Everhart and Pearlman, "Stability of Patient Preferences Regarding Life-Sustaining Treatments."

35. L. J. Schneiderman, "Exile and PVS," *The Hastings Center Report,* Vol. 20 (Jan. 1990), p. 5.

36. G. J. Annas, "Precatory Prediction and Mindless Mimicry: The Case of Mary O'Connor," *The Hastings Center Report,* Vol. 18 (1988), pp. 31-33; M. Angell, "Prisoners of Technology: The Case of Nancy Cruzan," *The New England Journal of Medicine,* Vol. 322 (April 26, 1990), pp. 1226-1228; J. Lynn and J. F. Childress, "Must Patients Always Be Given Food and Water," *The Hastings Center Report,* Vol. 13 (1983), pp. 17-21: R. F. Weir and L. Gostin, "Decisions to Abate Life-Sustaining Treatment for Nonautonomous Patients: Ethical Standards and Legal Liability for Physicians After Cruzan," *Journal of the American Medical Association,* Vol. 264 (Oct. 10, 1990), pp. 1846-1853.

37. *Cruzan v. Director of Missouri Department of Health,* 109 S. Ct. 3240, 1989.

38. D. Callahan, *What Kind of Life: The Limits of Medical Progress* (New York: Simon & Schuster, 1990).

8

Can We Set Limits
and Enhance Autonomy?

Lawrence J. Schneiderman

Introduction

Two social movements over the past decade of health care in the
United States have attracted the particular attention of ethicists.
One, in response to soaring costs, is the urgent call for rationing and
resource allocation that is more specific and consistent than the
haphazard socioeconomic forms now in place. The second movement
is the rising tide of patient autonomy including demands to be
involved in terminal health-care decisions even after the loss of
mental competence. By now nearly every state has legalized some
form of advance directive, such as the living will or durable power
of attorney, specifically designed for health-care decisions.

Until recently these movements have carried on without any
apparent recognition of each other. Those who proposed rationing
criteria to hold down costs rarely considered patient preferences;
those who advocated patient autonomy rarely referred to cost
considerations. Daniel Callahan, in fact sees them on a collision
course, accusing the "powerful, unremitting public demand for better
health and a longer life," of being the major obstacle to cost
containment.[1] "Most of the growth in health-care expenditures," he
says "has come about because of the growth of public demand, a
demand insulated for the most part by third-party payments,
allowing individual health needs with little worry about the
personal financial cost to themselves or the collective cost to
society."[2] Note how often Callahan uses the word "demand" rather

than "utilization." True, there is ever-mounting health-care utilization. That is an empirically supportable observation. But that all utilization is due to public demand is an unchallenged assumption.

What Does the Public Demand?

I concede that there *is* a public demand for many of medicine's marvels, which range from dermatological treatment of wrinkles and baldness to in vitro fertilization and organ transplantation. But these are the choices that are offered, choices not made within the context of alternative choices, such as, Would you rather have treatment for baldness or funding for home health care? Nor is the public demand entirely selfish. High impact media events, like that provoked by the poignant story of a child seeking a potentially life-saving bone marrow transplant, become televised dramas in the intimacy of our homes and arouse deep and laudable impulses of sympathy. Why don't they *do* something for the unfortunate child? The state of Oregon, by *not* doing something--that is, by refusing to fund the bone marrow transplant under its Medicaid--program was deemed by many to be cruel and callous.

But, as Larry Churchill says, "It is the role of reason to render our sentiments more public and social--to extend beyond the range of our immediate encounters."[3] In other words, reason should permit us to see the hundreds and thousands of children who do not get on television, whose lives depend on prenatal care and immunization, and are bartered for the child receiving the transplant.

It is true that medicine is becoming more complex, technological, miraculous and expensive. But how much is due to public demand? Many observers have pointed out that, in fact, it is physicians who determine the supply and demand market. Increase the supply of physicians, and you increase the utilization and cost of medical services. This is so because physicians largely generate their own business. As Churchill states, "They are simultaneously the experts who decide who needs care, how much care, and what kind of care patients need (gatekeepers) and the recipients of the financial rewards."[4] Medicine is, in the words of Paul Starr, the "sovereign profession."

So, it is time to point out that there is evidence for quite a different kind of public demand than that assumed by Callahan and others. Almost every survey of elderly people shows that they do *not* want aggressive medical intervention in the face of terminal illness. Ironically, what has stirred the movement to develop advance directives has not been the demand for *more* care but the demand for *less* care. At its most extreme, this movement is calling for the right to active euthanasia. And the propelling images are not bodies resurrected to life, but insensate bodies entangled in a morass of wires and tubes--images that have come to characterize unrestrained technological power over more humane considerations.

What have been the practical consequences so far of this movement for advance directives? Much and yet remarkably little. Today living wills and durable powers of attorney are widely available, yet only a small fraction of people, healthy or ill, have executed such documents. This leads to the question: If patients really do not want high-technology, expensive life-saving care, what would happen if greater efforts were made to make such advance directives available to patients? Would this implementation of autonomy result in fewer unwanted procedures and reduced medical costs? One could also imagine other goods coming from more patient involvement in medical decision-making: better communication and greater satisfaction and well-being, for example. But one could also imagine harms, particularly if patients put a brake on physicians' drive to cure: neglect, abandonment, and other more subtle forms of diminished medical attention.

In any event, these questions are serious enough to merit addressing. If enthusiasm for advance directives is misguided, we should know that. If the consequences of using such directives are good--that is, if health care is improved and, at the same time, costs are reduced--then the focus of thinking currently prevalent among health policy makers might be encouraged to shift. The solution to rising health costs--at least with regard to high-technology terminal care--could be seen less in terms of imposing limits by rationing and more in terms of enhancing patient autonomy. This would be a more universally acceptable ethical solution; it would be a solution that would not require a frontal assault on the country's sacred values of individual rights. Even if it seems outrageous, the question is worth addressing: Is it possible that ethical individualism does not invariably lead to destruction of the medical commons?

But, says Callahan, there is, as yet, no good evidence that giving people more choice about their manner of dying will save money. He is correct since without good research there can be no good evidence, only speculation and extrapolation. For example, he points to the fact that although hospital care constitutes the single largest component of total health care costs, approximately 40 percent, Medicare data collected in the late 1970s show that the large burden of medical care costs at the end of life were *not* disproportionately due to aggressive intensive treatment of moribund patients. Since then, however, hospital costs have continued to soar, and intensive care unit activities have become more complex and expensive. Economists now estimate that advances in high-technology medicine have contributed at least one-fifth of the growth last year in health-care spending. Might not efforts to reduce aggressive treatment in terminal care have more impact today?

A Study of the Use of Advance Directives

With these thoughts my colleagues, Robert Kaplan and John Anderson, and I embarked upon a randomized, longitudinal, experimental trial of the effects of advance directives on the health care of 200 patients with life-threatening diseases (defined as having no better than a 50 percent five-year survival). The diseases included cancer, chronic renal disease, chronic pulmonary disease, cardiovascular disease and AIDS. Since offering an advance directive to patients was not standard care, we were able to assign patients randomly to two alternate groups: one group offered the California's Durable Power of Attorney for Health Care, and a control group not offered an advance directive. We used the official form supplied by the California Medical Association which includes provisions for naming a surrogate and for specific instructions, as well as a summary portion which enables the patient to indicate one or another of the following three choices:

1. I do *not* want my life to be prolonged and I do *not* want sustaining treatment to be provided or continued if the burdens of the treatment outweigh the expected benefits. I want my agent to consider the relief of suffering and the quality of life as well as the possible extension of my life in making decisions concerning life-sustaining treatment.
2. I want my life to be prolonged and I want life-sustaining treatment to be provided *unless I am in a coma* which my doctors reasonably believe to be irreversible. Once my doctors have reasonably concluded I am in irreversible coma, I do not want life-sustaining treatment to be provided or continued.
3. I want my life to be prolonged to the greatest extent possible without regard to my condition, the chances I have for recovery, or the cost of the procedures.

The patients also summarized their instructions in a single page "Notice to My Health Care Providers." This notice was inserted in

The patients also summarized their instructions in a single page "Notice to My Health Care Providers." This notice was inserted in the patient's chart and checked at every hospitalization in order to insure that physicians had access to the patient's advance directive instructions at all times. The patients were interviewed in their homes at regular intervals to obtain data with respect to their general well-being, satisfaction with health care, health status, and health-care utilization. If a patient died, a close family member was interviewed to obtain data on these measures just prior to the death. Medical records of all the patients were also reviewed to document procedures and hospital costs.

Results of the Study

This study is still in progress; therefore, our data collection and analyses are not complete. But here are some of the highlights so far:

1. At the time of first contact, only 2 percent of patients had previously executed any form of advance directive. These patients, it should be remembered, were all aware they had a serious illness with a high probability of mortality.

2. Only 23 percent of patients contacted refused entry into this study. This is a gratifying sign that the vast majority of patients--sick as they are--are willing to participate in clinical research, even when it involves emotionally difficult questions.

3. Approximately 70 percent of patients offered the Durable Power of Attorney for Health Care and asked to participate in the study, returned the notice confirming that they had executed the document. These patients had to overcome at least three obstacles: (1) executing the Durable Power of Attorney for Health Care, (2) returning the notice to inform us of this, and (3) agreeing to participate in our study, which involved repeated interviews. Thus, the high percentage choosing to participate reveals, I believe, a strong interest in advance directives--if they are offered.

4. Of those executing the advance directive, 80 percent selected option one described above. In other words, they specified that they do not want life prolonged if the burdens of treatment outweigh the expected benefits. They do want

their agent to consider relief from suffering and the quality of life as well as the extension of life in making life-sustaining treatment decisions. Another 18 percent stated they wanted life-sustaining treatment to be provided unless they are in irreversible coma (option two). Thus a total of 98 percent of these patients executing the advance directive wanted to *limit* life-sustaining medical treatment under certain conditions. So much for the "powerful unremitting public demand for a longer life."

5. Only two patients stated that they wanted their life prolonged to the greatest extent possible without regard to their condition, the chances for recovery, or the cost of the procedures (option three).

6. We were relieved to note that there were no apparent adverse consequences of executing the advance directive. That is, there were no significant differences between the two groups in general well-being, satisfaction with health care, health status and mortality.

7. Although there was a strong correlation between general instructions on the California Durable Power of Attorney for Health Care form and specific wishes with respect to procedures, in individual cases the relationships between general instructions and specific procedure preferences were inconsistent. Most patients who executed the advance directive did not want artificial nutrition to sustain them for a lengthy period of time in the hospital. On the other hand, most patients *did* want cardiopulmonary resuscitation in the event of cardiac arrest and hospitalization in the event of pneumonia. Unfortunately, it appears that the instructions offered on the California Durable Power of Attorney for Health Care do not provide reliable guidance to physicians in the event of loss of patient decision-making capacity.

8. Advance directives and preferences regarding specific procedures proved stable over time except for the two individuals who at entry wanted highly aggressive treatment under all medical circumstances. Within a year, the one survivor had become uncertain about all these choices.

9. Finally--and again emphasizing that we are still in the midst of our study--we have found no significant differences in life-saving procedures or medical costs between the group offered the advance directive and the group not offered the directive.

Further Questions

So, at this point we agree with Callahan that there is no good evidence that giving people more choice about their manner of dying saves money. Or more precisely if there is an effect, it is not large enough to be captured by our data collection and analyses so far.

But we are already beginning to ask why? How can this be? If patients are claiming that they do not want expensive life-saving medical procedures, why are there not more obvious measurable effects, such as reduced days in the intensive care unit, fewer days on the ventilator, less cardiopulmonary resuscitation (CPR), and so forth? Are patients changing their minds? (Our information so far does not support this.) Are patients in the control group communicating their wishes just as well as those in the advance directive group? (We do not know.) Is it possible that comfort care is just as complex and expensive as aggressive life-saving care? (Possible, but not likely.)

We have begun to carry out additional investigations in a slightly different direction. Following the lead of other investigators, who showed that physicians and spouses have poor insight into patients' wishes, we took the next step and asked physicians to do two things: not only *predict* their patients' choices but also indicate what choices they would make for *themselves* if they were in the same circumstances as their patients. In other words, we wanted to find out not only how well physicians knew of their patients' wishes, but also whether the physicians' wishes for themselves *influenced* their perception of their patients' wishes. Some of these effects were large. In line with others, we discovered that physicians have little insight into their patients' wishes. With the exception of CPR, all their predictions were significantly different from the choices their patients actually made. Moreover it appears that the physicians' self-preferences account for these differences.

Already this line of inquiry shows some hope of unlocking the problem. In contrast to Callahan's assumption that patients' demands are accounting for inappropriate and extravagant use of medical resources, it may well be that patients' demands are sometimes being ignored and that physicians themselves are driving such utilization. We should be clear, however, that our study does not involve persons who are for the most part healthy and who may indeed want to draw as extensively as possible on medicine's resources to preserve their good health. Our study involves patients who know they have a mortal illness and who have become accustomed over time to dealing with the risks as well as the benefits of what medicine has to offer, with all the pain, suffering, and burdens that result from the ravages of not only the disease, but the treatment. It does not seem to be an unreasonable hypothesis to pursue further, however, that when people become sick most of them come to terms with the notion of their mortality, that the goals they seek are not longevity as much as comfort and dignity, and that, therefore, they would prefer the simple measures of compassion to the harsh (and more expensive) technology that is often applied against their wishes.

Conclusion

In any event, whether or not enhancing patient autonomy serves as a cost-cutting measure it would be more compatible with our current traditions of ethical individualism, or as Callahan views it, "the pervasive beliefs in our culture that it is good to live a long, even longer life; that it is good to use the mind and the economy in devising ways to cure disease and control death; and that it is good to give people choice about the fate of their health and their bodies . . ."[5] All this, he says--in what seems little more than a cry of despair--will cause reform efforts to fail unless there is "a ready willingness to change, modify and compromise those values."[6]

But perhaps we do not understand those values as well as we think. What I am suggesting of course is that if we want to have it both ways, that is, setting limits through enhancing autonomy, we have to involve the cooperation of that most powerful agent, the physician. To begin with, the physician will have to seek to understand and be more responsive to the patient. I hope that this is not also a cry of despair.

Notes and References

1. Daniel Callahan, *What Kind of Life? The Limits of Medical Progress* (New York: Simon & Schuster, 1990),
2. Ibid.
3. Larry R. Churchill, *Rationing Health Care in America*, (Notre Dame: University of Notre Dame Press, 1987),
4. Paul Starr, *The Social Transformation of American Medicine* (New York: Basic Books, 1982).
5. Callahan, *What Kind of Life?*
6. Ibid.

PART FOUR

Economics and Public Policy

9

Is Global Budgeting the Way to Set Limits on Health Care for the Elderly?

Michael D. Reagan

Introduction

Ethical principles and propositions, no matter how rigorously or elegantly delineated in the discourse of ethics, do not implement themselves. To reach the doctor and patient, they must be applied through policy-making institutions and the organizations that constitute the health-care "delivery system." In the realm of health care for the elderly, those institutions are dominated by the federal government's Medicare program. Since political science focuses strongly on public sector institutions, their internal governing structures and their external relationships to constituencies and client groups, a political scientist may thus be able to contribute to the discussion.

To make this more concrete, consider the provocative, seminal writings of Daniel Callahan, who argues that we are overspending on health care for the elderly relative to other societal needs, and that limits should be set on such spending.[1] Very specifically, he advocates a flat age limitation in the late 70s or early 80s, by which time one is assumed to have lived a "natural life-span." Since the purpose of the limits is to free up funds for use in other high priority areas (perhaps health care for children, or housing for the homeless, or educational reform, to choose some widely-advocated needs), implementation questions arise: *How* is the trade-off (the transfer of funds) to be accomplished? By *whom*? What institution or individual will set the policy that establishes the priorities implied by the very concept of limits?[2] In other words, have we an adequate, appropriate societal mechanism for accomplishing the trade-off? How do we get from the concept to the practical reality?

Callahan does not provide an explicit answer to such questions. Rather, he calls for a shift in attitudes and values--among health-care professionals and the general public--that would lead to public acceptance of a policy of age-based limitations. By inference, we can see that acceptance of this new ethic would still require an institutional context in which to transfer the funds from lower to higher priority uses. What Callahan tells us directly, however, is simply that even though a "reduction of spending on the elderly in no way guarantees that the money saved would be spent wisely or well," to spend more on the elderly "almost ensures" inadequate budgets for other needs.[3] He would, therefore, reduce the expenditures (which has to mean, concretely, the Medicare budget, because it is the largest source of resources for elderly health-care) in order to make the resources available for other needs.

Norman Daniels, another medical ethicist, also sees a need to set limits, including rationing by age on the basis of a concept he terms the "prudential lifespan account." He departs sharply from Callahan, however, when it comes to the conditions under which such rationing (in the sense of denying potentially beneficial care) may be justifiably imposed. Daniels argues that individual physicians should not say "No" to some patients in order to save resources for others until we have in place a closed system in which explicit trade-offs could be made with some assurance that what would be saved on the aged would go to support socially-determined higher priority uses, and would not just be released for adding to investors' profit (in a for-profit hospital chain) or for additional military weaponry.[4]

The concept of a closed system brings me to the central focus of this essay: Is "global budgeting," made possible by a closed system, the way to set limits on health care for the elderly?

Global Budgeting

Global budgeting in health care can be defined as an institutional arrangement that has a single payer, comprehensive in both demographic scope and medical care coverage. Putting it less formally, global budgeting means a single buyer for all, or nearly all, health-care services for the entire population. Britain's National Health Service fits this definition; so does Canada's universal health insurance system--though the global budgeting is done by each of the ten provinces, using a unified combination of its own tax revenues and a formula grant from the national government in Ottawa.

In Canada, all patients are eligible for care, and all bills are paid by the province. Individual physicians may opt out of the system entirely, but few do because those who do may not provide services offered by the public system. The cost in Canada is less per person (in 1989: U.S., $2,354; Canada, $1,683) and a substantially lower share of gross domestic product than in the United States (1989: U.S., 11.8 percent; Canada, 8.7 percent). It is thus understandable that Canadian global budgeting has received much attention in this country as an overall key to effective cost control without denial of necessary care or leaving 15-18 percent of the population out of the insurance system, as we now do.

The Canadian system provides an effective way to implement--some might say, enforce--a national policy that primary care for all takes precedence over expensive, high-tech elective care for some. Thus Canadians (like the British) face waiting lists for things like hip replacements in the elderly. If, however, policymakers (health ministry officials acting with the approval of the Parliament) should decide tomorrow that priorities should be reversed, they have an institutional means for accomplishing that.

Analogously, *if* the United States had a global budgeting system like Canada's, and *if* it covered almost all of the population, then there would be a context for the kind of inter-generational and inter-program shifts discussed by Callahan and Daniels. But the "ifs" are too great. Global budgeting for health is not a politically practicable approach for us.

Why not? The short answer can be given in two words: *pluralism* in our society; *fragmentation* in our governmental structure. Let me spell these out.

Trouble With Global Budgeting in the U.S.

The United States and Canada are both representative democracies, but Canada has a much more disciplined political system than ours--one that is far more capable of centralizing decision-making. By more disciplined I mean both in governmental structure and political party characteristics. Canada's parliamentary system, in which the executive leadership is drawn from the majority party in the legislature (nationally and in each province) ensures executive-legislative cooperation with few exceptions. Partly because of this, and partly contributing to it, is a party system of more homogeneous ideology in each party and stronger levers of party leadership with which to enforce the party position than in the U.S.

The United States is characterized, on the other hand, by loose, undisciplined parties with diverse internal ideologies, and a governmental system built on decentralizing and thwarting power, constitutionally separating the executive and legislative branches. Furthermore, our political culture encourages a kind of "group individualism," by which I mean that each group goes its own way, seeking to avoid subordination of its narrow interests to the broader compromises that a stronger party structure might be able to impose.

Another major difference in politico-economic culture is the U.S. emphasis upon economic individualism and the use of the market to distribute services that are socially (i.e., governmentally) distributed in Canada and most of Europe. In health care, this translates into the fact that in the U.S. 58 percent of health care is financed in the private sector and only 42 percent flows through public budgets. In Canada, 90 percent flows through government budgets. This difference is crucial to explaining why a global budget is feasible there but not here: No one payer is even close to being a single dominant buyer of health care here. To change that would mean turning to a publicly sponsored national health insurance system, and the aforementioned market individualism of our culture has so far been an absolute bar against such a development.

U.S. pluralism (that is, the large number of diverse points of power and influence) is also strong within both the private and public sectors, further inhibiting any potential cooperative efforts to achieve something close to all-payer budgets on a national basis, as a close substitute for full global budgeting. Within the private sector, we have not-for-profit voluntary hospitals as the dominant organizational mode, but a few strong for-profit chains of hospitals have developed in recent years. Under the stimulus of federal controls over in-patient hospital charges, the 1980s brought free-standing out-patient surgical facilities into play as yet another interest group. Fee-for-service (FFS) individual practice by physicians is increasingly being challenged by various kinds of group practices, both FFS and prepaid (which we call HMOs or health maintenance organizations). Some of these changes represent positive innovations, but collectively their pluralism impedes any effort to impose a single set of priorities on health-care delivery.

Even in the governmental health sector taken alone, we are far from a global budget. The two major health insurance programs are operated as separate entities on separate distributional principles and with varied financing. Medicare is a national government program (whose day-to-day operation is in the hands of private intermediary groups), financed by payroll taxes (the hospital segment) and by a mix of general tax revenues and premiums paid by the elderly who are the beneficiaries (for the physician segment). It is a universal program for all those 65 and over in age, plus the disabled. Medicaid was established by national legislation, but is jointly financed by the national and state governments, and most of the decisions of what and whom to cover are made by the 50 states. National law requires that the states provide Medicaid coverage to everyone eligible for means-tested income assistance (that is, Aid to Families with Dependent Children--AFDC). But each state sets its own income limit for AFDC and thus, effectively, for Medicaid as well. And those limits range from an income 83 percent of the poverty level down to about 20 percent.

Putting all these elements together, we see the enormity of the task of creating a global budget out of long-established partial programs that reflect and give continuing support to a plurality of systems, not *a* system. We will not soon have global budgeting as a base for trade-offs in the use of health-care resources.

This seems like an appropriate place to dispose of a related matter. It is often argued that we should not ration or limit health care for the elderly (or for anyone else, in most such arguments) as long as we spend many billions of dollars on tobacco, liquor, drugs and gambling. While I would agree with the values this argument espouses, we must ask, How would we make that shift of resources? If one really wants to see society insist on such a trade-off, it could only be done by a kind of society-wide global budgeting in which the government imposed that set of priorities on the population. Even if done after due deliberation by Congress, I think most of us would call that an unacceptable denial of personal freedom. This would not be global budgeting but dictatorship. If the argument is a plea that citizens should give up such wasteful or harmful expenditures in order to pay higher taxes to support a stronger health-care system, then it may serve as a conscience prod toward incremental change, but clearly is not going to accomplish much in the short run.

If I have argued convincingly that a national--or even a state by state--global budgeting closed system is not foreseeably feasible, then what other options might we suggest as ways of achieving some of the Callahan goal of making funds available for other needs by reducing elderly health-care expenditures?

Other Options

Two general points should be made before citing specific approaches. First, *any* health-care expenditure reduction--whatever the age of the patient involved--that can be made without reducing necessary treatment or the quality of medicine (and we do know that there are many unnecessary tests and procedures) will serve to free up funds for higher priority needs. This is based on the premise that our pluralistic institutions choose to use the funds released in that way, rather than just as more for everyday consumer expenditures. Thus all the resource-releasing limits need not necessarily be imposed exclusively on the elderly. Second, institutional changes in the delivery system that produce more effective use of resources (that is, making the same amount stretch further) can, even without expenditure reduction, accomplish some of the primary objective of doing more to meet total needs.

Now let's get more specific.

Many of the cost containment measures adopted in recent years by third-party payers--both governmental and business--follow an economic model: They are based in financial analysis and attempt to change financial patterns without, ostensibly, limiting useful care. Most obvious among these is the greatly increased level of cost-sharing called for in employer-provided health plans. Where once there was "first-dollar" coverage (that is, the entire charge by hospital or physician was insurance covered) there is often now a co-payment (say, 20 percent), to be paid by the patient, with the insurance covering 80 percent. Where the employer once paid all of the tab for insurance, now the employee pays part of the insurance premium if choosing a plan that costs more than the fixed sum contribution set by the employer. And some employers are no longer covering dependents at all, thus reducing the company's costs (if not society's), by throwing people into the uninsured group. In the public sector, we have the diagnosis-related groups (DRGs) system of prospective payment, in which Medicare has set fixed fees for some 480 in-patient hospital treatments.

Quite different--and I think much less likely to endanger the quality of care or deny necessary care--are what I call medical model cost controls. These are measures that start by analyzing a characteristic of medical practice and assessing its necessity, or the specific conditions for which it is appropriate, or finding the most cost-effective mode of treatment.[5] Among these medically-grounded ways to save money are included technology assessment, utilization review, practice guidelines, and a relative value scale for setting physician fees. Let's look briefly at each of these.

Technological improvements--from heart transplants to medications that make transplant rejections much less likely, and from knee and hip replacements to the drug AZT for AIDS patients--constitute a great source of pride in American biomedical research and practice. We have certainly done much that is amazing and contributes greatly to life extension and to improved quality of life. But most of the high-tech advancements, unfortunately, come with a high price tag. In many cases, an assessment will lead to consensus that the expense is worthwhile; but not always. Electronic monitoring of the heartrate of premature infants has not been found to be more effective than monitoring by stethescope; the coronary by-pass is said to be over-used. And one new drug for dissolving bloodclots in heart attack patients costs almost 12 times as much as an older one that a large research study found to be just as effective. If we spent as much thought and money in determining when a new technology was cost-effective as we do on basic workability, we might save both money and patients' lives.

Still, the technological thrust need not, in principle, always produce greater expenditure. A renal transplant reduces by two-thirds the cost of maintaining a patient with end-stage renal disease. Could not the National Institutes of Health adjust priorities to encourage a focus on cost-reducing innovations?

Utilization review (UR) is, understandably, an unpopular term among physicians, for it means someone looking over their shoulders, second-guessing them. UR takes several forms. One is prospective, requiring second opinions before performing selected procedures, for example. Another is after the fact, reviewing the rates of procedures done by physicians practicing in a given hospital, or community, and providing them all with printouts for self-comparison--sometimes followed up by discussion with those whose rates are far higher than the norm.[6]

While much UR has been cost-stimulated, it is increasingly being focused on quality, as measured by effectiveness. Medicare has an "effectiveness initiative," and a system of "outcomes management" is being developed by Ellwood and associates.[7] Medicare is pushing UR through contractor organizations called PROs (Professional Review Organizations). California Medical Review, the PRO for that state, has reported that its prior authorization program for just four programs avoided 6,022 operations in a year, without denying them to anyone who needed one of them, and that its total program saved Medicare $114 million in the year ended March, 1990.[8]

There is considerable evidence justifying UR in some form. We know that there are great practice variations: differences in the rates at which various medical procedures are performed on comparable populations. For example, in adjoining Maine communities, Wennberg[9] found that prostatectomies had been done on 60 percent of men reaching age 85 in one, but only 15 percent in the other. For children's tonsillectomies, the variation was from 8 percent to 70 percent. Given this, and after ascertaining that the health outcomes were as good in the low as in the high rate towns, it makes both medical and economic sense to reduce use of such procedures toward the lower rate.

There has been a major stumbling block to cost-effectiveness in the uncertainty, the lack of professional consensus, that has existed regarding what is the optimal treatment for a given diagnosis. However, the effectiveness research mentioned above is directed toward an end-product of "practice guidelines," which the American Medical Association, the American College of Physicians and other organizations are now developing.

Medicare is in the process of augmenting a new mode of physician payment beginning in 1992. It will set a fixed fee (rather than starting from the individual doctor's historical charges as in the past) for each of several thousand services, all based on what is called a Relative Value Scale (RVS), which takes into account the time, effort, and skills involved. Overall, the RVS will increase compensation for "cognitive services" such as office visits and diagnoses, and decrease it for surgery and other procedure-oriented medical treatments. One potential by-product (though not the primary reason for developing the RVS) is that overall Medicare costs may be cut because the incentives to physicians will be turned somewhat away from the procedural mode, which generally also means the more expensive treatment.

One other medical model change--a much more sweeping one-- needs to be mentioned. The dominant ethic of American medicine has long been to "Do something!"--without too much regard for what it costs or whether it has much chance of really helping the patient. (My brevity oversimplifies, of course, but the point is generally recognized.) If that were to change to "Do what will contribute to a quality of life for the patient," then a lot of expenses might be avoided.

Closely related, of course, is the individual's own role in using the doctrine of informed consent, via such advance directives as living wills and durable powers of attorney for health affairs that put on record what extraordinary measures many of us may wish to avoid if they can, but keep us technically alive without a meaningful life.

Partial Global Budgeting

Finally, I return to the concept of global budgeting, in order to suggest that what I will call *partial* global budgeting can help to make health-care distribution more rational and more equitable, as well as more cost-effective, in particular patient segments of the population. For example, every health maintenance organization (HMO) can be seen as a partial global budgeting system. Because its income is derived from predictable per capita monthly payments, the payment amount times the number of subscribers anticipated for a given year equals a prospective budget for that year. The incentive for an HMO is to work hard to avoid providing unneeded services, since its financial well-being depends on spending less to provide services than its budget. The HMO, unlike the fee-for-service provider, cannot gain more by doing more. Analysis of established HMOs has shown a significantly lower rate of hospitalization, and thus a reduction of costs and of the risks of hospital-induced illnesses.[10] All-payer hospital regulatory systems, as in New York state, are somewhat analogous. And Oregon is planning a controversial Medicaid experiment that would create a global system to cover all those whose incomes are under the federal poverty line. It would do this (instead of covering only 58 percent of the poor as now) by establishing a prioritized list of medical services within a specified state Medicaid budget. Services below the budget line that could not be afforded within the state budget would not be covered.[11]

This proposal--not yet federally approved as I write in the summer of 1991--has been attacked on the basis that it applies explicit rationing only for the poor. But the fact is that we are already doing that in perhaps less defensible fashion, in my view, by providing all services, but for only half the poor. The Oregon global budget might at least ensure cost-effectiveness among all of the poor. This would be accomplished by providing an institutional framework in which everyone would be eligible for primary care before funds were allocated for very expensive tertiary care. On the other hand, a number of serious practical problems of implementation do cast doubt on what seems sensible at the conceptual level.[12]

Conclusion

In short, we have too diverse, pluralistic and fragmented a system to provide an assured trade-off between sacrifices that might be made by or to the elderly and the gains of others. Yet we do have a number of incremental, medically-grounded approaches worth pursuing in the interests of both a more humane and a more cost-effective health-care delivery system.

Notes and References

1. Callahan's pertinent writings include: *Setting Limits: Medical Goals in an Aging Society* (New York: Simon & Schuster, 1987; Touchstone edition, 1988; *What Kind of Life? The Limits of Medical Progress* (New York: Simon & Schuster, 1990); "Old Age and New Policy," *Journal of the American Medical Association*, Vol. 261 (February 10, 1989), pp. 905-906.

2. Please note that I write in a context that asks what to do if one approves of Callahan's age-limitation concept. Personally, I do not accept that as the appropriate way to set limits on care, although I do agree that some limits must be (and are being) set.

3. Callahan, *Setting Limits*, p. 128.

4. Norman Daniels, *Am I My Parents' Keeper? An Essay on Justice Between the Young and the Old* (New York: Oxford University Press, 1988), Chapter 4 and pp. 146-147.

5. The most cost-effective way to do something is that which accomplishes the most with a given expenditure, or achieves a given level of service at least cost. This is different from cost-benefit analysis, which asks the almost impossible question (given the intangibles in defining medical benefits), "Does the benefit exceed the cost?" before authorizing an expenditure.

6. As of Fall 1990, the Health Care Financing Administration (the Medicare agency) began a system of Comparative Performance Reports, which will pick out from Medicare data 0.1 percent of physicians who exceed the norms of utilizing certain proceedures in their specialities and areas. HCFA will provide these "outliers" with information about their own rates of doing certain procedures and the statistical norm for others in the same

speciality and area. The information is termed educational, rather than regulatory--at least as the system starts.

7.   P. M. Ellwood, "Outcomes Management: A Technology of Patient Experience," *The New England Journal of Medicine*, Vol. 318 (June 9, 1988), pp. 1549-1555.

8.   R. Steinbrook, "Report Shows Drop in Surgeries for Elderly," *Los Angeles Times*, July 30, 1990.

9.   J. E. Wennberg, "Dealing With Medical Practice Variations," *Health Affairs*, Vol. 3 (Summer 1984), pp. 6-32

10.   Such findings are not as certainly true of the more recent Independent Practice Associations.

11.   H. G Welch, "Health Care Tickets for the Uninsured," *The New England Journal of Medicine*, Vol. 10, No. 3 (Summer 1991), pp. 28-51.

12.   L. D. Brown, "The National Politics of Oregon's Rationing Plan," *Health Affairs*, Vol. 10 (Summer 1991), pp. 28-51.

10

Counting the Costs of Lifesaving Interventions for the Elderly

Paul T. Menzel

Introduction

The escalating cost of health care has forced us to confront the possibility of rationing--foregoing beneficial care for patients in order to use the resources either to care for other current or prospective patients or for entirely other things in life than health care. Rationing is usually thought to pose a moral dilemma between meeting the needs of the individual patient and attending to the welfare of the larger society.   On the one hand, do *not* ration-- deliver all medically-appropriate care portending net benefit for *the patient.* Yet on the other hand, *do* ration--reserve resources for other things more important in *the larger social order.*

If this is the way we frame the issue, it will be a long and difficult time indeed before our society comes to any kind of reasonably secure and ethical satisfaction with selectively restricting medically beneficial care because of its expense. Rationing care will be accused, plausibly, of assaulting our most vulnerable citizens--the sick and disabled--so others can retain their desired level of amenities.

There is a very different way, however, of looking at the entire matter.   Suppose the "welfare of society" side of the conflict represented people's own hard judgment about the kind of society in which--on balance, in the long term, and considering all the realities of cost and scarcity--*they* wished to live.   And suppose that commitment to individual patients were seen as involving much more than maximizing their welfare *as patients.* I have argued elsewhere that precisely here lies the promising line of moral analysis about rationing.[1] The conceptual point that provides the actual reconciliation of respect for individual patients with the larger welfare of society is essentially simple: if individual patients have consented beforehand--or clearly would have--to substantive and procedural policies for rationing care of relatively high expense per benefit, the appeal of those policies will rest not merely on attachment to the morally controversial goal of increasing aggregate societal welfare but on respect for patients' own will.[2] Rationing will be an essential, constitutive part of any successful attempt of people to control the resources of their lives.

People of integrity, and a society of people of integrity, will thus be concerned about the relationship of cost to likely benefit in their medical care. Ahead of time, even considering their later possible plight as needy patients, they will agree that high cost (in relation to low benefit) care takes a back seat to low-cost procedures for all later, contingent maladies. (This conclusion will not hold, however, for individually foreknown maladies, such as many congenital conditions.) People may well agree, even for their own cases, to restrict some very high ticket items or diagnostic procedures of modest nominal cost that only rarely uncover actually treatable problems.

If low benefit-per-cost care is generally thus the main target of our reflections about what we would choose to ration out of medical practice, it is absolutely crucial, of course, to get straight what the true costs of care really are. Otherwise the whole business of trying seriously to decide what to spend will not make remotely any sense. For example, take the real policy decision in our society of whether to fund and provide flu vaccine for elderly nursing home residents. We tend to think of such a life-saving measure's cost as just the money we have to lay out for it directly. One noted economic analysis of influenza immunization for the U.S. Medicare population portrayed direct medical cost, as only $13 per year of healthy life saved.[3] At that bargain price we correctly wonder how any sane Medicare administration could fail to cover routine immunization. According to the same study, including the costs of later unrelated health care (but not long-term nursing home expenses) for patients whose lives are thus prolonged increases the cost to $800 per year of healthy life, still an exceptional bargain as medical life-saving goes. There are, however, two other (and big) hidden costs of such life-saving: The later nursing home expenses of the longer lives of the residents whose lives are thus saved, and the pension benefits paid to them in their added years of life. Altogether, the inclusion of longer years of Social Security payments and medical and nursing home bills ($35,000 a year, perhaps) may bring costs-per-year-of-life-saved to a level where the argument for passing over vaccination becomes very plausible indeed. I have heard, in fact, several notable experts in influenza immunization policy express the opinion that behind-the-scenes worries about precisely these hidden costs are the real explanation of why the Medicare administration and Congress have been so reluctant to pay for routine vaccination. In the film, *Love and Death*, Woody Allen quips, "Death's a great way to cut down on expenses." Maybe we have acted that out already.

Types of Cost

So what are the real costs of life-saving? How should we count them? I will pursue this first through a somewhat different comparative example of life-saving, anti-smoking programs, and then get back to the context of common life-saving treatments for elderly nursing home residents.

In analysis of any particular human behavior or service we should first note several fundamental types of cost that need to be distinguished. (See Table 10.1.) With these distinctions in mind we can understand some of the widely varying estimates of the economic cost of an activity like smoking. (See Table 10.2.)[4]

TABLE 10.1 Types of Costs

External Costs (ECs):	costs paid by others
Foregone Contributions:	what would have been paid to others
External Savings (ESs):	savings or benefits for others (negative external costs)
Net External Costs:	ECs + Foregone Contributions - ESs

(continues)

TABLE 10.1 (*continued*)

Internal Costs (ICs):	costs paid by those engaging in the behavior or by recipients of the service
Internal Savings (ISs)	savings or benefits for those engaging in the behavior or receiving the services
Net Internal Costs:	ICs - ISs
Total Societal Costs:	costs to everyone (net ECs + net ICs)

TABLE 10.2 Major Estimates of the Costs of Smoking

Study	Estimate	Notable Omissions	Notable Inclusions
OTA 1985	$65b	later h.c. $, pension payouts, EC/IC distinction	lost earnings, and worktime
Rice 1986	$53.7b (1984)	same as OTA 1985	lost earnings, and worktime
DHHS 1990	$52.3b (1985)	same as OTA 1985	lost earnings and worktime
Warner 1987	nil	value of life left unmonetarized	later h.c. $, pensions, lost earnings, and worktime
Manning 1989	$5b ECs $73b ICs	alternatives to $1.66m value of life in ICs (high)	EC/IC distinction, later h.c. $, pensions, lost earnings, and worktime

Sources for this table are listed in note #4.

The "nil" estimate of smoking's economic cost by Warner and the $5 billion estimate of external cost by Manning provide the interesting, surprising contrast here. Their estimates come out that way precisely because they include later health-care expenditures and later pension payouts as costs of quitting. If it is hard to believe that the net health-care costs of smoking are that low, one must remember to distinguish *per-year* costs from the *life-time* costs on which a full accounting should focus. Leu and Schaub's well-known 1983 study first brought home the importance of considering lifetime costs; for males age 35, it found that subsequent lifetime medical care expenditures came out lowest for smokers, and regular non-smokers' lifetime expenditures were higher even than the lifetime expenditures of "non-smoking smoker-types."[5] This general direction has been borne out again in more recent calculations by Warner,[6] and it led Wright to conclude that even after accounting for smokers' lost years of earnings and smaller tax contributions, the average smoker who completely and forever quits at age 45 thereby costs the U.S. Medicare fund a net $1495.[7] The typical non-smoker hardly lives healthily to 85 only to be hit by a bus and die instantly.

The full effect of both later health-care expenses and retirement pension benefits on smoking's cost is graphically captured by Manning's 1989 estimate of the costs to others of a smoker smoking a pack of cigarettes:[8] Assuming a 5 percent discount rate and altering assumptions about the scope of external costs to include fires and passive smoking, Manning's final estimate of the net external cost of smoking a pack of cigarettes is $0.38.[9] Since this is virtually the current (1989) average tobacco tax of $0.37 per pack, Manning concludes that smokers already pay their own way and that the case for higher excise taxes on tobacco products is very questionable.

It is important to note that such a factual analysis does not pose a serious objection to *non-coercive* (and otherwise reasonably designed) anti-smoking programs; those programs may not save "us" (nonsmokers) money, but whatever small net expense we may incur from them seems well justified by the value of the life itself that gets prolonged. An estimate, for example, of the total societal costs (not just "external" ones) must include the subjective value to smokers of the 28 minutes of life they lose per pack they smoke. Manning then calculates this total cost at $5.00 per pack, using a valuation of life rate to smokers of $10 per hour, or $1.66 million per 20-year life.[10]

TABLE 10.3 External Costs Per Pack of Cigarettes (1986 $)

		(real discount rate)	
		0 percent	5 percent
1. External Costs			
	a. medical care	$0.38	$0.26
	b. sick leave	$0.01	$0.01
	c. group life insurance	$0.11	$0.05
	d. fires	$0.02	$0.02
2. Foregone contributions -- income taxes not available due to smokers' lower earnings		$0.65	$0.09
3. Negative external costs (savings)			
	a. nursing home care	-0.26	-0.03
	b. retirement pensions	-1.82	-0.24
4. Total net external costs		-0.91	$0.15

Now let us shift this discussion toward the elderly. Consider, for example, the real costs of curing pneumonia in elderly patients in nursing homes. Here a number of things are immediately different. We are no longer concerned to keep external costs distinct from internal ones, as we would naturally be when we are clarifying costs amidst a discussion of excise taxes. Pneumonia, unlike smoking, is not a lifestyle, so there is no behavior to tax. Thus total costs ("total societal costs") in relation to benefits, not just external costs, properly dominate the discussion. Here in the nursing home context, however, such a shift in focus from external to total societal costs does not greatly change the dollar figures as it does in the smoking case. Though, as a matter of empirical fact, total societal costs may be very low in relation to total benefits in the smoking case, here in the nursing home context they are not. Total costs can easily, for example, be $35,000 per year of life saved: $24,000 for nursing home care, $3000 for medical care, and $8000 in additional pension payouts.

There are other differences, too, between counting the costs of smoking reduction programs and those of curing pneumonia in elderly patients in nursing homes. Just as a matter of fact, in the nursing home case there are seldom lost earnings to recoup, and pension payouts and later health-care expenditures get only modestly reduced when discounted back to present value (those costs occur not nearly so far into the future). These comparisons are summarized in Table 10.4.

The policy implications of all this should not be missed. The roughly $35,000 real cost for extending life one year by the simple measure of treating pneumonia in elderly nursing home residents stands in sharp contrast to the low nominal expense of the required antibiotics that we commonly think of as the cost of treatment. Such a $35,000 figure then puts antibiotics for treating pneumonia in elderly nursing home residents into the same cost-benefit ballpark of questionable care as kidney dialysis, open heart surgery in the high risk elderly, or certain transplants.

TABLE 10.4 Comparison of Nursing Home and Smoking Cases

Nursing home case	Smoking case
1. Pneumonia is not a life-style	1. Smoking is a chosen life-style

a. No behavior to tax
  b. Total cost/benefit, not just external cost, seems relevant
	a. A behavior to tax
	  b. Recoup net external cost with excise tax

2. No lost earnings to recoup	2. Lost earnings to recoup
3. Pensions and later health care $ get only modestly discounted	3. Pensions and later health care $ get heavily discounted (further into future)

This claim depends, of course, on the assumption that pension benefits are real costs, and that costs for essentials like later medical care should be counted in weighing up the net load on an economy that life-saving treatment creates. I will now defend both of these assumptions. Despite the counter-intuitive look of counting later nursing home care and pension benefits, I will argue both that they are real costs and that we should count even the costs of life's essentials, taking full responsibility for what we really will be paying before we decide to save lives.

Pension Benefits as Real Costs

In a very important and relevant sense, pension benefits are real costs. This runs counter to the view especially common among economists that pension benefits are merely costless transfer payments that should therefore not be counted into total societal costs in contexts like the treatment of pneumonia for elderly nursing home residents. As I have previously explained, in such contexts our proper focus is on total societal costs, not just external ones. The common argument among economists then simply notes that though someone, through taxes or premiums, pays pension benefits to someone else and a pension is thus a cost of the payer, "society" (everyone together) incurs no net cost. When older people die, for example, they have lost a pension benefit but others have saved a roughly equal expense. That is, there is no net *societal* cost.

But though the above argument is correct for static populations (people who live for a certain length of life whether or not the transfer is made), it does not hold when the *number* of people changes. To see this, compare two courses of events:

Course A: I am alive to receive a payment from others.

Course B: Others save that expense, not because I do without the benefit but because I am not around at all.

Someone somewhere down the economic line is going to have more in B than in A, without anyone else in B getting less. In a per capita income sense, then, A is a loss compared to B.

The per capita sense of resources is one perfectly good sense of "societal" cost. In figuring it, after all, all costs are considered before dividing by the number of people. Most citizens (though probably not typically most economists) think in per capita societal terms. Particularly in a resource trade-off situation, people are trying to decide whether their lives will be better or worse off by incurring this or that life-saving expense. They try to keep in focus their own per-person likely cost, not some abstract "total good" or "total cost." Then, knowing that cost, they try to decide whether the extra life it buys is worth it--a query not about whether it is worthwhile at all, but whether it is worth that cost.

The key conceptual focus here is the same that I began this essay proposing as crucial in rationing medical care in general. Economic resources are not just "available" somehow from some big pot of resources. They are produced by people, and it is largely only through some such production that they are available to anyone at all. Given what we produce, then, we have so much, and only so much, to use in our lifetimes. The longer we live without producing proportionately more, the further we will have to stretch those resources. Thus, in competition with other things in life, we naturally have to see the added pension benefits as a cost of living longer just as much as we see the other things we need in added years of life as real costs. That has to be the case once we get the least bit into this business of trying to gain control over the resources of our lives. In fact, then, from the very perspective we already occupy simply by the fact that we are discussing limiting what we should spend on health care, we are compelled to consider pension benefits for the added years of life as a real cost of lifesaving care.

In addition to the objection that pension benefits are not real costs, one also hears objections to the *moral* propriety of counting pensions or later health-care expenditures as costs of life-saving. One objection centers on an alleged parallel between later health care expenses, on the one hand, and essentials like food and clothing on the other. If someone proposed counting food and clothing costs in deciding whether to save a life, would we not object? Food and clothing are basic needs or rights--just part of what everybody needs to live. People should not be held accountable in society's allocation calculus for using financial resources for the bare essentials of life. But then this is as true for health care and for pension benefits as it is for food and clothing.[11]

An adequate reply to this objection rests on the key distinction between providing things to people when it is *already assumed* that they will continue to live, and providing things to them so that their lives can be *extended*. Just because we believe that people have a right to food, shelter, and medical care in the time that it is already assumed they will be living, we do not have to ignore these items' cost when the issue is explicitly the extension of their lives. If we had a shortage of food, for example, we would probably allocate sufficient food first to avoid debilitating malnutrition to people who were going to live anyhow, and last to those who needed large amounts just to stay alive. That is, we would count food consumed in figuring the cost of saving people's lives. Today life-saving health care is parallel: Given its expense, we see it as scarce. That is, we distinguish decisions to extend life from decisions in which the affected persons are going to be alive in any case.

So added years of pension benefits are real costs of life-saving, and it is not morally objectionable to count later medical and nursing home care expenses as we enter into considering what to spend to save our lives. The $35,000 per year-of-life-saved expense of some routine treatments in old age puts them in the same candidate-for-rationing ballpark as kidney dialysis, the most expensive transplants and open heart surgeries, and diagnostic tests of statistically small return.

Age-Rationing

Once we thus see the cost of certain life-saving medical procedures for the elderly as much more robust than most of us heretofore usually have, it may seem that we will end up with age-rationed health care: We will provide much less health care than presently to people in their last years of life. This, I will argue, is not "age-rationing." In this context the charge of age-rationing is a red herring that works on our persuasions only to the extent that we fail to understand the rationing process upon which we have embarked.

Look at the following choice. You are 30. You can purchase coverage for any of three treatments for $5 per month each, paid from age 30 to 65 (whether you ever need the treatment or not):

Treatment A: for a disease generally striking at age 30-50.

Treatment B: for a disease generally striking at age 50-70.

Treatment C: for a disease generally striking over age 70.

If your likelihoods of needing A, B, and C are equal, would you not buy coverage first for A, then for B, and lastly for C? Furthermore, will you not verify that priority's wisdom even when you are 70?

To control the resources of our lives, virtually all of us will be willing, if we once think about the issues, to bind ourselves to limits on the lowest benefit-per-cost items of care. To be sure, such precommitment is abused by those who do not reflect seriously on their future vulnerability. Indeed we should discount the choice of a 30-year-old not to invest in *any* policy that provides life-prolonging care in his or her eighties. But on the other hand, none of these observations are reason to take the octogenarian's word as controlling, either.[12]

Note, of course, that if we are wisely trying to manage available resources for our lifetimes, we will clearly *not* commit ourselves to doing without palliative or chronic care no matter how old we may become. That is one of the signs that it simply is not *age*-rationing that is going on here. We might discount the relative priority of lifesaving rescue care as old age sets in, yet not at all because of old age itself but because of the care's low benefit-cost characteristics *in* old age. Moreover, we will hardly condemn ourselves to misery and lack of care for any time when we will be alive, regardless of our age. Long-term and palliative care stay as high priority as they are at any age. People who worry that rationing care for the elderly or terminally ill will lead us to deny them palliative or chronic care, not just life-extending measures, simply do not understand the prior consent basis for rationing to begin with.

Age-rationing is simply not the prospect or the issue once people see that rationing health care can reflect their own wise and prudent allocations of resources over their lifetimes.

Conclusion

There is no general or abstract way to decide whether $35,000 per year of life saved at 80 is too high a cost to pay for penicillin for pneumonia or vaccine for influenza. Everything will depend on all the other things we want to do with the resources of our lives-- yes, *all* the other things, from second chickens in our pots, to better education and lower burdens of national debt for our children, food for the starving, third world economic development, homes for the homeless, a start on rebuilding our economic infrastructure, adventurous traveling, and on and on. What is clear is that people of integrity, appreciating all the ages they might live into, will not hide their heads in the sand about what the real costs of lifesaving are, including later health-care expenses and added years of pension benefits. There's seldom a free lunch, and life-saving care in old age is certainly not one of them. We can no longer pretend that we do not have to make hard trade-off decisions about finite resources. Something as apparently inexpensive and common as a lifesaving antibiotic for pneumonia can pull huge amounts of resources away from other things we think are important in our lives. Recognizing these costs, and at times being willing to reject incurring them, is a paramount responsibility of persons of integrity.

In effect we have already decided to engage in the difficult trade-off game of rationing care when we adopted a public program like Medicare for the bulk of care for the aged. Since then the context of our thinking about care for the elderly has necessarily had to become what we might call "congressional"--seeing ourselves as legislators, responsible for the use of resources over our larger lives. And in old age, the longer we live the more we cost. Whether to pay that real cost of saving life is always an open question, but whether to face up to those real costs is not. Facing up is not a requirement of a tyrannical or collectivist society, but a reflection of the integrity of not hiding the consequences of our decisions.

Notes and References

1.   Paul T. Menzel, *Strong Medicine: The Ethical Rationing of Health Care* (New York: Oxford University Press, 1990), especially Chapter 1.

2.   Ibid., pp. 3-21 and 45-53, especially pp. 10-15.

3.   Michael A. Riddiough et al., "Influenza Vaccination--Cost-Effectiveness and Public Policy," *Journal of the American Medical Association*, Vol. 249 (June 17, 1983), pp. 3189-3195.

4.   It should be noted that a dated dollar estimate is in that year's dollars, not the publication year's dollars. The studies that serve as the basis for Table 10.2 are as follows:

Office of Technology Assessment (OTA), "Smoking-Related Deaths and Financial Costs" (Staff Memorandum). Washington, D.C.: U.S. Congress, 1985.

Dorothy P. Rice et al., "The Economic Costs of the Health Effects of Smoking, 1984," *Milbank Quarterly*, Vol. 64 (Fall 1986), pp. 489-547.

Department of Health and Human Services (DHHS), *Smoking and Health, A National Status Report*, 2nd ed., HHS Publication #87-8396 (Washington, D.C.: Government Printing Office, 1990).

Kenneth E. Warner, "Health and Economic Implications of a Tobacco-Free Society," *Journal of the American Medical Association*, Vol. 258 (October 16, 1987), pp. 2080-2086.

Willard G. Manning et al. "The Taxes of Sin: Do Smokers and Drinkers Pay Their Way?" *Journal of the American Medical Association*, Vol. 261 (March 17, 1989), pp. 1604-1609.

5.   Robert E. Leu and Thomas Schaub, "Does Smoking Increase Medical Care Expenditure?" *Social Science and Medicine*, Vol. 17 (1983), pp. 1907-1914.

6.   Warner, "Health and Economic Implications of a Tobacco-Free Society."

7.   Virginia Baxter Wright, "Will Quitting Smoking Help Medicare Solve Its Financial Problems?" *Inquiry*, Vol. 23 (Spring, 1986), pp. 76-82.

8.   Manning et al, "The Taxes of Sin."

9.   Ibid.

10.   The $1.66 million per 20 years of life rate may be high. Manning takes it from a willingness-to-pay estimate by Shepard and Zeckhauser, "Survival vs. Consumption," *Management Science*, Vol. 30 (1984), pp. 423-439.

11.   Russell has broached this argument in briefer form. Louise B. Russell, *Is Prevention Better Than Cure?* (Washington, D.C.: Brookings Institution, 1986), pp. 35-36.

12. The general argument pursued here is similar to that of Norman Daniels, *Am I My Parents' Keeper? An Essay on Justice Between the Young and the Old* (New York: Oxford University Press, 1988), especially Chapters 3 and 5.

11

Cost Containment
and Conflicts of Interest
in the Care of the Elderly

Charles E. Begley

Introduction

Over the past few years, the federal government has been considering whether to prohibit Medicare-participating health maintenance organizations (HMOs) and other comprehensive medical plans (CMPs) from offering financial incentives to physicians for reduced medical costs. In 1986, Congress passed a law prohibiting hospitals, HMOs, and CMPs from making direct payments to physicians as inducements to reduce or limit services for Medicare beneficiaries. The law was in response to a case in Florida in which physicians were receiving a cost-containment kickback from a hospital. Recognizing that such inducements are common in the physician payment arrangements used by the HMO industry, Congress delayed applying the law to Medicare-participating HMOs and CMPs until further study could be conducted.

At present, the law has still not been applied to HMOs and CMPs although it is in effect for hospitals. A modified version proposed by the Department of Health and Human Services (HHS) would bar Medicare from contracting with prepaid health plans which put physicians at full financial risk for patients. Instead of banning all incentive arrangements, the amended law would require HHS to review the characteristics of a potential contractor's system of payment and bar only those that put physicians at "excessive risk."[1] The importance of this issue arises out of the unprecedented growth in the number of aged Americans and the accompanying increases in the costs of medical care. It is well known that the elderly are the biggest users of health care in our society, accounting for 40 percent of the days spent in acute care hospitals, 25 percent of all prescriptions drugs purchased, 50 percent of the federal government's health budget, and 30 percent of the nation's overall health expenditures.[2] These percentages undoubtedly will rise with the changing age structure of the population.

The prospects for insolvency of the Medicare program have led the government to explore alternative health-care delivery systems as a cost-saving strategy. Prepaid health plans offered through HMOs and CMPs are being promoted through the Medicare risk contractor provisions of the Tax Equity and Fiscal Responsibility Act of 1982. Under the risk-contracting program, HHS pays HMOs a set fee in advance to care for a predetermined number of Medicare beneficiaries. The payment is raised annually, based on increases in medical and administrative costs. At the present, about 1.5 million people are enrolled in such plans, representing about 4 percent of the 34 million enrolled in Medicare.[3] Most plans attempt to pass on a portion of the risk for the costs of care to participating physicians in the form of risk-sharing payment arrangements. Banning the use of such arrangements among risk contractors could eliminate the access of Medicare beneficiaries to all forms of prepaid care.

Both the initial and revised proposals reflect a general concern that cost-containment incentives may have an adverse effect on the physician-patient relationship and may lead to lower standards of care. This essay analyzes this concern on two levels. An argument is made that the ethical basis for concern--the potential conflict of interest between the physician's financial gain and his or her obligations to patients--fails on two grounds. First, it fails to recognize that such conflict is inherent in all payment mechanisms and that the nature and extent of conflict posed by such incentives may be no greater than already exists under the prevailing fee-for-service system. Second, the concern is based on uncertain assumptions about the relationship between negative financial incentives and physician behavior, and the extent to which changes in physician behavior lead to changes in the quality of care. The second part of the paper provides a review of empirical research related to the second set of issues: What is the structure of incentives in HMOs? What is the relationship between such incentives and physician behavior? What is the relationship between the quality of care in HMOs and in fee-for-service settings?

The Conflict of Interest Debate

The traditional, normative model of clinical ethics argues that a physician ought to be motivated primarily by consideration of the patient's welfare.[4] The vulnerable position of the patient who must rely upon the physician to diagnose and provide services, and who (in many instances) cannot judge performance, provides the rationale for this ethic. This view explains that the physician/patient relationship is properly understood as a trust relationship in which the patient delegates decision-making authority to the physician and the physician acts as the patient's agent by providing all beneficial care without regard to cost.

In recent years, the traditional model has been challenged by those who would advocate the principle of patient autonomy over medical welfare.[5] Because of the paternalism implied by the traditional model, many have concluded that the physician should recognize the patient's right to refuse medical care even if that care is considered to be in the patient's best interest. Under this principle of autonomy, the physician's obligation shifts from pursuing the patient's best medical interest to serving the patient's beliefs and values. The obligation remains patient-centered and includes costs only when the patient's wishes include financial considerations.

Many ethicists who support this model are concerned that financial incentives to reduce cost will create conflict with the physician's traditional obligation to serve patients.[6] The ethic of the doctor as patient agent--either acting in the patient's best medical interest or serving the patient's preferences and financial situation--would be compromised. The concern is with the potential for conflict when physicians have a personal financial stake in conserving resources while serving their role as patient agent.

In a related article on diagnosis-related groups (DRGs) for hospitals, Veatch argued that, in effect, physicians are being asked to remove the Hippocratic Oath from their walls and replace it with a sign that reads, "Warning, I will generally work for your welfare, but if benefits are marginal and costs are high, I will abandon you in favor of society."[7] Morreim, who has written extensively on this subject, has suggested that "financial incentives [to reduce cost] represent a profound challenge to physicians' fiduciary commitment to honor patients' interest above their own."[8] The incentives not only encourage physicians to withhold care, but to withhold information about the financial structure designed to influence their decisions. Relman wrote in 1985, "Financial incentives ignore the basic social role of the physician, which is to be an agent and trustee for the patient."[9]

What is missing from these expressions is recognition that, in their social role as agent and supplier, physicians have always had to face such conflict. In his classic treatment of the medical marketplace, Arrow describes the inherent conflict in the physician's dual role as the patient's agent and supplier of services.[10] The physician/agent not only provides advice about what tests and procedures a patient needs or desires (agency role) but also supplies some of those tests and procedures (economic role). On a national basis, services provided by physicians were 22 percent of personal health-care spending in 1988.[11] Most of the remaining 78 percent was for services obtained on the basis of the recommendations of physicians.

A physician faces negative or positive incentives under all types of payment arrangements that can potentially create conflict with patient interests. Prospective payment arrangements that are common in HMOs and CMPs create the potential for conflict by encouraging physicians to limit or restrict the level of services. Salaries also create a negative incentive. If the costs of a health-care plan consistently exceed the plan's income, salaried physicians would find themselves either unemployed or with reduced salaries in the future. In fee-for-service systems, third-party payments result in financial rewards to physicians, thus exposing patients to unnecessary risk through the provision of excess services.

The traditional normative model of clinical ethics, emphasizing fidelity to the patient, can be justified because of its role in limiting the power of financial incentives to affect physician behavior adversely. The model does not rule out the existence of conflicts of interest, but leads to the behavioral principle that, in the face of such conflicts, a physician ought to be motivated primarily by consideration of the patient's interests.

Some argue that the positive incentives created by the fee-for-service mechanism create less potential for conflict because physicians are rewarded for ordering treatments and tests which patients need or desire.[12] The incentive for excess service from the incremental increase in income is alleged to be relatively weak given (1) the relative scarcity of physicians (ensuring that each has plenty to do), and (2) the patient's prerogative to obtain a second opinion about any proposed intervention.[13] Proponents of negative incentives, however, maintain that the strong positive financial incentives under fee-for-service arrangements have led to excessive use. They contend that negative incentives would reduce conflict by rewarding physicians for providing an efficient mix and quantity of service.[14]

Recognizing that conflicts of interest are an inherent part of all payment mechanisms, the key question regarding the ethical implications of cost-containment incentives shifts from whether conflict is created to whether the nature and extent of conflict created poses more of a threat to patient interests than that created under positive incentives. Unfortunately, this question is difficult to answer because empirical research has not established a clear relationship between financial incentives and physician concern for their patients. There are no studies showing that a particular payment arrangement increases or decreases a physician's tendency to over- or under-prescribe services.

However, there is a growing body of literature which attempts to identify precisely the structure of incentives in HMOs and compare their effects on physician behavior and standards of care with that in fee-for-service settings. In the following section of the paper, a review of this literature considers a number of complicating questions: (1) What is the precise nature and extent of negative financial incentives created by a particular HMO payment arrangement? (2) What is the influence of different types and strengths of incentives on physician behavior? (3) What is the link between physician behavior and the quality of care?

Effect of Financial Incentives in HMOs

Over the past few years, largely as a result of the federal government's interest, a number of surveys have been conducted to determine the nature of incentive arrangements offered to physicians by HMOs and CMPs.[15] The surveys suggest that there is wide variation in the nature and strength of incentive structures being used. While the surveys did not attempt to directly measure the strength of incentives, a typology was developed to classify incentive arrangements according to some major structural factors that are associated with strength. These include the method of compensation (salary, fee-for-service, or capitation), the proportion of compensation withheld for later distribution, and the method for distributing year-end surpluses and deficits (tied to individual or group performance).

This classification leads to an estimate of the number of plans using incentive arrangements which have the potential to produce excessive risk for patients. Those plans with capitation payments covering a broad set of services, large withholds, and a scheme for distributing surpluses or deficits on the basis of individual physician performance were classified on one end of the spectrum as having the potential to produce the strongest financial incentives. At the other end of the spectrum were plans in which physicians are paid on a fee-for-service basis, withheld amounts are a small percentage of payments, and fund losses and surpluses are shared equally by all physicians.

The surveys indicated that only a small number of plans-- between 14 and 20 percent--use arrangements that have the potential to create strong incentives for physicians to reduce service. This result was based mainly on whether the plan used group incentives or individual incentives. The central issue was whether physicians' individual decisions about their patients significantly alter their income or whether their income was tied to the performance of all physicians in the group.

A 1987 survey of 302 HMOs (representing 51 percent of all operating HMOs in the nation) indicated that 18 percent of plans which withhold payments distribute the withheld amounts on the basis of individual physician performance.[16] A 1986 survey which included 145 HMOs contracting with Medicare on a risk basis, and a random sample of federally qualified HMOs without Medicare risk contracts, found that about 14 percent of the plans distributed withheld amounts on the basis of individual physician performance.[17] A second survey, conducted in 1986 by the Group Health Association of America (GHAA), found that individual physician risk arrangements were evident in three-fifths (60 percent) of 104 GHAA member plans and 71 Blue-Cross/Blue Shield plans.[18] A reconciliation of GHAA's findings with those of the first survey indicated that about 20 percent of plans with Medicare risk contracts produce strong negative incentives for physicians by using individual incentive arrangements in their compensation mechanism.[19]

It is still not clear, however, whether the observed differences in hospital utilization between HMO and non-HMO plans reflect physicians' decisions to treat patients differently or differences in the way treatment is provided. Are differences in rates of hospitalization due to fewer diagnostic and surgical procedures being performed? Or are more of these procedures done on an out-patient basis? The first question implies that services are being reduced in response to incentives, while the second suggests that greater efficiency in service delivery is the likely response. Obviously, the implications for the quality of care would be different in each case.

Hillman and colleagues were the first to look at the relationship between specific types of incentives and rates of service (for hospitalization, primary care visits, and visits for outpatient services per enrollee) as a proxy for physician behavior.[20] They found lower rates of hospitalization were associated with HMOs using capitation or salaries, in comparison with fee-for-service. Placing individual physicians at risk and imposing penalties for deficits in the HMO's hospital fund were also associated with fewer outpatient visits and days of hospitalization. Physicians in for-profit HMOs and group-model HMOs also tended to hospitalize patients less often. However, no single type of financial risk was found to be significantly associated with reductions in all the measures of utilization. Furthermore, one analysis in the Hillman study found that an increase in case loads for physicians enrolled in the HMO (which strengthens incentives for less care) was associated with more visits per enrollee and had no relationship to hospitalization.

If services are reduced in response to negative incentives, a third question that must be addressed is whether the reductions lower the quality of care. If a significant amount of the procedures, tests, prescriptions, and hospitalizations currently being provided to patients are unnecessary or contribute little to patient outcomes, then reductions in service would not violate an ethical obligation. On this question, the relevant literature provides no support for the hypothesis that quality of care is being compromised by cost-containment incentives.

Reviews of the limited number of studies on the quality of care in HMOs find no evidence that their quality of care differs from that provided in the fee-for-service sector.[21] The studies suggest that the lower rates of in-patient utilization that have been documented are achieved with no reduction in quality. Several recent studies have looked at differences in treatment for specific conditions in the elderly and other high-risk populations, and have compared outcomes in a broader range of financial incentive plans to those in fee-for-service settings.[22]

Unfortunately, methodological problems with these studies combined with the rapidly changing HMO environment make it impossible to generalize results. Luft has argued that it is unclear whether or not the average quality level in HMOs is higher or lower than other types of health-care plans.

Various research studies found quality of care in selected HMOs to be at least as good as the community average, and the HMO industry seems to have taken refuge in those findings. Unfortunately, the generalizability of those findings was limited even when they were undertaken, and the major changes in the competitive environment make them even less useful today.[23]

Industry changes include the growth in network or Independent Practice Association (IPA) HMOs in the market. The success of IPAs has been accompanied by their strong efforts to contain costs through the adoption of financial incentives similar to those used in traditional HMO plans. However, many IPAs do not have the peer review and other quality assurance capabilities of the traditional HMO plans. It may be that medical practices incorporating peer interaction, such as staff/group HMOs, are more effective in maintaining professional standards of care in the face of incentives to reduce utilization. Also, in the early IPAs the great bulk of a physician's practice was fee-for-service patients, whereas physicians practicing in contemporary IPAs frequently have a large part (one-third or more) of their clientele enrolled in the IPA.

Conclusion

The risk of inappropriate reliance on strong financial incentives to reduce cost must remain a matter of concern. However, the evidence that exists at the present is not consistent with the conclusion that cost-containment incentives are accompanied by a cost-quality trade-off. These findings challenge those who would use conflict of interest as an argument against the use of financial incentives to encourage cost-containment. The burden of proof is on them to show that such incentives lead physicians to reduce services and that such reductions lower the quality of care.

Cost-containment incentives have the potential to create conflict between the financial interests of the physician and the best medical interests of patients. However, such conflict is inherent in all payment mechanisms and the effect of different payment mechanisms is not known with certainty. Further, there is reason to believe that equal or better care can be provided with lower levels of service and cost. For these reasons, it seems fallacious to criticize cost-containment incentives on the basis of conflict of interest. For those who recognize the inherent conflict in all payment mechanisms, a decision to restrict the payment arrangements in HMOs can be viewed as a judgment that the risks of underservice resulting from the negative incentive structure outweigh the potential for greater efficiency in service delivery. The available evidence indicates it would be premature for the federal government to make that judgment. The federal government should monitor the quality of care provided to HMO beneficiaries who participate in the Medicare program. Because cost-containment incentives could result in the inappropriate reduction of services, effective quality assurance programs have a key role in ensuring that Medicare enrollees receive quality health care. The same standards of necessity, appropriateness, and quality that are applied for Medicare fee-for-service health care should be established for HMOs. Further restriction or requirements on Medicare HMOs are not warranted at this time.

Notes and References

1. "House Panel Modifies Physician-Incentive Law," *Managed Health Care*, July 17, 1989, p. 1.

2. U. S. Department of Health and Human Services, National Center for Health Services Research, *Prescribed Medicines: Use, Expenditures, and Source of Payment*. National Health Care Expenditures Study (Washington, D.C.: U. S. Government Printing Office, 1982).

3. "Washington Watch," *Health Week*, July 30, 1990, p. 5.

4. T. L. Beauchamp and J. F. Childress, *Principles of Biomedical Ethics*, 2nd ed. (New York: Oxford University Press, 1983).

5. H. T. Engelhardt, *The Foundations of Bioethics* (New York: Oxford University Press, 1986).

6. E. D. Pellegrino, "Medical Morality and Medical Economics," *Hastings Center Report*, Vol. 9, 1978, pp. 8-11. See also D. Mechanic, "Cost Containment and Quality of Care: Rationing Strategies in an Era of Constrained Resources," *Milbank Memorial Fund Quarterly*, Vol. 63 (1985), pp. 453-475.

7. R. M. Veatch, "DRGs and the Ethical Reallocation of Resources," *The Hastings Center Report*, Vol. 17, June 1986, pp. 32-40.

8. E. H. Morreim, "Cost Containment: Challenging Fidelity and Justice," *Hastings Center Report*, Vol. 18 (1988), pp. 20-25.

9. A. Relman, "Dealing with Conflicts of Interest," *The New England Journal of Medicine*, Vol. 313 (1985), pp. 749-751.

10. K. J. Arrow, "Uncertainty and the Welfare Economics of Medical Care," *American Economic Review*, Vol. 53 (1963), pp. 941-973.

11. U. S. Department of Health and Human Services, Health Care Financing Administration, Office of National Cost Estimates, "National Health Expenditures, 1988." *Health Care Financing Review*, Vol. 11 (1990), pp. 1-41.

12. Relman, "Dealing with Conflicts of Interest."

13. Morreim, "Cost Containment."

14. R. H. Egdahl and C. H. Taft, "Financial Incentives to Physicians," *The New England Journal of Medicine*, Vol. 315 (1986), pp. 56-91. See also J. E. Wennberg, "On Patient Need, Equity, Supplier-Induced Demand, and the Need to Assess the Outcome of Common Medical Practices," *Medical Care*, Vol. 23 (1985), pp. 512-520.

15. A. L. Hillman, "Financial Incentives for Physicians in HMOs: Is There a Conflict of Interest?" *The New England Journal of Medicine*, Vol. 317 (1987), pp. 1743-1748. See also ICF, Inc., "Study of Incentive Arrangements Offered by HMOs and CMPs to Physicians: Final Report," Unpublished report prepared for the Office of the Assistant Secretary for Planning and Evaluation, Department of Health and Human Services, Washington, D.C., 1988; and M. Gold and I. Reeves, "Preliminary Results of the GHAA-BC/BS Survey of Physician Incentives in Health Maintenence Organizations (HMOs)," in *Research Briefs*, No. 1 (Washingtion, D.C.: Group Health Association of America, Inc., November, 1987).

16. Hillman, "Financial Incentives for Physicians in HMOs."

17. ICF, Inc., "Study of Incentive Arrangements."

18. Gold and Reeves, "Preliminary Results."

19. U. S. Department of Health and Human Services, Assistant Secretary for Planning and Evaluation, "Incentive Arrangements Offered by Health Maintenence Organizations and Competitive Medical Plans to Physicians," (Washington D.C.: U.S. Government Printing Office, 1990).

20. A. L. Hillman, M. V. Pauly, and J. H. Kerstein, "How Do Financial Incentives Affect Physicians' Clinical Decisions and the Financial Performance of Health Maintenance Organizations?" *The New England Journal of Medicine*, Vol. 321 (1989), pp. 86-92.

21. H. S. Luft, "Health Maintenance Organizations and the Rationing of Medical Care," *Milbank Memorial Fund Quarterly*, Vol. 60 (1982), pp. 268-306. See also F. C. Cunningham and J. W. Williamson, "How Does the Quality of Heath Care in HMOs Compare to That in Other Settings--An Analytic Review of the Literature: 1958-1979," *Group Health Journal*, Vol. 1 (1980), pp. 4-25.

22. A. L. Sui, R.H. Brook, and L. Z. Rubenstein, "Medicare Capitation and Quality of Care for the Frail Elderly," *Health Care Financing Review*, Annual Supplement (1986), pp. 57-63. See also E. H. Yelin, M. A. Shearn, and W. V. Epstein, "Health Outcomes for a Chronic Disease in Prepaid Group Practice and Fee-for-Service Settings," *Medical Care*, Vol. 24 (1986), pp. 236-247; and S. M. Retchin and B. Brown, "The Quality of Ambulatory Care in Medicare Health Maintenance Organizations," *American Journal of Public Health*, Vol. 80 (990), pp. 411-415.

23. Luft, "Health Maintenance Organizations and the Rationing of Medical Care."

12

Changing the Debate
About Health Care for the Elderly

Edward L. Schneider

Introduction

After two decades of increasing entitlements for older Americans, we are experiencing the first substantial cuts in these programs. Since the number of Americans covered by these entitlements is expected to grow rapidly, there will be increasing pressure on Congress to reduce further both Medicare and Medicaid expenditures.

What are the potential consequences of our nation's failure to fund health-care entitlement programs for the increasing number of older persons? Will public hospitals and nursing homes be overwhelmed as vast numbers of older patients are turned away by private hospitals and nursing homes? Will American industry be further imperiled by the number of employees, mostly female, leaving their jobs to take care of disabled older friends, relatives, and spouses who are no longer provided with federally-supported long-term care? Will increasing numbers of older Americans fall below the poverty level as they struggle to pay for their health-care costs?

In this article, I will address the magnitude of future increases in our older population, the consequences of these increases on future health-care costs, the long-term failure of cost containment, and the spectre of health-care rationing. This will be the context for a proposal to increase support for research directed towards eliminating those diseases and disorders which have the greatest impact, both personally and economically, on our entire population.

More Older Americans: Good News and Bad

Unprecedented numbers of Americans are reaching older ages.
In 1900 there were 3 million older Americans, defined as 65 years of
age or older, comprising 4 percent of the population. Today, there
are over 30 million people in this age group, comprising 12 percent
of the population. In the upcoming decades, the numbers of older
Americans may reach as high as 87 million or close to 25 percent of
the population. In 1988, federal programs paid for over $100 billion
in health-care costs for older Americans. Even without inflation of
health-care costs, the increasing numbers of older Americans could
cause this figure to rise to $300 billion in 1988 dollars.

Increasing numbers of older Americans, per se, do not represent
a challenge to our economy or to our federal budget. The critical
issue in regard to health-care costs is not the increase in absolute
numbers of older Americans, but, it is the quantity of health care
needed by this age group.

Can We Afford Health Care for the Elderly?

There are several factors that will substantially affect the health-
care costs of older Americans. The first factor, and the one that has
received the most attention, is the average cost of health care. The
average cost for health care for older Americans has paralleled the
health-care costs for the general population, increasing at a rate of 10
percent per year over the last decade, almost double the increase in
the Consumer Price Index (CPI). Later, I will argue that we may be
able, at best, in the future, to slightly reduce average health-care
costs per disease or per procedure. However, these savings will be
more than offset by the increasing number of older Americans.

Another factor that will influence health-care costs is the aging
of the older population itself. Today, the fastest growing age group
in America is the group comprised of those individuals 85 years of
age and older. In 1990, there were over 3 million Americans ages 85
and older. By 2040, there may be as many as 24 million Americans
at these vulnerable ages. The next fastest growing age group is
those ages 75 to 84. In the upcoming decades we will have
unprecedented numbers of Americans in their eighth, ninth, and
even tenth decades of life. While individuals in their 60s require
very little medical care (less than 5 percent), those in their late 70s
and 80s have substantial medical and social needs. The oldest old,
those 85 and above, have the highest per capita health-care costs,

closely followed by those 75 to 84 (See Figure 12.1). The per capita Medicare costs in 1987 for those 85 years old and over is $9,178 compared with $3,728 for those 65 to 69 years of age. Therefore, the aging of the older population itself will have a substantial effect on health-care costs for an aging population.

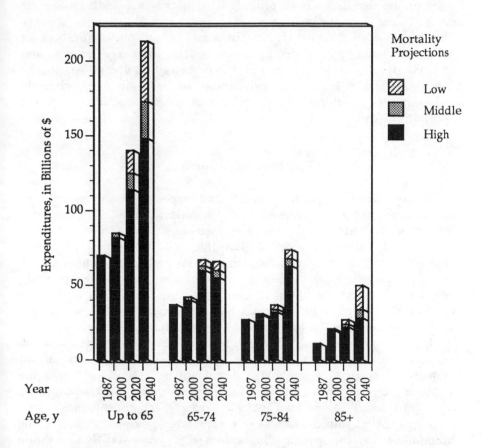

FIGURE 12.1: Actual (1987) and Projected Medicare Expenses in 1987 Dollars by Age Group. Average Medicare expenses per person were obtained from data from the Health-care Financing Administration. Cost projections are based on low- (series 9), middle- (series 14), and high- (series 19) mortality assumptions from the US Bureau of the Census.

Source: Spencer, G. *Projections of the Population of the United Sates by Age, Sex and Race: 1988-2040.* U.S. Bureau of the Census; 1989, *Current Population Reports,* Series P-25, No. 1018.

The last factor impacting on future health-care costs is the average health of the older population. A healthier population could be expected to generate less health-care costs. Unfortunately, there is no evidence that the average health of our older population is improving. In fact, the majority of studies indicate that the extra years of life that have been provided to the average individual over the last few decades include more years of disability and disease. Therefore, with projected future increases in absolute numbers of older Americans, with more of them in the oldest age groups, and with no significant change in health-care costs or average health, we will undoubtedly experience substantial increases in both absolute and relative health-care costs for our older population in the upcoming decades.

The Present Approach

Today, faced with the current and expected hemorrhaging of health-care costs, governmental agencies, health providers, corporations, and individuals are focusing their efforts on cost containment. Before I propose that this is not the best long-term approach, it is necessary to confirm that cost containment is an important and necessary response to the present and future spiralling of health-care costs. Our health-care costs are among the highest in the world, 12 percent of the gross national product (GNP), compared with 9 percent for Canada and 6 percent for Great Britain. No doubt, our system could benefit from efficient cost containment. However, cost containment in this situation is a Band Aid; it can slow the hemorrhage temporarily, but it will not stop it! During the 1980s, a number of highly innovative cost-containment approaches were introduced to reduce Medicare costs. Perhaps the most well-known is the introduction of perspective payment system for hospitals, based on specific diagnosis-related groups (DRGs). While this approach had a major effect on hospital costs for the first few years after its introduction, the cost savings have slowed. In addition, hospitals and physicians have responded by shifting many of their services and attendant costs to the outpatient setting. For example, elective surgery for cataracts, which previously occurred in hospitals, is now performed in outpatient facilities or in physicians' offices.

Even if health-care costs per disease or DRG could be reduced, the success of a pure cost-containment strategy is unlikely in the face of projected future three- to five-fold increases in health-care costs for age-dependent conditions, such as hip fractures or Alzheimer's disease, based entirely on the growing number of individuals susceptible to these conditions. A 25 percent reduction in cost for the care of each Alzheimer victim, which would be considered a great victory, would still result in a net 225 to 375 percent increase in health-care costs for all those affected by this disease. Therefore, while cost-containment has an important place in restraining health-care costs, it is clearly not the cure for the enormous projected increases in health-care costs for older Americans.

Rationing Health Care by Age

Faced with the failure of cost-containment to stop the current and projected increases in health-care costs for older Americans, desperate solutions are now being proposed. Richard Lamm, former governor of Colorado, seized the nation's attention when he proposed that we may not be able to afford so much medical care for older Americans. The argument for rationing health care by age has been more fully presented by Daniel Callahan, Director of The Hastings Center. Concerned about the lack of health-care for infants and children, Callahan proposes that federal funds be shifted from health-care for the aged to health care for younger Americans. He proposes that after individuals have completed their natural life-span, which he defines as the period of health and productivity, their health care would be limited to the relief of pain and suffering. He does not set a specific age limit for health care, but rather indicates that one could be set in the upper 70s or lower 80s. He believes that, in time, such a limit would be accepted by older Americans and their health-care providers.

Today, health care is rationed in the United States by wealth, in South Africa by color, and in Great Britain by age. None of these criteria is medically justifiable. However, there are sound medical and ethical criteria for rationing health care that could reduce health-care costs. An example would be decisions to withhold high-technology life-support systems for individuals of all ages with terminal, irreversible conditions which severely compromise the quality of life.

Aging, per se, is a poor criterion to use for rationing health care. It is not a homogeneous process; everyone ages at different rates. The enormous heterogeneity of aging makes chronological age an unreliable indicator of an individual's biologic age. Some 75-year-old individuals have the appearance, productivity, and actions of individuals in their 60s, while others resemble 90-year-olds. Therefore, if 75 were selected by the advocates of health-care rationing as the age to ration care, it would be difficult to justify withholding antibiotic therapy to treat the pneumonia of an otherwise healthy and vigorous 75-year-old woman while we would pay for the same treatment for a 74-year-old Alzheimer victim with dubious remaining quality of life.

Furthermore, if rationing of health care by age were to become a part of our entitlement regulations, the result would be rationing of health care for poor older Americans. The vast majority of older individuals with financial means, if denied health care by federal entitlement, would either pay directly for their health care or seek assistance in paying for this care from friends and family members. Thus, rationing of health care by age would place further strains on those already burdened with providing social care for older spouses, parents, relatives, and friends.

One of the important foundations for the arguments of advocates of rationing health care by age is that this nation has limited resources to pay for health care for all Americans. Thus, according to their arguments, dollars spent for health care for older Americans must come at the expense of resources to provide health care for younger Americans. They point to the increasing poverty among children and the decreasing level of poverty among those aged 65 and above, and suggest a cause and effect relationship. The fallacy of this argument has been demonstrated by Richard Easterlin and Eileen Crimmins, whose research showed that the increasing poverty among children is directly related to the increasing number of single-parent families and not to the diversion of resources to the elderly.[1] This argument is also weakened by the recent inclusion of all those aged 18 and under within Medicaid entitlements. Furthermore, the argument of fixed resources for health care is a difficult one to support when this nation continues to spend billions to support subsidies to farmers who produce substances, such as tobacco, that are harmful to health and lead to substantial health-care costs!

A Rational Alternative to Rationing

The proposed solutions for the impending rise in health-care costs for older Americans have been largely negative: rationing health care and cost containment through decreasing entitlement benefits or reducing provider payments. I would like to present another, more positive approach. One of the major factors determining health-care costs is the average health status of our older population. If we could improve the average health of older Americans at a rate faster than the growth of numbers in this group, we might actually reduce total health-care costs for older Americans.

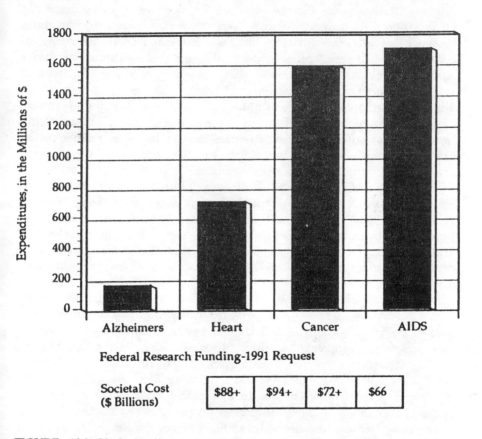

FIGURE 12.2 Underfunding of Alzheimer's Research Compared to Other Major Diseases, in Millions of Dollars. *Source: National Institutes of Health, 1990.*

Much of the rationale for the pessimistic view of those focusing on cost containment or on rationing is the belief that the health-care needs of older Americans are an inevitable consequence of the aging process. Aging research over the last decade has revealed that many of the physiologic decreases believed to be associated with aging do not significantly impair the functioning of older Americans. The major causes of disability and the need for health care among older Americans is not aging processes per se, but specific diseases and disorders that are more common at older ages. For many decades we believed that the major cause of dementia was aging and the condition was even called "senility." Today, it is clear that a specific disease, Alzheimer's disease, is the major cause of dementia. Furthermore, Alzheimer's disease can occur in individuals in their 50s and 60s and not occur in others who reach their 80s and 90s. Examination of the other major disabling conditions of older Americans reveals that osteoarthritis, not aging, is the main cause of arthritis; macular degeneration, not aging, is the main cause of blindness; osteoporosis (the thinning of bone that leads to fractures of the spine, hip, and wrist), not aging, is the main cause of hip fractures, and so forth. These diseases should be as amenable to the development of effective preventive and therapeutic approaches as diseases that afflict younger Americans.

For the first five decades of this century, large amounts of health-care resources were devoted to two major disabling illnesses--tuberculosis and polio. Millions of Americans feared contracting these conditions, which severely taxed the resources of families. Today, millions of older Americans fear that they will develop one of the chronic diseases of aging: Alzheimer's disease, Parkinson's disease, osteoarthritis, or osteoporosis.

In the 1940s and 1950s a national campaign, the "March of Dimes," was organized by a private foundation to conquer polio. Backed by the President of the United States, who was paralyzed by this disorder, mothers marched door to door soliciting funds. During the same period, "Easter Seals" were sold by another foundation to fight tuberculosis. Today, in response to the challenges presented by the diseases of aging, policy makers focus on cost-containment and make desperate proposals to ration health care. There is no reason to believe that the diseases of aging are any less amenable to prevention and cure than polio or tuberculosis. However, we must place the necessary resources behind research on the diseases and disorders of aging. The National Institutes of Health spend over $1 billion per year for research on cancer, heart disease and AIDS. The diseases of aging desperately need this level of attention. In comparison to the enormous cost of Alzheimer's disease, we spend a trivial amount on research for this condition: between one-tenth and two-tenths of a cent for research for every dollar spent for the *care* of individuals with Alzheimer's disease. We must place our national resources behind a campaign to abolish

Alzheimer's disease and other costly conditions of aging with the same vigor with which we conquered polio and defeated tuberculosis.

A Dream That Could Come True

This is obviously not the ideal time to initiate a program that would cost additional federal monies. However, if we examine the potential national costs of just one disease of aging, it is clear that the old adage--penny wise, pound foolish--rings true. Alzheimer's disease is projected to cost Americans between $1 trillion and $2 trillion in constant 1987 dollars over the next two decades. If, by increasing expenditures now, we could either delay the onset of Alzheimer's disease for five years or reduce the number of people who get the disease by 50 percent, this would result in savings of as much as $500 billion per decade.

There are many examples of the billions of dollars saved each year through biomedical research. The elimination of tuberculosis and polio as major causes of disability are two examples of the applications of biomedical research. Perhaps the best example of the potential benefits of large investments in biomedical and epidemiological research is the impressive progress that has been made in responding to AIDS. While this disease was first described in the medical literature in 1981, funding for research reached a level of over $100 million in 1985, over $500 million in 1987 and $1.3 billion by 1989. In the brief time of less than a decade, a successful, but not curative drug, azathymidine was introduced and tested, and today, forty-three federally funded centers are established and are conducting clinical trials of vaccines and second generation drug therapies. There is little doubt that AIDS research has been accelerated by this massive investment in research and that millions of lives and billions of dollars may be saved.

First Step Toward a Realistic Budget

On March 2, 1990, the Pepper Commission, a bipartisan congressional commission on comprehensive health care, recommended that federal funding for research and development related to long-term care, move towards a level of $1 billion annually. Pressure to convert this recommendation to legislation was exerted by the Alliance for Aging Research, an organization comprised of scientists and corporate executives, and by the Alzheimer's Association. In October 1990, under the bipartisan leadership of Congressmen Harkins, Roybal, Hatch, Waxman, Hatfield, Snowe, Stark, Downey, Oakar, Rinaldo, Regula, Bruce, Metzenbaum, Pressler, Grassley and Graham, the Independence for Older Americans Act of 1990 was passed. This action resulted in an increase of the appropriations for aging research to the National Institute on Aging (NIA) from $239 million in 1989-90 to $324 million in 1990-91, the largest increase in its budget since its inception in 1975. This increase in funding to the NIA at a time when many federal programs have received sizable cutbacks, reflects the recognition by Congress of the need to accelerate research on aging.

Can the government spend over $1 billion per year efficiently and effectively for research on aging? Before funding decisions are made, the National Institutes of Health (NIH) conducts an exhaustive, in-depth review of all research projects. In 1989, the NIA, like the other institutes comprising the NIH, funded the lowest percent of applications in its history. Thousands of high quality scientifically approved grants were not funded due to lack of available funds. If the budget of the NIH were increased to over $1 billion per year for aging research, there is little doubt in the scientific community that the funds could be effectively spent.

Remaining Steps

Expenditures for aging research at the NIH, which includes the NIA, were approximately $426 million in 1989-90. With the passage of the Independence for Older Americans Act, this figure is now approximately $520 million. To reach the level of $1 billion per year for federal support for aging research, an additional $480 million is needed for the NIH. How would these additional funds be spent and what could be the results of this additional research effort? Let me provide a few examples of promising research areas where these funds could be profitably invested.

Basic Biomedical Research

A foundation of knowledge is needed about the mechanisms of normal aging to provide a basis for understanding the many diseases and disorders of aging. A similar approach to the understanding of the normal control of cell growth and differentiation is providing valuable clues to the origins of human cancers. The molecular, genetic approaches which have provided enormous insight into the mechanisms of cancer can also be utilized to understand aging processes. One example of this approach is the work on identifying genes that regulate aging processes, or "gerontogenes."

Some of the cell types within our body are constantly dividing while other cell types rarely, if ever, divide. The decline in the rate of replication of immune cells with normal aging may contribute to the increased susceptibility of older individuals to infectious diseases. Many of the genes that are involved in the control of cellular division have been found to be related to genes, called oncogenes, which control the development of cancers. Some gerontogenes may act opposite to these oncogenes by inhibiting cellular replication. Future research which identifies, isolates, and characterizes these genes may lead to the development of drugs that restore replicative capabilities to immune cells and thus protect older individuals from bacterial and viral diseases.

A key non-dividing cell, the brain cell, also called the neuron, plays an important part in aging. Aging of the brain leads to the loss of neurons in certain brain regions which may be responsible for the normal decline in functions, such as short term memory, that occurs with aging. When this loss of brain cells is accelerated, it can lead to the development of two important age-dependent diseases, Alzheimer's and Parkinson's diseases. The recent identification of proteins, called nerve growth factors, which can restore function to damaged neurons, provides the exciting possibility that these proteins or their derivatives may be able to prevent some of the declines in brain functions that occur with aging. These nerve growth factors are currently being assessed for their use in Alzheimer's disease.

Studies of the Normal Processes of Aging

We know far more about many human diseases than we know about the normal processes of aging. Most studies of human aging have been cross-sectional, defined as measurements of a parameter on individuals of different ages at one point in time. Longitudinal studies, where the parameter is measured in the same individuals over many years, may provide a more accurate assessment of normal human aging. The problem with cross-sectional studies is illustrated by the aberrant results of a hypothetical cross-sectional study of births and deaths in southern Florida, which might reveal that most individuals in this region were born Hispanic and die Jewish.

Longitudinal studies, such as the pioneering program of the Gerontology Research Center in Baltimore, should provide valuable insights into the extent of variability, as well as the patterns of normal aging. These studies may also reveal factors that will enable "successful aging."

Research Aimed at Preventing or Treating Diseases of Aging

Recent research in Alzheimer's disease has revealed several promising areas for further efforts. At least one gene has been identified that is involved in the familial form of Alzheimer's disease. Using classic molecular genetic techniques, in the upcoming years, this gene can be isolated and its function elucidated. This approach has been successful in determining the molecular defect in other diseases that have a genetic component.

There is also evidence of an altered protein, called beta amyloid, being deposited in the brains of Alzheimer's disease victims. Recent research indicates that altered metabolism of this protein may play a key role in the development of the disease. Further research on the nature of the alteration should provide a pathway to correct the defective metabolism and perhaps arrest the progression of the disease. These are just two examples of the many promising research directions that are being conducted as a result of increasing research funding related to Alzheimer's disease.

While the nation's attention is being drawn to the plight of Alzheimer victims, other diseases of aging, such as Parkinson's disease, adult onset diabetes, hearing and vision losses, osteoarthritis (the arthritis of aging), and osteoporosis (the loss of bone with aging) need increased research attention.

Social, Behavioral, and Epidemiological Research

Many of the diseases and disorders of aging may be prevented or ameliorated by alterations in health behaviors, such as stopping smoking, diet modification, and exercise programs. For example, while we know that exercise programs can delay osteoporosis (the loss of bone with aging) and prevent hip fractures, it would be helpful to identify which types of exercise and what frequency of exercise can minimize bone loss.

Epidemiological research is needed to identify risk factors as well as populations that are at increased risk and need special attention. An example of the potential of this research is the need to educate fair-complexioned, older caucasian women who are at increased risk for hip fractures. One area that needs more support is the identification of psychosocial factors that impact on aging. For example, while we have many anecdotes about the effect of stress on health, there is a great need for experimental data to determine how stress modifies aging and how successful coping strategies can be developed.

Finally, there is a critical need for more investigators to enter the various fields of aging research. The many challenges of aging research will occupy scientists for decades to come. Their work in the upcoming decades will add more life to our years.

Conclusion

We are in the final decade of a century where we have witnessed the conquest of many acute diseases, diseases that predominantly cause death rather than disability. Through the application of preventive measures, medications, vaccines, and therapies developed through research, we have witnessed a twenty-five-year increase in longevity since 1900. The next century will be dominated by an aging population at risk for chronic, disabling diseases.

The entitlement programs developed to support older Americans did not consider the long-term consequences of an aging population and rising health-care costs. Faced with massive projected future increases in health-care costs for older Americans, we have several options. Unfortunately, until recently, most attention has focused on the negative approaches of cost containment and rationing. While the 101st Congress was making major cutbacks in Medicare programs and increasing Medicare taxation, it also took the first step towards a positive approach by substantially increasing funding for aging research. By investing now to conquer the disabling diseases of an aging population, we are providing the dual benefits of reducing future federal entitlement spending for health-care, while ensuring for ourselves and future generations a long and healthy life-span.

Notes and References

1. Richard A. Easterlin and Eileen M. Crimmins, *The Fertility Revolution: A Supply-Demand Analysis* (Chicago: University of Chicago Press, 1985).

Note: A much shorter version of this article was published in *Issues in Science and Technology*, Vol. VII, No. 4, 1991.

Special thanks to Donna Polisar and Gitta Morris for their special technical assistance.

PART FIVE

Gender, Equity, and Distributive Justice

13

Achieving Equity and Setting Limits: The Importance of Gender

Bethany Spielman

"The problems of old age in America are largely the problems of women."[1]

Introduction

Much of the attention given Daniel Callahan's *Setting Limits*[2]--by feminists and non-feminists alike--has focused on Callahan's proposal to ration health care for the elderly.[3]   But in addition to recommending age rationing, Callahan has a great deal to say about broader cultural and social issues.   He critiques the technological mind-set that views old age as a disease to be conquered; he invites us to consider aging and death as natural phenomena to be lived, not fought.   Further, Callahan urges the elderly to adopt a new role; he claims that they have become increasingly hedonistic, and calls them to service to the young.   He would argue that we cannot fully understand or begin to evaluate age rationing apart from its social and cultural context.

The goal of this essay is to make the gender issues in these contextual aspects of *Setting Limits* more visible.   Women make up the majority of the elderly, and that majority becomes even more pronounced as the elderly get older.   The majority of professional and home caregivers are also women.   A discussion about aging that discounts these demographic and social facts risks distorting important aspects of aging.

A perspective that highlights these facts generates several questions about Callahan's proposal, and about the health-care system and cultural attitudes he wants to change: What consequences for women might result from Callahan's proposal for a new social role for the elderly? Would the social role Callahan proposes increase or decrease the likelihood of attaining equitable security--a precondition, in Callahan's scheme, for rationing? A gendered, feminist perspective suggests a departure from, or at least some reservations about, Callahan's proposal for a new social role for the elderly. But if those reservations can be adequately addressed, there are important enough similarities between Callahan's critique of medicine and feminist thought that his constructive proposal, including age rationing, ought to be seriously considered by women.

A Social Role for the Elderly Within Gendered Life Courses

Why a Gendered Perspective on the Social Role of the Elderly

Callahan proposes that the elderly, who he believes have a unique capacity to link past, present, and future, strive to become "moral conservators." By serving the young and future generations the elderly would gain not only a sense of meaning but also greater social significance. It is not entirely clear what Callahan means either by "moral conservator" or by "service to the young." As Callahan describes the role, a moral conservator somehow links past, present, and future, and from this perspective--which Callahan believes is uniquely accessible to the elderly--serves the young.

There are problems with Callahan's assertion that only the very old are able to link time and see the cycle of generations: For example, how could a middle-aged woman caring for both her frail, widowed mother and her young children avoid thinking about the cycle of generations? Equally problematic is Callahan's suggestion that the elderly would be fulfilling an age-distinctive role by giving advice and counseling to younger friends and family members, or by working to ameliorate conditions that reduce the possibility of living a decent life: Many young and middle-aged adults regularly do precisely these things.

But what Callahan wants the elderly to strive towards is most unclear and potentially problematic: service to the young and future generations. What does Callahan mean by this? Service to the young might include just about anything that is not consumptive self-absorption. One could hardly argue against Callahan, at least from an ethical perspective, if that were all he meant. But if we take Callahan to be saying something more intentionally specific about how the elderly should behave--that they should intentionally direct their time, energy, and resources toward the young--then we need to ask some questions that arise from a consideration of gender.

There are three reasons why we cannot safely ignore gender here. First, whatever role Callahan carves out for the elderly will disproportionately affect women, since they make up the majority of the elderly. Second, as John and Matilda Riley remind us, every alteration in one phase of a person's life can have consequences not only for that particular phase, but for other phases as well; in fact, a change in one phase can conceivably reshape the entire life course.[4] We need to ask, "What would be the impact on a woman's life course if the last stage of life were defined by the role of service to the young? What would be the impact on a man's life course?" Finally, the social role Callahan proposes may actually conflict with another of his aims--to achieve equitable security.

Callahan has not made any links between the social roles filled in earlier adult life and what he proposes for old age. But the gendered nature of the roles preceding old age could make a great deal of difference in how the role in old age is played out. And anticipating a particular role for old age affects how earlier roles are played. Earlier stages are quite different for men and women with respect to links to generations other than their own, and particularly with respect to service links to the young. A gendered description of the stages of life is necessary to understand adequately the implications of Callahan's new role for the last stage of life.

The Cumulative Effect of Multiple Service Roles

Women have a wealth of experience serving the young. They have been socialized to think of themselves as good when they live lives of service, and to think of themselves as selfish when they do not. Religion is one vehicle of this gendered socialization, but there are many other vehicles. Matilda Gage wrote 100 years ago: "The whole theory regarding women, under Christianity, has been based upon the conception that she has no right to be for herself alone.

Her duty to others has continuously been placed before her and her training has ever been that of self-sacrifice."[5]

From Matilda Gage to Beverly Harrison[6] and Barbara Andolsen,[7] religious feminists have agreed that women's servant role has been applied in a remarkably one-sided way to women. The moral training of women for service--by religious and other social institutions--has been effective. Carol Gilligan has shown that women's moral thinking is more typically oriented toward care and toward relationship than is men's moral thinking.[8] Often women become developmentally "stuck" at a stage in which they are unable to distinguish caring for themselves from "selfishness."

At the heart of women's socialization into service is motherhood--the paradigmatic role of service to the young. The cultural script for the good mother is a selfless one.[9] When children are small, women are almost always the primary parent. Even fully employed women dutifully perform their "second shift,"[10] including long hours of household chores for their children.

Women are expected to sacrifice--their jobs, if necessary--for the sake of even unconceived children. Fetal protection policies in the workplace illustrate how extreme the demand for women's service to future generations has become--and how it affects women's entire adulthood. For example, because exposure to lead may present health risks to as yet unconceived children of its Battery Division workers, Johnson Controls gave women an ultimatum: get sterilized or lose your jobs. That sacrifice was not demanded of men, though the potential risk of the lead to unconceived children may be as great for men's offspring as for women's.[11] Fetal protection policies have been applied against women as old as 70.[12]

But women's strong intergenerational links are not limited to their children or potential children.[13] As Emily Culpepper points out[14] in *Ageism, Sexism and Health-Care: Why We Need Older Women in Power*, grandmothers in some ethnic groups are under significant pressure to provide childcare to their grandchildren. Throughout their lives, women find it easier than do men to cross age and generation boundaries--making links with generations that precede and follow their own.[15] Women serve as the linchpins of their widowed mothers' support systems, and provide more parent care than men when either parent becomes needy. Women now spend as many years caring for elderly parents as they do caring for young children. They move from the "mommy track" to the "daughter track." Women move from one set of intergenerational commitments to another

Contrast these role patterns with men's intergenerational roles, particularly those involving service to the young. Though the media have stressed gender equality in the family, there are sharp contrasts between men's and women's intergenerational connections at every stage of life. In childhood, boys regard age differences as more important than do girls; they exhibit a greater tendency to orient themselves toward relationships with age peers.[16] In part because of the increasing number of divorced parents and single mothers, adult males of all educational, racial, and geographic categories have spent much less time during recent decades living in families with young children.[17] Men's lives are now organized so that children occupy a smaller proportion of their adult years. And during the years they live with children, men are rarely primary parents or even equally involved parents. They have more tenuous ties with their children after divorce, and with their grown children; they do not serve as linchpins of support for their widowed mothers; and they give less parent care than women.

In what ways might these gendered role patterns make a difference in our assessment of Callahan's proposal? When applied to women, Callahan's proposal should be viewed in the context of at least two other life stages of heavy intergenerational service: first to their children (usually in women's young adult lives, but occasionally--as is the case with some fetal protection policies--all through adulthood) and, second, to their parents (usually in women's middle age). What if women were socialized to expect *three* or even *four* stages of life in which their energies were consumed by service to other generations? Callahan's proposal seems to call for repeating in the last stage of life what women are already well socialized to do in earlier stages. On one hand, we might view this string of intergenerational service roles favorably if women wanted or needed little role flexibility but a great deal of role continuity.

On the other hand, we might worry that many women, by the time they reach old age, have already spent a considerable number of years serving the young, and that they have also spent a considerable number of years serving the generation that preceded them. Three or four stages of expected intergenerational service could crowd out other life projects, as child rearing and parent care often do now. To frame the contribution of elderly women yet again in terms of service to the young, rather than, say, service to the poor, caring for the environment, or improving the material conditions of women, would be to risk seriously constricting women's life options. The cumulative effect of multiple stages of costly intergenerational service--in young adult life, middle age, and old age--might be to significantly affect women's development.

There would be no cumulative socialization, or concomitant risk, for men. Adopting an ideal of service to the young could be far more voluntary and far less constricting for men than for women, since men are not usually expected to devote other life stages to direct service to the young (or to the old).

Extending and Intensifying the Service Role While Achieving Equitable Security

This gendered description of intergenerational links accounts only for service to family members. Callahan wants to distinguish service to the family from service to the young in the public context. The elderly need to serve the young in the larger public world, he believes, if they are to achieve meaning and significance. Can women's strong intergenerational commitments be translated or extended to a commitment to serve the young in the public realm? Should they be?

One answer is that many women have already extended their service to the young to the public realm. Feminist writers including Gilman,[18] Ruddick,[19] and Okin[20] have described women's obligation to the next generation in terms that encompass, but extend far beyond, family life. One need not resort to theory, though, to observe women's commitment to young other than their own. A greater percentage of women than men are personally involved in direct aid to the needy and to friends and neighbors; a greater percentage of women than men help the handicapped, the sick, the poor and the homeless.[21] Women--even elderly women--are more willing to raise taxes for children's education than are males among their cohorts.[22] Callahan's call for service to the young may be redundant, if it is directed at women.

But this is only a partial answer. The obstacles to participating fully in both family life and paid work may not be as high for all women as they were for the women of Johnson Controls, but they are still very high. Women who do confine their service to family life may do so because employed women are so poorly supported in this country. Unlike many of their European counterparts, American women have no national day-care policy, or family leave policy that would help them and their children achieve economic security.[23] American women have no long-term care policy that would help them keep jobs while caring for parents. They have a Supreme Court hostile to their claims of sex discrimination in the workplace.

Women's public role is uneasy at best; they have a precarious presence in public life.

It is in the public arena, which is so difficult for women throughout their adult lives, that Callahan would have the elderly intensify their service. To make demands upon elderly women for greater public service before more public support is available to women in younger adult life could be premature--in the same way that Callahan thinks that asking health-care sacrifices of the elderly before they have better health-care benefits would be premature.[24]

Callahan touches on this general point in his discussion of equitable security, which he views as a precondition of the rationing scheme. He remarks that "women could make more demands." Surely he is correct. The feminization of poverty has deepened during the last decade, and more women in poverty means more children in poverty.[25] But Callahan's brief comment is limited to health-care benefits, and does not address the fundamental conflict between women "demanding more" (even from younger generations) in order to achieve equitable security--and serving more in order to achieve meaning and social significance. Encouraging women to further commit themselves to a service role may make them less disposed to insist on the economic security they and their children need, and therefore more poorly positioned to achieve the equitable security Callahan desires. Before women--old or young--begin aspiring to Callahan's intensified service role, the scope and legitimacy of women's needs deserves much more public discussion.

Women have been excluded for so long from Western political, philosophical, and ethical thought[26] that our culture has few intellectual resources to begin to fill in the gaps and solve this problem. Feminism is one resource. It speaks to the enlarging of women's roles; to a significant extent it speaks for those attempting to become public beings. Women who identify themselves as feminists have developed distinctive views about the split between public and private life, and one's obligations to others in each. The political values of feminists reflect both strong public support for the disadvantaged and a desire for more public support for women's own needs as parents and workers.[27] Feminist consciousness may therefore be a mechanism suited both to extending the value of service to the young from the private to the public sphere and to enabling the servants in this scheme to make enough demands, effectively enough, to achieve the equitable security Callahan desires. But only extended public discussion among feminists and nonfeminists alike will begin to fill the lacuna in Callahan's, and our culture's, thinking about women and equity.

Callahan's proposal requires extending values heretofore associated with domesticity and femaleness into the public realm. That transition requires a better solution to the problem of equitable security than Callahan offers. As a first step, it requires abandoning a gender-neutral posture. Only then can we examine carefully the cumulative effect of multiple stages of intergenerational service on women's lives, and begin to explore how women can achieve equitable security while they intensify and extend their efforts on behalf of future generations. If these problems are solveable, it would not be far-fetched to think that feminists could support Callahan's constructive proposals for health-care. The common ground between feminists and Callahan is considerable.

Common Ground: Critique of Medicine

The Quest for Immortality

Three fundamental aspects of Callahan's work--his view of mortality, his view of technological progress, and his view of medical needs--are part of a critique that he holds in common with feminists. Callahan criticizes the modernizers of aging, who aggressively resist the physical process of aging, viewing it as a new "frontier" to conquer. He believes that death has a place at the end of life that ought not to be denied. Though extending the lives of the elderly may seem attractive, we ought to learn to accept death after a natural life-span--in part, because doing so will allow us to spend our resources more wisely on the young. Both Western religion and Western medicine have been preoccupied with transcending finitude. Modernizers hope that if medicine is technologically successful enough, eventually it will be able to prolong life so that we need not die at all. In the meantime, it tries to prolong life as long as possible, while we derive some comfort from religion's promise of an afterlife. The link between death-denying medicine and death-denying religion is clear to Callahan, and to Gerald Gruman, whom he cites:

> The principal source of the prestige that modern biomedicine enjoys is the fact that it was the one professional group that seriously took up the imperative of meliorist progress from the Enlightenment . . . for biomedicine carries forward the transcendent Judeo-Christian quest for salvation from evil and death.[28]

With few exceptions,[29] feminist thinkers place a low value on immortality and life extension. In fact, for almost a century, feminists have criticized religion's preoccupation with death and immortality, and its distrust of bodily life. Seventy-five years ago Charlotte Perkins Gilman distinguished what she called men's religion ("death-based religion") from women's religion ("birth-based religion") on just this basis:

> The death-based religions have led to a limitless individualism, a demand for the eternal extension of personality. The birth-based religion is necessarily and essentially altruistic, a forgetting of oneself for the good of the child, and tends to develop naturally into love and labor for the widening range of family, state, and world.[30]

Although contemporary feminists would challenge some aspects of Gilman's description, they almost uniformly share Gilman's disinterest in immortality and life extension. Rosemary Ruether, for example, argues that feminists do not have the same stake in denying their mortality as men do. Focusing on immortality distracts attention from our present responsibility: to create a "just and good community for our generation and our children."[31] Nel Noddings' analysis of evil does not even count death as a fundamental evil.[32] The pain, separation, and helplessness that accompany dying are evil, but death itself need not be.

The Technological Promise of Human Perfectibility

The second, and closely related, idea on which Callahan builds his critique is that medical technology can be socially dangerous. It creates constantly rising expectations about the perfectibility of human life--expectations that crowd out other social goods and reduce our commitment to giving humane care. Constant technological innovation and refinement demand more resources than society can afford, and displace sympathy and compassion in healthcare. Callahan hints at the importance of caring in *Setting Limits*[33] and develops his theory of caring more fully in *What Kind of Life*,[34] arguing that attention to pain and suffering should always receive high priority in health care.

Feminists share this wariness of medical technology and this commitment to caring above curing. The ways in which reproductive technology pushes society are painfully clear to them:

Technology has contributed to the expectation of ever more perfect babies, ever more controlled labors and deliveries, and ever more in vitro fertilization among the infertile.[35]   For feminists, high technology is a double-edged sword, at best. It ought to be scaled back and replaced in part by lower technology combined with a more caring health-care setting, one marked by responsiveness to pain and suffering. Since at least the nineteenth century, women in health-care have committed themselves to an ethic of caring. From the "sympathy and science" of physicians such as Elizabeth Blackwell[36] to the theories of caring developed by contemporary nurses such as Jean Watson[37] and Sara Fry,[38] to Nel Noddings' theological ethic of care,[39] feminist attempts to improve health-care have been focused on human caring and sympathy, not on high technology or an aggressive contest against finitude.

Cultural Influence on the Definition of Medical Needs

A third criticism of medicine is one Callahan has voiced since his early writings:[40] that medical needs are culturally shaped. The level of technology available in a society determines what it perceives as medical need. Those "needs" are always expanding. We constantly upgrade them; the more we get, the more we want. Callahan insists that many medical "needs" of the elderly reflect only social expectations and the quest for individual happiness; fulfilling them does not necessarily contribute to the common good.

Feminist thinkers, too, have observed that technological "solutions" are developed for socially-shaped medical "needs". Again, reproductive medicine provides striking examples of this pheno- menon: The "need" for infertile couples to have genetically related children gives rise to elaborate and costly medical enterprises. The "need" for genetically "perfect" children and the "need" for many hysterectomies are socially created expectations that grow from and result in medical-technological solutions.   Feminists, along with Callahan, urge us to reject widely touted technologies that exchange long-range social values for short-term individual wish fulfillment.

Conclusion

Callahan and feminists agree in fundamental ways about the dangers of current medical trends. Feminists are unlikely to have a stake in the kind of death-denying technological "progress" that

Callahan wants medicine to forego, and they have a significant stake in a health-care system focused on human caring, as Callahan advocates. However, women cannot be expected to support wholeheartedly his proposal for age rationing because he has not resolved the conflict between an intensified service role and equitable security for women, which Callahan says is a prerequisite to age rationing. In fact, his gender neutrality presents significant obstacles to understanding the impact on women's lives of multiple stages of intergenerational service, and to exploring the means to equitable security.

Notes and References

1. Robert N. Butler, preface to U.S. National Institute on Aging, *The Older Woman: Contributions and Discontinuities* (Washington, D.C.: U.S. Government Printing Office, 1978), p. 1.

2. Daniel Callahan, *Setting Limits: Medical Goals in an Aging Society* (New York: Simon & Schuster, 1987).

3. Janet A. Coy, "On the Alleged Sexism of the Age-Rationing of Social Resources," Paper presented to the SHHV [Society for Health and Human Values], Chicago, November 10, 1990.

4. Matilda White Riley and John W. Riley, Jr., "Longevity and Social Structure: The Potential of the Added Years," *Our Aging Society: Paradox and Promise*, edited by Alan Pifer and Lydia Bronte (New York: Norton, 1986), pp. 53-79.

5. Matilda Joslyn Gage, *Woman, Church, and Society: The Original Expose of Male Collaboration Against the Female Sex* (Watertown, Mass.: Persephone Press, 1980 [c. 1893]), p. 239.

6. Beverly Harrison, "The Consciousness of Women: A Socio-political Resource," *Cross Currents*, Vol. 24 (Fall, 1975), pp. 445-462.

7. Barbara Andolsen, "Agape and Feminist Ethics," *Journal of Religious Ethics*, Vol. 16 (Fall 1988), p. 273.

8. See Carol Gilligan, *In a Different Voice* (Boston: Harvard University Press, 1982); and "Reply by Carol Gilligan," *Signs*, Vol. 11 (Winter, 1986), pp. 324-333.

9. J. Attanucci, "*Mothers in Their Own Terms: A Developmental Perspective on Self and Role*," Unpublished Doctoral Dissertation, Harvard Graduate School in Education, 1984.

10. Arlie Hochschild and Anne Machung, *The Second Shift: Working Parents and the Revolution at Home* (New York: Viking, 1989).

11. *International Union, United Automobile, Aerospace and Agricultural*

Implement Workers of America, UAW, et al. *v. Johnson Controls, Inc.* 111 S. Ct 1196 (1991).

12. Carol Kleiman, "Women Challenge 'Fetal Protection' Policy," *The Washington Post,* September 2, 1990, H3.

13. James L. Peterson Furstenberg et al., "The Life Course of Children of Divorce: Marital Disruption and Parental Contact," *American Sociological Review,* Vol. 48 (Oct. 1983), pp. 656-668.

14. See Emily Erwin Culpepper's chapter in this volume.

15. Gunhild O. Hagestad, "The Family: Women and Grandparents as Kin-Keepers," *Our Aging Society,* edited by Alan and Lydia Bronte (New York: W. W. Norton, 1986), pp. 141-160.

16. Furstenberg, et al., *The Life Course of Children of Divorce."*

17. David Eggebeen and Peter Uhlenberg, "Changes in the Organization of Men's Lives: 1960-1980," *Family Relations,* Vol. 34 (April 1985), pp. 251-257.

18. Charlotte Perkins Gilman, *The Living of Charlotte Perkins Gilman* (New York: Arno, 1972 [c. 1935]).

19. Sara Ruddick, *Maternal Thinking* (Boston: Beacon Press, 1989).

20. Susan Moller Okin, *Justice, Gender and the Family* (New York: Basic Books, 1989).

21. Diane Colasanto, "Americans Show Commitment to Helping Those in Need," *The Gallup Report,* Vol. 290, 1989, pp. 17-24.

22. Roper Center for Public Opinion Research, Data prepared by the Roper Center, Storrs: The Roper Center, 1986.

23. Sylvia Ann Hewlett, *A Lesser Life: The Myth of Women's Liberation in America* (New York: William Morrow and Co., Inc., 1986); Roberta A. Spalter-Roth and Heidi Hartmann, *Unnecessary Losses: Costs to Americans of the Lack of Family and Medical Leave* (Washington, D.C.: Institute for Women's Policy Research, 1990).

24. Callahan, *Setting Limits.*

25. Diana Pearce, *The Feminization of Poverty: A Second Look* (Washington, D.C.: Institute for Women's Policy Research, 1989).

26. Okin, *Justice, Gender and the Family.*

27. Pamela Johnston Conover, "Feminists and the Gender Gap," *Journal of Politics,* Vol. 50 (November 1988), pp. 985-1010.

28. Gerald Gruman, "Cultural Origins of Present-Day 'Ageism': The Modernization of the Life Cycle," *Aging and the Elderly: Humanistic Perspectives in Gerontology,* edited by Stuart F. Spicker, et al. (Highlands, N.J.: Humanities Press, 1978), p. 379.

29. Molly Sinclair, "Shedding Light on Mystique of Aging Women: Feminists Say Issues Are Becoming Inextricably Linked as Life Expectancy in U.S. Grows," *The Washington Post,* February 19, 1989, A21.

30. Charlotte Perkins Gilman, *His Religion and Hers: A Study of the Faith of Our Fathers and the Works of Our Mothers* (New York: The Century Co., 1923), pp. 46-47.

31. Rosemary Ruether, *Sexism and God-Talk: Toward a Feminist Theology* (Boston: Beacon Press, 1983), p. 258.

32. Nel Noddings, *Women and Evil* (Berkeley: University of California Press, 1989).

33. Callahan, *Setting Limits*.

34. Daniel Callahan, *What Kind of Life: The Limits of Medical Progress* (New York: Simon & Schuster, 1990).

35. Barbara Katz Rothman, *The Tentative Pregnancy: Prenatal Diagnosis and the Future of Motherhood* (New York: Viking, 1986); *The Woman in the Body: A Cultural Analysis of Reproduction* (Boston: Beacon Press, 1986); Patricia Spallone and Deborah Steinberg, editors, *Made to Order: The Myth of Reproductive and Genetic Progress* (Oxford: Pergamon Press, 1987).

36. See Regina Markell Morantz-Sanchez, *Sympathy and Science: Women Physicians in American Medicine* (New York: Oxford University Press, 1985).

37. Jean Watson, *Nursing: Human Science and Human Care* (New York: Appleton Century Crofts, 1985); Jean Watson, *Nursing: The Philosophy and Science of Caring* (Boulder: Colorado Associated University Press, 1985).

38. Sara T. Fry, "The Role of Caring in a Theory of Nursing Ethics," *Hypatia*, Vol. 4 (Summer, 1989), pp. 88-103).

39. Noddings, *Women and Evil*.

40. Daniel Callahan, *The Tyranny of Survival and Other Pathologies of Civilized Life* (New York: Macmillan, 1973).

14

Ageism, Sexism, and Health Care: Why We Need Old Women in Power

Emily Erwin Culpepper

Introduction

This essay focuses on the insights of activists working for social change regarding sexism and ageism. As a feminist I am committed to placing these voices in the midst of scholarly and public discussion of social issues. Too often issues first raised by committed activists are taken up in academic and public forums, studied, legitimated, polished and promoted in ways that leave behind the original wisdom that first raised the cry of alarm.

I am interpreting health care very broadly. Oppressive social power imbalances must be addressed to create real change in the delivery of health care to the elderly. Without attention to political context, we will achieve only partial reforms--what one feminist activist against ageism has castigated as "patch up services" that still stereotype, segregate and disempower the elderly.[1]

The feminist method I use here involves a three-fold task. The first step comes from the practice of consciousness-raising: listening to those directly involved, to the voices of old women. The second step is social critique, bringing into visibility the interwoven pressures that form the context of women's lives as we age. Making visible such issues is crucial because it is the repeated experience of women and minorities that their lives and needs are made invisible by this society. Invisibility takes many forms: outright erasure and denial, token lip-service without serious sustained attention, misrepresentation, and distortion through stereotyping. Invisibility can be crushing. Becoming visible, while essential, is not easy. Our society's discomfort with this first essential step is often manifested by labeling those who speak out as "strident," "shrill" or "extremist." (Or, more tastefully, "inappropriate," "marginal," or "unrealistic.") These perspectives sound dissonant and loud because they are demanding to be let in. They reflect the anger and anguish of exclusion. Their presence will transform our understanding.

The third step is our obligation to make positive suggestions for change--proposing and implementing experiments, inventions, and visions. Without this constructive dimension, critique can become disheartening, subverting its intent. Even small steps for change can relocate our angle of vision, opening up further insight and action. These tangible positive steps include the practical and the seemingly implausible. Massive social problems demand a wide range of approaches.

Baba Copper, a ground-breaking activist in addressing ageism, has written:

> I can remember the day when I would use the phrase "over the hill" to describe an old woman. The implications of the phrase, and my complicity in those implications never crossed my mind. Now, from experience, I understand that someone "over the hill" is metaphorically out of sight.[2]

And "the hill," she shrewdly observes, "is a hill of power." Ageism turns aging into a slippery slope, down which the old--both men and women, but especially women and minorities--can slide into increasing powerlessness. Ageism and sexism intersect in women's lives with terrible force, accelerating and intensifying our marginalization. Hardships caused by race, class, sexual orientation, lack of education, and disability all increase with aging. Examining her own experience of aging and ageism, Copper formulated a fundamental contribution to feminist analysis: "One of the primary definitions of patriarchy is the absence of old women in power."

Old women are threatening to the interstructured oppressions of patriarchy. Feminist activists identify several major themes we need to examine, if we are to understand and address this absence of old women in power: (1) attitudes towards aging that are deeply negative, (2) the place of women in the elderly population, (3) the impact of women's traditional roles, (4) women's economic situation as unpaid and paid workers, and (5) suggestions for change. Let us look at each of these in turn.

Attitudes Toward Aging in the U.S.

As Beverly Harrison has noted, "this society's basic social myth is that ours has been the greatest social experiment in human history and that here the possibilities for human fulfillment have come to fruition as never before."[3] Evidence to the contrary is strongly resisted, producing that familiar phenomenon of blaming the victims. If they are marginalized and in difficult circumstances, if care is difficult to find, there must be something wrong with the way they lived and prepared (or failed to) for old age. Our national passion for independence does not compare well with the situation of most of the elderly, therefore attention turns away from them and fixes more strongly on asserting the myth. It helps to repress this knowledge if the elderly are isolated, out of sight, especially those who are least able to confirm the American Dream. The elderly come to represent those who need or will soon need care and who are dependent. Thus, many symbolic meanings collapse upon them. The more isolated they are, the more the elderly symbolically function as reminders of infirmity, decay and death. The dream of eternal pioneering progress does not have room for them. Our fixation on adventurous adolescent heroic energy as the paradigm for the American psyche is so strong that taboos around aging begin quite early, long before old age, long before frailty or infirmity are even present.

Feeding this delusion is the American equation of worth with usefulness, with what one does and earns. Our economy, geared to capitalistic production, strongly shapes our cultural values. I agree with Harrison that this system of production glorifies persons seen as full-fledged producers who add to the goods and services of our economy, and earning enough to consume lots of these same goods and services. This ideal producer/consumer is not old. The emphasis is on what is new--in people and in things. Old means obsolete (something to discard, to reject); something that has failed to remain useful. Youth is new and exciting. Adulthood is only "thirty-something." The middle-aged are on the way out. Our lives are considered boring and we know it. Mid-life crisis over these realizations has become a veritable national pastime, spawning whole new industries to help us cope and stay young.

The elderly are expected to step aside, and genteelly fade into the background where they are welcome to play supporting roles for the nuclear family and the economy, when convenient. With our virtual worship of advanced technologies and rapid social change, the knowledge and skills of older generations are quickly devalued. They are yesterday, and we are living not just in today but in the future shock of tomorrow already here. Conservative forces trumpeting the nuclear family further marginalize the elderly. The idealized U.S. family is young adults raising children, preferably with mother in the home full or at least part-time. Harrison criticizes the involvement of the churches in promoting this distorted emphasis as "Christian complicity in ageism."[4]

Our language about aging betrays our ageism. The designation "old" is euphemistically avoided. One is older, elderly, a senior, or in the retirement set. Copper is typical of many activists who are reclaiming the word old as an important step for self-esteem and facing issues clearly. At sixty-six, she wrote:

> Part of the reason I self-identify as *old* is a need to escape the prissy
> category of "older woman"--which covers women from thirty on up.
> If I don't embrace *old*, how am I to speak of myself.[5]

I have begun using the word *old* straightforwardly, in order to join old women in breaking the terrible, negative power of this word.

This broad sketch of sources of ageism in our society alerts us to the many forces aligned against full human relationship with the elderly, the old. If health care for the elderly is to be ethical, we must not only become conscious of the distortions of ageism, we must learn to be actively anti-ageist. Without this commitment, health care is delivered as a condescending top-down arrangement, with basic causes of inequity unaddressed.

The Place of Women Among the Old

The face of the majority of aging Americans is a female face. Issues of age are predominantly women's issues, yet in our society the male is the norm, the subject of most attention, the reference point for most research. Women's health, and especially our needs around aging, are much less researched than men's health. (This is also true for men who are not white.) For example, there is very little knowledge of normal menopause. Numerous health studies exclude women, relying on a male norm that may or may not apply to women's bodies.[6] The famous study showing positive cardiac health benefits from an aspirin a day was based on men only. Even to understand men's issues clearly, we must relocate our perspective on who the elderly are and how they are interrelated. As men age, they live increasingly in a world of women. Their social context becomes more female, which in a male-dominated society is one of lower status.

Up to age forty-five the percentage of women and men in the United States is virtually equal, and then a gap begins and widens continually. Over age 65 the population shifts to 59 percent women and 41 percent men. Women over age 65 are the fastest growing part of our population. In the population over 75, two-thirds are women and one-third are men.[7] Since women's longevity is increasing relative to men's, these figures will probably increase.

Looking more closely at the circumstances of women over age 65; about 50 percent are widows. More than 80 percent of all Americans over 65 who live alone are women. Women 65 and older make up 72 percent of the elderly poor, 13 percent more than their share of the over 65 population. If we break these figures down by race and ethnic groups, we find familiar and deepening disadvantages for minorities. While 15 percent of all women over 65 live below our insanely low poverty level, this figure jumps to 25 percent for Hispanic women and up to 35 percent for Black women.[8] Looking further at Black women 65 and over, 60 percent are still working mostly in low paying jobs, with no pension and often no Social Security.[9] The situation for most women over 65 is not life as "golden girls." The realities of aging contrast sharply with popular media attention to affluent older consumers.

Improving health care for the elderly cannot progress very far until we place fundamental changes in the status of women on our agenda. The social and economic oppressions that women face are formidable barriers to adequate and ethical health care.

The Impact of Women's Traditional Roles

Sexual Objects and Age-Passing

Women's familiar patriarchal role as sex objects is directly connected with ageism. Women are not only expected to define themselves sexually, but as sexually young. Ever younger slimmer bodies are the model for attractiveness. We are judged by these standards with increasing harshness as we age, and we are pressured to judge ourselves by them. Many people do not see any prejudice in regarding women's aging bodies as ugly. This highly conditioned response is usually defended as simply "natural." Feminists recognize this claim as a familiar part of patriarchal ideology, what de Beauvoir called the "disguise" of oppressive attitudes and conditions as "natural."[10]

The pain that this causes was addressed in one of the earliest feminist articles about ageism and sexism, bluntly titled "It Hurts to Be Alive and Obsolete." The author used a pseudonym for fear of mockery, humiliation, and possible job loss.

> What, fat and 43 and I dare to think I'm still a person? No, I am
> an invisible lump. I belong to a category labelled *a priori* without
> interest to anyone. I am not even expected to interest myself. A
> middle-aged woman is comic by definition. . . . Every day in 70,000
> ways this society tells an older woman that it is her sin and her
> guilt that she has a real living body.[11]

Such painful pressures lead women to age-passing, which is the effort to appear younger in order to be treated fairly and seen as attractive, desirable, interesting. As with any kind of passing, this strategy is framed by power relations. Passing is the submission of the powerless in an attempt to survive. Age-passing is a chronic source of stress and its damage to self-esteem is inexorable. For passing means lying--not only to others but, if it occurs often enough, it becomes a habit of lying to one's self, denying who we really are and what we need.

Let us not forget that age-passing is big business. The promise of creating a youthful appearance drives a considerable part of the economy. The cosmetics industry, fashion advisors, cosmetic surgery (the fastest growing medical specialty), and the diet industry all trade in the need of women to create the self as young or "young for her age." Just this last business, dieting, takes a tremendous toll on women's health. It is normal for the majority of women to gain weight with age. Yet our society is so fat phobic that large numbers of women are chronic dieters and increasing numbers are anorexic and/or bulimic. Many health problems formerly associated with being overweight are now being reevaluated as resulting from stresses on the body from constant dieting and repeated weight gain and loss. The damage this does to women's health carries into old age and leads to more need for medical care.

Intertwined with women's status as sexual objects is the related belief that women are "the weaker sex." As we age, this expectation and enforced role leads to the view that women are frailer, more prone to health problems--in short, that women are naturally sicker. As but one example, misogynist attitudes toward menstruation and menopause play a major role in the ideology of female instability. One of the tragedies of oppression is that societies construct restrictive conditions reinforcing these beliefs which become, in effect, self-fulfilling prophecies. Oppressed groups often succumb to internalizing and living out the socially constructed inferior roles assigned to them. These conditions set up aging women to be seen as victims--as troubled patients in need of a lot of medical and psychological care.

Women are simultaneously rewarded and punished for voicing our health concerns. Patriarchy both expects us to voice health needs and denigrates women (when we do) as complaining, whining old women. The cult of female illness, described so well by Ehrenreich and English,[12] is with us still for a significant part of the female population and their caretakers. Such attitudes introduce dangerous distortions in perspective as we attempt to provide ethical health care.

Motherwork and Women in the Middle

As we age, women experience a shift away from being seen as a sex object and toward being regarded as a mother-object and eventually as a grandmother object. Patriarchy in general expects women to serve--to nurture, to listen, to support, to console, to care-- and to give more than we expect to receive in these regards. Our economy and our health-care arrangements are based in major ways on women's unpaid work in the home--"motherwork" as sociologist Jessie Bernard has called it.[13] Whether or not we are or have been mothers, simply aging itself brings to women more expectations that we do motherwork. Our agreement is not required. Motherwork becomes a demand. (Many older women have expressed frustration with this objectification by wearing T-shirts and making buttons that proclaim, "I am not your mother.")

As part of motherwork in the home, middle-aged and old women are expected to assume major work roles in caring for older relatives. Women are nine to ten times more likely than men to care for an aging spouse, parent, spouse's parent or other relatives.[14]

Gerontologist Elaine Brody has named them "women in the middle."[15]
They are daughters, daughters-in-law, and nieces. All this hidden
work is work for which we are well socialized, but it is unpaid,
carries no health benefits or pension plan and does not even count
in the GNP. Barbara MacDonald has observed: "As long as society
is able to have the care of the elderly done in the home as women's
invisible work, you can be sure it will."[16] She has aptly termed this
situation "exploitation by compassion." The average woman spends
17 years caring for children and another 18 for aged parents, and
often an older husband. Most women in the middle are in their 50s
or older. In a growing number of families, the women (and
sometimes men) in the middle are in their 60s and 70s. Currently,
35 percent are over 65.[17]

        This caretaking work by women is necessitated by the gaping
lack of adequate options for chronic care. Family care for the
elderly often stretches past the breaking point due to lack of support
options and attempts to avoid institutionalization. The American
fixation on the heroic self has produced overdevelopment and
overuse of heroic medical measures, to the neglect of caregiving
practices that would address ongoing and long-term needs. The
elderly are marginalized, but the seriously chronically disabled
elderly are virtually ghettoized. While only 5 to 8 percent of the
elderly are in nursing homes at any one time, about 25 percent of
the elderly over 65 will spend some time there.[18] Seventy-five
percent of the elderly over 65 in nursing homes are women,[19] which
is a rate 16 percent greater than women's share of the over 65
population. Men, as they age, are much more likely than women to
be cared for in the home, often by their wives. Sometimes these
wives are themselves elderly, but frequently they are much younger
second wives. For the elderly over age 85, 50 percent of women live
alone compared to only 20 percent of the men.[20]

        The longer women live and outlive husbands, lovers, children,
relatives, and friends, the more we are likely to live alone or to need
institutional care. It is not surprising in our economy to find that
nursing home work receives low status and low pay. Nursing home
care is an extension of motherwork into the barely paying public
economy. In both nonprofit and for profit nursing homes, staffing
relies heavily on aides who are overworked and underpaid, usually
working at or only slightly above minimum wage. Most aide
positions pay less than fast-food service. Many aides are women,
especially minority women, the marginalized caring for the
marginalized.

Grandmother Work and Powerlessness

Eventually patriarchal perception of older women shifts from mother object to grandmother object, and the stresses from ageism and sexism intensify. Very old age often brings a further decrease in simple affectionate touch--basic caring contact which is literally lifegiving. I hear old women speaking of a deep hunger in this regard. Deprivation of touch is often particularly acute in nursing homes. My partner's mother has severe Alzheimer's disease. When we visit her nursing home, I am always shaken by the feeling that I am in a concentration camp of untouchables. I try to do my small part, stroking her arm, shaking someone's hand, mostly summoning the courage to look people in the eye and acknowledge their human presence. But these acts are small drops on an endlessly parched field. Standard ethics and care are pitifully inadequate to address the problems here. The oppressive social power arrangements that construct this awful situation--in what is, let me assure you, a "good" nursing home--demand a deeply political awareness and an analysis of what must change.

Old age for women is too often an increasingly rapid slide into further powerlessness and invisibility. Old women are expected to metamorphose into quiet non-demanding grannies who are cute and powerless. As grandmother objects, old women often discover that they are expected to do what I call "grandmother work." While this includes non-reciprocal listening, nurturing and emotional caretaking; child care is often a major task. While grandmothering can certainly be a fulfilling role that enhances self-esteem and brings many pleasures, a little recognized problem is the over-reliance on grandmothers in the face of inadequate child-care options.

Many older women placed in this stressful, overworked position have begun to speak out, despite considerable taboos against doing so. The more economically disadvantaged a community, the greater the need to rely on grandmothers for child care, often for full-time child rearing. Seventy-six percent of Black women over 65 care for a young child in their home part- or full-time.[21] In a study of elderly Chicano widows, the majority expressed frustrations with the strong expectation that they virtually focus their lives on grandmother work, far beyond their desire or perceived abilities. Many of these Chicano grandmothers described pressure to be totally available, including stigmatization of remarriage or involvement with new sexual partners. The ideal grandmother is a single widow focused on support of her children's children.[22] For white women who are middle-class and above, there is much less pressure to do grandmother work, while the situation of poor and working-class white women is similar to that of racial and ethnic minority women. In the last decade, there has been a huge jump in the number of grandmothers having to assume total care of the offspring of their adult children who are drug addicted or HIV-positive. Many of these grandchildren are themselves born drug addicted or HIV-positive and face many health and emotional problems as they grow up. The 1990s will see increasing, overwhelming pressures on elderly women to fill in the gaps of our social programs. Such demands for grandmother work are a primary stress on the health of these women.

Fear of Crones

As the harsh realities of ageism take their toll on women and the reasons for female anger build up, the pressures on old women to be nice, sweet and nurturing increase. A strong, assertive and sometimes angry old woman sounds very different from "sweet little old lady." Herein lies a further critical dimension undergirding rejection of old women--patriarchal fear of women's anger (actual and *potential* anger) at our oppression. The older women get, the greater is our ability to discern the false promises of patriarchy, the contradictions, and traps in women's roles. And the lie is long-standing. As Melanie Kaye-Kantrowitz has said of women's oppression, "our emergency is so ancient."[23]

Gloria Steinham has said that women as a group become more radical as we age, less patient with the tricks, deceptions and cruelties of patriarchal arrangements. And, I would add, more bored by them. Certainly not all women become more radical and angry with injustice. Many women are broken, or bought off by some measure of racial or economic privilege, or beaten into pessimistic support of reactionary values in fear of how much worse our lot might be. But the potential for seeing through patriarchy is there. For increasing numbers of women, this potential is being actualized. This is what patriarchy deeply fears and resists--independent, wise, bold, angry and passionate women who love ourselves and the vision of a loving and just society enough to act on our accumulated knowledge and power. Patriarchy frames this as a fear of "matriarchy"--their name for old women in power, as though our imaginations were so small as to want to imitate the status quo. Feminists understand this reaction as the fear of women joined in collective, intergenerational solidarity. Such sisterhood requires the return of Crones, an ancient title of respect for powerful and wise elder women.[24]

Fear of Crones is a deep structure of patriarchy. It is channeled into rejection, abuse and neglect of old women, who represent a possibility of women's escape from male domination. Especially threatening are women past childbearing, women who have outlived or left men, spinsters, lesbians, and women who are not submissive. In this way fear and scapegoating of all old women resembles that of lesbians, who also represent women not fully under patriarchal control. Thus, our elder women bear the brunt of a special kind of literal and mythical scapegoating, lest they break free and become the furies whom guilty male dominators fear. The liberation of old women would require a transformation of society that would create fuller health and life for everyone. But patriarchy, in one of its typical reversals,[25] turns this life-enhancing potential upside down and sees not life but death. Patriarchy conditions us to recoil from aging in women as a disturbing embodiment of mortality. Many men leave wives whose aging reminds them too closely of their own.

Women's Economic Situation

Women are significantly behind men in earning power and the consequences of economic discrimination follow women into old age. Fifteen percent of women aged 65 and older live in poverty, compared to 9 percent of men. Women's median income after 65 is 57 percent of men's. Lack of equal participation in the paid labor force carries serious economic consequences for most women over 65. Over three-quarters have *no* pension from any source (their own or a husband's). Women 65 and over are the majority of recipients of Supplemental Social Security Income (SSI) on the basis of age. Medicare pays for a much smaller percent of women's total health-care expenditures, especially if they are unmarried.[26] In a vicious double bind, women's lower earning power often reinforces the sex role expectation that they are the "better" choice for unpaid caretaking work in the home. This catch-22 sets up women for fewer years in the job market, interrupted work histories, and part-time work (often with few or no benefits).

The rising divorce rate is having a profound impact on women economically. After divorce, women's standards of living drop an average of 42 percent, while men's rises 73 percent. This drop in economic resources disastrously affects the circumstances of these women when they reach old age. For widows, there are also particular financial problems. Only 5 percent collect any benefits from a husband after his death. Many men select retirement plans that pay a higher benefit during their lifetime, rather than a lower benefit for the lifetimes of both spouses. Far too many women do not have sound financial plans for old age. Exacerbating these problems is the still prevalent practice that husbands handle any financial planning that occurs. It is not uncommon for a widow to have no real understanding of her economic situation, including that her husband's benefits may only be for his lifetime.

Poor and minority women often have jobs without health and retirement benefits. When married, their husbands often lack such benefits. Two-thirds of elderly Mexican-Americans worked in jobs with no pension *and* no Social Security. Many of these jobs are in the secondary job market of undocumented work such as field hands, domestics, cannery service, and garment workers.[27] Diminished access to resources arising from differences in race, education, class, and sexual orientation, worsens with age. As an example of this last difference (sexual orientation), same sex partners are not eligible for spouse benefits from health-care or retirement plans. Same sex partners also must make special legal arrangements to have the right to participate in their partner's health-care decisions when the partner is incapacitated. Unmarried women in general are more likely to depend on Social Security for all or almost all of their income after age 65.[28]

All these factors add up to mean that aging itself puts women at greater risk of poverty. Women's economic situations are not only stressful; they translate into hard differences in access to health care. Elderly women are more likely to be unable to pay for care on their own, and more likely to need government assistance. They are more likely to self-treat and delay treatment for health problems and less able to pay for supplemental help in their homes. In a capitalistic economy, where access to care is drastically affected by access to money, most elderly women are multiply marginalized and cared for inadequately.

Suggestions for Change

Feminist method must include positive envisioning and concrete suggestions for social change. Properly understood, the detailed work of criticism is part of this constructive process, offering essential clues and helping us identify where to begin. Feminism has been burdened with the media stereotype of being the bearer of bad news. This familiar sexist image of whining, bitter women can unleash a powerful denial response, wanting to kill the messenger. But feminism's fundamental message is good news: Feminism means being *for* women, and includes bringing attention to the positive features of women's lives, their strengths, and their strategies for change.

Work for a more ethical situation involves becoming activists for the changes we need. My years as an activist and an academician have shown me that we must pursue a holistic continuum of changes--from individual to communal, from personal to political, from temporary Band-Aids to revolutionary restructuring. Activism has several dimensions and we may concentrate on those where we are most able to work with energy and integrity.

The most basic activism begins with the self. Especially for women who have been trained to put others first at the expense of ourselves--becoming advocates of our own needs--standing up for ourselves is paramount. Activism for one's self includes gaining basic information and finding support networks. It begins with women breaking silence, speaking out about the genuine conditions of our lives. If one of the primary definitions of patriarchy is the absence of old women in power, one of the primary signs of change is the growing presence of old women in power. Patriarchy does exact a terrible toll on old women but women's lives have always been larger than patriarchal lies and oppressive limitations.

As we take the activist step of listening to old women, we also hear them celebrating. They are naming what is good in their lives and their strategies for surviving and thriving. MacDonald speaks of discovering some very taboo feelings of pleasure in her aging.

> I like growing old. I say this to myself with surprise. I had not thought it could be like this. There are days of excitement when I feel almost a kind of high with the changes taking place in my own body. . . . I say to myself frequently in wonder, "This is my body doing this."[29]

Older women speak of the release of energy and insight that comes with leaving youthful illusions behind. I hear new models of old age as a second chance, a time of increased confidence. For many women who have had major work responsibilities in the home, aging can bring more freedom--for work, for education, for personal growth, for political action. Older women are, for example, a fast growing part of the college population.

In the reexamination of our lives prompted by feminism, many women have identified strengths developed within traditional roles that are invaluable for creating a more equitable world. Perhaps foremost among these are relationship skills, both interpersonal and those employed in weaving networks for support. In *Number Our Days*, a study of elderly Jews, anthropologist Barbara Myerhoff noted that these skills directly enhanced the abilities of older women to cope with the changes of aging. Men often had more trouble forming new friendships in changed situations.[30] Women were also more likely to have diverse roles, and therefore more varied sources of self-esteem. Knowing the skills of making a home often better prepared women for new living situations in old age.

As more and more old women speak out and find their way into print, we have a growing record of some thrilling models for being old women. A personal favorite of mine is this statement by dancer, Louise Mattlage.

> So I'll be 80. 80! Great heavens, I've passed four score and ten. I'm old. Old? . . . 50 . . . now that's youth. At 60 one worries. Age is creeping up. At 60 one is taught to be careful. One is advised to watch out. But I mustn't leave out 70--70 is bursting with imaginative energy. I started a new career. And 80--have I said what 80 has to live for? There is so much. And it fills me--this disbeliever in her dotage, in her old age, with great longing for its wonder.[31]

Older women are sharing stories about PMZ (Post Menopausal Zest) a phrase I have heard attributed to Margaret Mead. Heterosexual women describe the relief from worry over contraception. As more and more women refuse to succumb to "patriarchally-induced female senility," as Janet Lake has termed it, the possibilities for immediate improvement in the present open up.[32] The power of inspiration from such women is both instructive and contagious. Many old women are not waiting, or working simply for changes to benefit subsequent generations.

More and more women are rejecting age-passing, and the inner self-hate it feeds. Despite real risks in refusing to pass for being younger, growing numbers of women realize that this enforced hiding undermines us. As we have clearer, more diverse ideas about the ways 60, 70, 80, 90 and 100 can be, we are better equipped to embrace and plan well for our own aging. Breaking through racial and ethnic separations, women are sharing stories of strong old women from many cultures. Feminist spirituality is creating a new inner imagery for the Crone.[33]   Crones, as Mary Daly has observed, are the long-lasting ones.[34]   Increasing numbers of women are creating Croning rituals, eclectic and diverse, for menopause, retirement, or a significant birthday.[35]   There are no rigid rules and creeds.   Such rites of passage honor and empower oneself and old women, and say of aging: This is part of me and it is good.

I feel particularly blessed to have grown up in a matrilineal context in which I saw strong, proud, witty and irreverent old women.   Such positive role models of female aging are essential for our self-esteem, wholeness, and health.

Another dimension of activism is the step of connection. Breaking patterns of isolation, women are increasingly joining together to help each other.   There are old women's support and action groups, and menopause and women's health self-help groups. This bonding ranges from helping just one other woman to joining or starting small and large organizations focused on ending ageism and sexism.   There are groups such as the Grey Panthers, the Older Women's League, the Women's Initiative in the American Association of Retired Persons, and the recent National Conference of Old Lesbians which has met twice in the eighties.

The women's health movement is one major branch of this work for social change.   For women to know more about their own bodies and their health care, to be full agents in their own care, is radically transforming.   The classic, widely used self-help text, *Our Bodies, Our Selves* (available in thirteen languages) has massively expanded its information about menopause and aging.[36]   In addition, the authors sponsored a collective of older women who have written a companion book--a major resource for older women's health care called *Our Selves, Growing Older.*[37]   Rosetta Reitz went searching for nonmisogynist information about menopause and found almost none. So she started menopause consciousness-raising groups and ended up writing *Menopause: A Positive Approach*, based on women's experiences.[38]

Intertwined with the activism of standing up for one's self and bonding with others is political organizing and coalition building. There are, for example, increasingly diverse strategies to change the isolation of the elderly.   More than half of nursing home residents would be able to live in the community if there were adequate social supports.[39]   Intergenerational community building, shared elderly housing, and foster grandparenting are some new approaches. Institutions are being changed through advocacy programs for the elderly and ombudspersons in hospitals and nursing homes.   Tax breaks for smaller private nursing homes are another proposal to

make less institutionalized care more feasible. The National
Coalition for Nursing Home Reform brings together patients,
families, care providers and others to press for monitoring, higher
standards and legislative changes. In a very creative and pragmatic
step, union organizers of nursing home aides have placed better
patient care squarely in the middle of their agenda--an excellent
example of effective coalition building that has won some significant
improvements from large for-profit nursing home chains.[40]
    The broad range of legislative and other more radical proposals
to improve women's economic and social situation all have direct
bearing on the quality of old women's lives. Not only equal pay for
equal work, but equal pay for comparable work would significantly
improve women's financial resources for old age. Issues not often
connected with aging and health care do have a direct application,
such as enforcement of child-care payments. Flextime on jobs can
ease the immediate load on women in the middle who are caring for
elderly relatives, as would government support for such caregivers.
Raising the minimum wage, displaced homemaker programs,
expansion of women's Social Security eligibility, more equitable
pension and health benefit plans, and a national health insurance
program--all these would have tangible positive effects on the care
available to the elderly and especially elderly women and minority
men. Support programs that ease the load of grandmother work are
beginning to appear. Los Angeles County has a new program for
grandmothers raising children, especially those born drug-addicted.
Working to eliminate the many forms of violence against women--
incest and sexual abuse, rape, harassment and battering--will also
transform the quality of life and health for women in old age. All
these forms of violence compromise our health and well being.
Programs for support and healing should be available for women at
any age and are a vital form of activism. Programs that specifically
address elder abuse are essential.
    Some programs are temporary relief and by themselves are, of
course, not enough. But they help keep us going as we construct
the deeper social revolutions necessary to end destructive power
arrangements. We must confront and celebrate, criticize and
construct, tear down and build, rage and sing. As we perform these
tasks we are guided by the basic feminist insight of listening to
those whose lives are involved, in order to create anti-ageist
coalitions rather than a condescending kinder and gentler
paternalism. Not simply health care for the elderly, but health care
and social change *with* the elderly.

Women must take a leading role. Aging is a women's issue if ever there was one. We will be on the right track if we remember these words from Judy Grahn's poem "a plainsong from an elder woman to a younger woman":

> am I not elder
> berry
> brandy
>
> are you not wine before you find me
> in your own beaker? . . .
>
> are you not shamed to treat me meanly
> when you discover you become me?
> are you not proud that you become me?[41]

Notes and References

1. Barbara MacDonald with Cynthia Rich, *Look Me in the Eye: Old Women, Aging and Ageism* (San Francisco: Spinsters Inc., 1983).

2. Baba Copper, *Over the Hill: Reflections on Ageism Between Women* (Freedom, CA. Crossing Press, 1988).

3. Beverly Harrison, "The Older Person's Worth in the Eyes of Society," in *Making the Connections: Essays in Feminist Social Ethics,* edited by Carol S. Robb (Boston: Beacon Press, 1985), pp. 152-166.

4. Ibid.

5. Copper, *Over the Hill: Reflections on Ageism Between Women,* p. 44.

6. David J. Wheeler, "NIH to Require Researchers to Include Women in Studies," *The Chronicle of Higher Education,* Vol. 37, No. 3, September 19, 1990, pp. A1 and A32.

7. Boston Women's Health Book Collective, *The New Our Bodies, Ourselves* (New York: Simon & Schuster, 1984).

8. American Association of Retired Persons, *Facts About Older Women* (Washington, D.C.: American Association of Retired Persons, 1989).

9. Boston Women's Health Book Collective, *The New Our Bodies, Ourselves.*

10. Simone de Beauvoir, *The Second Sex,* translated by H. M. Parshley (New York: Alfred A. Knopf, 1949).

11. Zoe Moss, "It Hurts To Be Alive and Obsolete", in *Sisterhood is Powerful,* edited by Robin Morgan (New York: Random House, 1970), pp. 170-174.

12. Barbara Ehrenreich and Deidre English, *Complaints and Disorders: The Sexual Politics of Sickness* (Old Westbury, N.Y.: Feminist Press, 1973).

13. Jesse Bernard, *The Future of Motherhood* (New York: Penguin Books, 1974).

14. Boston Women's Health Book Collective, *The New Our Bodies, Ourselves.*

15. Lindsey Van Gelder, "Elaine Brody," *MS. Magazine,* January 1986, pp. 47-48 and 100-101.

16. MacDonald with Rich, *Look Me in the Eye: Old Women, Aging and Ageism.*

17. Grace W. Weinstein, "Help Wanted--The Crisis of Elder Care," *MS. Magazine,* October 1989, pp. 73-74 and 76-79.

18. Paula Brown Doress and Diana Laskin Siegal, *Ourselves Growing Older: Women Aging with Knowledge and Power* (New York: Simon & Schuster/Touchstone, 1987).

19. American Association of Retired Persons, *Facts About Older Women.*

20. Lissy Jarvik, *"Aging: A Woman's Issue,"* Paper delivered at Claremont Graduate School Conference on Women and Aging, Claremont, California, March 3, 1990.

21. Jean Griffin, *"Elderly Black Women,"* Lecture delivered at the University of Massachusetts, Boston, February 24, 1986.

22. Linda Facio, *"Living in Poverty and Pressured to Grandmother: Aging Among Chicano/Mexican Women,"* Paper delivered at Claremont Graduate School Conference on Women and Aging, Claremont, California, March 3, 1990.

23. Melanie Kaye-Kantrowitz, "Politics as an Act of Love," *Sinister Wisdom,* Vol. 8 (1979), pp. 26-29.

24. Barbara Walker, *The Crone: Woman of Age, Wisdom and Power* (San Francisco: Harper and Row, 1985).

25. Mary Daly, *Beyond God the Father: Toward a Philosophy of Women's Liberation* (Boston: Beacon Press, 1973).

26. American Association of Retired Persons, *Facts About Older Women.*

27. Facio, *Living in Poverty and Pressured to Grandmother: Aging Among Chicano/Mexican Women."*

28. American Association of Retired Persons, *Facts About Older Women.*

29. MacDonald with Rich, *Look Me in the Eye: Old Women, Aging and Ageism.*

30. Barbara Myerhoff, *Number Our Days* (New York: Simon & Schuster, 1978).

31.   Louise Mattlage, "Getting There," *Calyx: A Journal of Art and Literature by Women*, Vol. 9 (Winter 1986), pp. 79-81.

32. For example, Buffy Johnson, a feminist active in Boston, is the subject of a ground-breaking video on her old age called "It's Never Too Late." The title refers to Johnson's decisions at age 73 to begin a new, second career (in counseling), to become a lesbian, and then come out and help break lesbophobic stereotypes.   Micki Dickoff, *It's Never too Late: A Portrait of Buffy*, video (Los Angeles: Micki Dickoff Productions, 1982).

33.   Walker, *The Crone: Woman of Age, Wisdom and Power.*

34.   Mary Daly, *Gyn/Ecology: The Metaethics of Radical Feminism* (Boston: Beacon Press, 1978) .

35.   For example, The Feminist Institute distributes a flyer that describes Croning Celebrations two women created for their fiftieth birthdays and that encourages women to invent empowering rituals for our aging.   Jacquelyn Gentry and Faye Siefert, *The Croning Celebration* (Bethesda, M.D.:   The Feminist Institute, 1988).

36.   Boston Women's Health Book Collective, *The New Our Bodies, Ourselves.*

37.   Paula Brown Doress, Diana Laskin Siegal, and the Midlife and Older Women Book Project, *Ourselves Growing Older* (New York: Simon & Schuster, 1987).

38.   Rosetta Reitz, *Menopause: A Positive Approach* (New York: Penguin Books, 1979).

39.   Boston Women's Health Book Collective, *The New Our Bodies, Ourselves.*

40.   Paul Sweeney, "Now They've Got to Treat Folks Right," *Southern Exposure* (Special Issue: "Older, Wiser, Stronger: Southern Elders") March-June, 1985, pp. 113-115.

41.   Judy Grahn, *SHE WHO* (Oakland, Calif.:   Diana Press, 1979).

15

How Age Should Matter:
Justice as the Basis
for Limiting Care to the Elderly

Robert M. Veatch

Introduction

A 68-year-old man, the president of a mid-sized manufacturing corporation, had reached the end of his options for severe coronary insufficiency. He had had quadruple by-pass surgery two years previously, but was now confined to bed with no real medical option. Otherwise he was a robust man, a regular tennis player until his cardiac problems emerged. He had been physically active within the constraints of his cardiac disease. His cardiologist told him that a heart transplant was his only option.

Herein lay the problem: The organ procurement organization for his area--the group that controls the allocation of all organs for transplant--had a firm policy of no hearts going to anyone over age 65. The policy had its origins in the belief that older patients would not do well medically with transplant, but now we know that is an oversimplification. Medically, this man can be expected to do quite well. Of course, even a successful transplant will be in a patient who, because of his age, will have a shorter life expectancy than other potential recipients of the heart. Moreover, some might argue that it is simply unfair to give the heart to someone who has had a chance at most of his life when other, younger patients have not yet. On the other hand, is it ethical to use age as a basis for excluding this otherwise suitable heart-transplant patient from the recipient list?

At another hospital a 92-year-old woman lay almost immobile in a bed, a victim of a stroke, arteriosclerotic heart disease, and diabetes. She has heard of by-pass surgery and asks her physician whether it could possibly help her. After pointing out the obvious risks of major surgery in a woman of her age, he admits there is a chance it would make her more comfortable and might even restore some of her mobility. Of course, he points out, her age places limits on how long she is likely to be able to enjoy this benefit. She decides that, since her insurance company will pay for it, it is worth the risk. Should the physician refuse to perform the surgery? Should her insurance company pay for it?

These cases suggest the controversy over the use of age as a criterion on allocating scarce health resources. There are reasons based in calculation of expected consequences for and against using age. On the other hand, while appeals to justice or fairness seem to count against allocations based on age, there are reasons why justice might provide a more moral basis for using age as one of the allocation criteria. Here, I will argue that justice, rather than consequences, is the morally appropriate reason why age should be considered one factor in allocating certain health resouces.

Current Situation

It is fashionable in American medical circles and the press to ridicule British policy of excluding patients from dialysis at age 65. This is usually presented as an outrage that could never be contemplated in the United States, as if age, per se, ought never to be a factor in allocating scarce medical resources.

The facts are somewhat more complex. The British apparently do not have a firm, official policy limiting care for those over 65. According to one, somewhat dated study, 80 percent of British dialysis units exclude patients over 65, and 35 percent exclude those over 55.[1] But this is apparently only a general guideline. The real problem may be that if one has the clout to work the system, dialysis can be obtained at any age.

By contrast, in the United States similar informal age-based allocation policies have been in place for some time. Some are even official policies such as the age-based limits on organ allocation by some organ procurement agencies. Medicare's system of diagnosis-related groups (DRGs) for hospital reimbursement had, until recently, differential reimbursements based on age.[2] Usually, the age group over age 69 received higher rather than lower reimbursement under that system, but the principle is already in place, recognizing the legitimacy of different funding solely on the basis of age. There is no reason why the same system could not be used to provide lower or no reimbursement for the elderly.

Some might argue at this point that any such proposals to base allocation on age rest on the false claim that resources have to be rationed. Perhaps if the waste were removed from the system and individuals were allowed to exercise their autonomy in refusing treatment through advanced directives, there would be no need to limit health resources to the elderly or anyone else. This position, however, rests on a mistaken understanding of the nature of the problem. Living wills, advanced directives, and the principle of autonomy eliminate care perceived as useless by the patient or surrogate--when net benefits are perceived as no greater than detriments. That care is ethically easy to eliminate. No insurance should pay for care unless there is evidence that the patient or surrogate has consented. That, however, still leaves care for which the patient perceives that benefits slightly exceed expected harms. Some of that care is very expensive. It is irrational to fund all of this slightly beneficial, expensive care. Nevertheless that patient will want it; the physician committed to benefiting the patient will want to provide it. Autonomy in an insurance system cannot provide a basis for setting limits.

Resources in health care, as in all other sectors, are inevitably scarce. This conclusion is a logical correlate of our finitude as humans. Human desires are infinite while resources are obviously finite. It is the nature of the human condition that we will always have goods that we need or want no matter how wealthy our society. Even if we ignore the obvious problems of the claims of justice of those in less wealthy societies, the human imagination can always conjure more that might be done that appears worth doing. This is true in medicine as well as all other spheres of life. It is not a matter of minor misallocations of our national priorities. Even if the entire GNP were devoted to health care and all expenditures were limited to interventions that were really beneficial and desired by patients, there would still always be more that could be done. After we eliminate all care that does no net good, there will be care that produces a slight excess of benefit over harm. It is rational for patients to want that care. It is rational for clinicians manifesting the traditional Hippocratic commitment to benefit their patients to want such care delivered. Yet almost certainly it would be both foolish and immoral to fund all such care. Some care is so marginally beneficial that other potential uses of the resources have a much stronger moral claim.[3]

It is both inevitable and morally necessary that some benefits at the margin be subordinated to other benefits that have a higher moral priority. Is it possible that age could be a basis for deciding that some benefits are too low in the priority scale? Let us look at the moral arguments for and against the use of age.

The Role of Age in Age-Based Allocation

It is not as easy as one might think to figure out exactly what the role of age is in apparently age-based allocation policies. It could be that age is used as a crude predictor of the benefit from treatment. A policy committed to using resources where they will do the most good might include the view that in cases where older people will not do as well with an intervention, age should be used as an indirect, approximating measure of where resources will do the most good. Even if the medical benefit measured in terms of cure rates or incidence of side effects is the same for older patients, the benefit measured in years will predictably not be as great. The elderly will not benefit as long, if the treatment is a success. Allocators might argue that it would be impractical to assess outcomes on a case-by-case basis and choose, instead, to use chronological age as a predictor of benefit.

This raises the ethical issue of the use of sociological measures as predictors of outcome. In the United States, in many situations, it is considered unethical (as well as illegal) in allocating goods to use sociological categories to predict expected outcome. Law schools in the 1960s had firm data showing that years of education invested in males would predictably end up in more years of legal practice than those invested in females. Feminists properly argued that using sociological statistics from a class of people such as women could treat individual members of the class unfairly. Individual women might practice law as long or longer than their male counterparts. Likewise, even if members of a racial group can be shown to perform on average at a lower level in some competition, it is considered unfair discrimination to presume that all members of that group will perform poorly. We cannot use sex, race, or other sociological measures as a basis for excluding individual members of their groups even if we can show that the group as a whole will use the resource less efficiently. We need evidence for the individual.

Then can we insist that age be used only when we can show

that age is a predictor of a poor outcome in the case of the individual elderly person? If so, that would be almost impossible to show.

Consequentialist Argument Pertaining to the Use of Age

Consequentialist Arguments for Age-Based Allocation

The arguments that appear most readily are grounded in appeals to the consequences of allocating on the basis of age. These appeals necessarily look at the benefits and social costs of using age as a criterion in allocation. The argument begins with the conclusion we have just reached: Resources are inevitably scarce. Those committed to one or another version of utilitarian, normative ethical theory hold that in such cases the ethical imperative is to do the greatest good for the greatest number; we need to maximize the net good in aggregate. For health care the ethical imperative is the use of health planning and cost-benefit analyses to make sure we use our health-care dollars to do the most good possible. As we have seen, it is impossibly inefficient to measure the benefits for each individual patient. The process itself would have great disutilities. The prudent, efficient thing to do would be to opt for the allocation formula that will do the greatest good overall. If age is a reasonably good predictor of good, then it morally must be used according to utilitarian theory. The welfare of individuals may have to be sacrificed in certain cases in order to produce the greatest aggregate benefit. A true consequentialist would not be dissuaded from this conclusion by concern that such a policy might be unfair to certain elderly persons.

Many American health planners find this persuasive. They assume that if we must ration--and we must--then the rationing must be on the basis of maximizing the common or aggregate good. There are reasons, however, why these utilitarian reasons for using age as a basis for allocating health resources should be resisted.

Consequentialist Arguments Against Using Age

Some critics of the use of age buy the principle, but reject the moral calculation. They accept that the goal is to serve the aggregate good, but then reject the claim that using age as a criterion will maximize the aggregate good. Their arguments are as follows:

First, some elderly can be very productive citizens. A policy of allocation based on age would shut out some potentially useful citizens. Holders of this view insist, at least, that we use physiological age rather than chronological age so that those who are physiologically young would not be excluded.

That consequentialist argument against the use of age, however, overlooks the fact that statistically the elderly are not as productive as the young. Every dollar of resources, every transplantable organ, going to an old person comes at the expense of a young person. Statistically, it seems clear that more good will be done if the younger patients get the organs. Even the process of figuring out who is physiologically young could have severe disutilities both in terms of cost and in terms of inevitable conflicts.

Second, critics of the use of age might argue that the psychological burden of anticipating reaching old age without life-sustaining medical care would be a serious disutility of using age as a criterion. They could claim that in order to avoid the anxiety of knowing that one will not get needed care when he or she is old, we should avoid using age as a criterion.

But one must also take into account the psychological burdens that would result from knowing that younger people might not get the benefits of needed medical care if resources are going to the elderly. The agony of seeing infants die while the elderly get high-tech, life-sustaining care would have to be factored in. On balance, the argument from psychological burden seems to be about a stand-off.

Third, utilitarian critics of the use of age as a criterion might appeal to the psychological and economic burdens on families whose elderly members were excluded from health care that could offer at least marginal benefits. Once again, however, these would be offset by the psychological and economic burdens on families whose younger members would be deprived of care if resources went to the elderly.

On balance, the consequentialist case for using age as a criterion in allocating resources seems to be convincing, provided the utilitarian principle of maximizing aggregate net outcome is morally legitimate in the first place.

Recently, I presented this material to a group of German physicians. The ethical danger of subordinating the individual to the social good was more obvious to the Germans than it is to many Americans. The real issue seems to be whether maximizing aggregate utility is always morally legitimate. This is not the place to review that fundamental moral controversy. Suffice to say that the dominant conclusion of both contemporary moral philosophers and policy makers is that justice or fairness must sometimes take priority over maximizing aggregate utility. If use of age as a criterion fails the test of the principle of justice, it will be hard to conclude that its use is ethical. To the surprise of many, however, it may turn out that even if we move to nonconsequentialist (or deontological) ethical theory, age may be a legitimate basis for allocating health resources.

Nonconsequentialist Considerations

Some ethical systems hold that morality is not just a matter of producing good and avoiding evil consequences. This characteristic is shared by the ethics of Kant, the Jewish ethics of the Ten Commandments, and by much Protestant thought. It is central to secular, liberal political philosophy that places the rights of the individual over against the aggregate welfare at least in some cases. In the Ten Commandments, for instance, the command is "Thou shalt not." There is no clause added "except when it would produce good consequences."

It is important to realize that nonconsequentialist ethical systems need not be any more legalistic or absolutistic than consequentialist ones. There is a form of consequentialism that can be quite legalistic. Called, "rule utilitarianism," it affirms the rule or system of rules that can be expected to produce as much or more good than any other set of rules.[4] There is no room for maximizing the good in individual cases.

On the other hand, some nonconsequentialist ethics can be quite case specific. Several forms of deontology affirm multiple principles such as the principles of autonomy, fidelity, and justice. They might resolve potential conflicts on a case-by-case basis even without any appeal to consequences. The key feature of all such non-consequentialist systems is that right and wrong are determined, at least in part, by features of actions or rules other than aggregate amount of good consequences produced.

One such non-consequentialist principle is the principle of justice. It is social and allocational but, as an independent ethical principle, does not focus on the aggregate amount of consequences produced. It is the nature of morally interesting allocational problems that the pattern that produces the greatest aggregate good is not the same as the one that distributes the good most justly. The criterion for what is a just or equitable pattern of distribution is itself a controversy among those who are committed to justice as a patterned principle. One particularly appealing formulation recognizes distributions as just when they provide opportunities for net welfare that are equal among people. The policy implication is that resources should be allocated in such a way as to give people an opportunity for equality of well being.[5]

Often the conflict between utility and justice is an uninteresting one since distributing resources to those who are worst off will do the most good. That is what economists refer to as decreasing marginal utility. However, often in health care the worst off--the ones who have the strongest claims of justice--are the sickest and, as such, they are just the ones whom it is most difficult to benefit. They are chronically ill with incurable, perhaps hopeless conditions. Here spending resources on the worst off will do the least good rather than the most good. Thus in health care the conflict between utility and justice is often a real one. This is particularly true with the elderly. Thus it will be critical to see whether the principle of justice militates against using age as a criterion for allocating health resources.

Justice-Based Arguments Against the Use of Age

It seems at first like justice weighs in against the use of age as an allocation criterion. A number of commentators who are committed to justice as an allocational principle have criticized the use of age as a criterion.[6] The logic is that justice requires that resources be used to provide opportunities to have needs met. Elderly people are often precisely the ones who are most needy medically. Therefore, they deserve priority. They at least deserve to be treated identically to those younger people who are medically in equal need.

This appears to set a battle between consequentialists and non-consequentialists, with consequentialists arguing for the use of an age-based allocation criterion to promote efficient use of resources and non-consequentialists wringing their hands, screaming it is unfair and unjust.

Justice-Based Arguments for the Use of Age

There is, of course, one other possibility. One might mount a justice-based argument in favor of the use of age as a criterion.

That is precisely what I believe is called for and shall attempt to do in the remainder of this essay.

It should be noted that there have been other efforts along these lines recently. Philosophers Daniel Callahan and Norman Daniels have both made important attempts to argue for limits on health care for the elderly that have not been grounded exclusively in considerations of utility. I am now convinced that, while they are on the right track, their approaches fail. I shall briefly summarize what I consider to be the problems with their approaches before presenting my own version of a justice-based defense of the use of age as a criterion for allocating health resources. Finally, I shall return to the problem of the formula for allocating hearts for transplant, as well as bypass surgery, and propose a modification in the formula that takes age into account without totally excluding the elderly from any transplants.

Daniel Callahan's Setting of Limits. Callahan, in a now well-known book, has argued that the goal of ever-continuing life supported by medical intervention is at once impossible, foolish, and morally wrong.[7] His claim is that there is a natural end to the life-span. Medical resources should be used to get people up to that natural completion and then only to use resources for the elderly to provide comfort and inexpensive treatments of acute illness. He summarizes his position:

> Our common social obligation to the elderly is only to help them live out a natural life span; that is, the government is obliged to provide deliberately life-extending health care only to the age which is necessary to achieve that goal. . . . I believe an age-based standard for the termination of life-extending treatment would be legitimate.[8]

The result is that medical care needed to complete the major phases of the life cycle generates a higher moral claim than care to sustain life after the life cycle is completed. According to Callahan, "The old should step aside in an active way."[9]

To be fair, Callahan has sometimes been terribly misunderstood. He was not suggesting that we be cruel. At least in *Setting Limits* he was not suggesting that we abandon the elderly.[10] Rather his position was that all of us ought to have a realistic conception of what counts as a full life. It cannot be endlessly more and more of the same thing. There comes a time when life is complete. All of us should be humble in our appetite for endless years of life. He includes himself. While Callahan does not directly make his argument in terms of justice, it seems to be an appeal to fairness considerations rather than aggregate utility.

The problem with Callahan's approach is that it rests on a controversial stance regarding the value of life after what he takes to be the end of the natural life-span. Moreover, it rests on an even more controversial claim about life having a natural span. Elsewhere, I have argued that the idea of a natural end to human life is problematic at best and morally offensive at worst. His use of age as a criterion for limiting certain life-sustaining resources for the elderly rests on a conviction that life after some purported natural end point is not very valuable in any case. For him, it is, thus, all too easy to argue that it deserves low priority.

There is a more practical problem as well. The notion that life after its natural end point calls for a lower priority in health resource allocation seems to call for a precipitous cessation of claims for a certain group of life-sustaining services at some age--the age at which the life cycle has been completed. As one is "over the hill," there is a precipitous fall "over the cliff." Yet, even if we are willing to accept the notion of a natural life-span, many of us would be acutely uncomfortable with the idea that there is some identifiable end point at which, for public policy purposes, some health-care resources would no longer be funded.

Yet, we would need some easily administered, if arbitrary, age cut-off. We could not tell insurance companies and hospital administrators to cut people off whenever it appears they have completed their life span without giving them some specific age. Callahan, at one point early in the discussion, suggested that a life span of 75 years was as good as any.[11] In *Setting Limits,* he was slightly more conservative, identifying the range of the late 70s to early 80s.

Whether we pick 75 or 85, administrators and clinicians would have to have some specific, cut-off age. It is the precipitous cut-off that seems both necessary and implausible in a theory grounded in the notion of completing a life-span. Consider, for example, two patients medically similar in need of some high-tech, life-extending technology such as a transplant. If one were 74 and the other 76 (or 84 and 86), the former would get the full treatment (because he has not yet completed his life-span) while the latter would get no life-extending interventions. I doubt that such a cut-off would be tolerable, yet it seems appropriate based on a theory that differentiates people into two groups, one which has completed the life-span and one that has not.

There is one final problem with Callahan's theory. He readily acknowledges the continuing need for relief of suffering, basic nursing care for cleanliness and dignity, and so forth. What the "life-span completion" theory cannot explain is why we should spend resources on these when others will never reach their full life-span. If these lives are over, why do they have claims for even these services? Would not those whose life span is not over have claims for these resources as well. Keeping in mind that chronic, basic nursing care for all the elderly of the world is a major resource investment, would it not be more reasonable to dispose painlessly of those whose life-span is over in order to give attention to those who will not have a chance to make it to what nature has bestowed upon them?

Here Callahan's instincts are stronger than his theory. It is intuitively obvious that we should continue to provide comfort care. I do not think Callahan's theory can explain why.

Norman Daniels' Prudential Life-Span Account. The account of Norman Daniels attempts to rectify some of these problems.[12] Daniels first deals with the argument that setting limits based on age seems unfair just as allocations based on race or gender. Daniels argues that age is different. We need to adopt what Daniels calls an intrapersonal rather than an interpersonal perspective in dealing with age as an allocation criterion. Daniels says we should see our policy task as one of allocating our personal shares of health care over our own lifetimes rather than allocating care interpersonally among cohorts of different ages. He then argues that, whatever one's personal share, it seems to make no moral difference how it is allocated over one's lifetime. He points out that we need not have the same kinds of medical services available at different points in our lives. Allocation would plausibly be based on what he calls an "age-specific normal opportunity range."[13] Allocations would provide what people need to function well at a particular age: to play sports in our youth, reproduce in early adulthood, pursue a vocation in middle age, and pursue active retirement in old age. It is a matter of prudence how one allocates his or her share of health care. Hence, he refers to his scheme as "a prudential life-span account." We can choose to structure our health insurance in any prudent way.

He goes on to point out that not all allocations would be ethical. In order for health insurance allocations to be ethical we need to correct for certain problems in people's choices about their insurance. We need to ensure that the choices are adequately informed, empathetic, willing to take other people's life plans into account adequately, and so forth. He, therefore, imposes a veil of ignorance-- after the fashion of John Rawls' theory of justice--on those making a prudent allocation of their health resources. He claims they would, under these conditions, save a prudent amount for old age and not more.

There are problems, however, with Daniels' account as well. It is not clear that people choosing their health-care allocation behind a veil of ignorance can simply choose any allocation that they find prudent. It is not obvious that it is only a matter of prudence how the resources get allocated to different stages of one's life-cycle. Even if it is prudent for people to save for their old age, it may not be just or fair.

The problem is especially acute when one takes into account the fact that not all people will reach old age. Daniels implies at one point that a prudent allocation would be one in which an equal portion of each age-specific need was met.[14] That seems reasonable, provided we are dealing with a group who will live through all stages of the life-cycle. The Rawls-Daniels scheme is based on a model in which rational, self-interested heads of households (blinded as to their specific interests and needs) are viewed as the ones making the allocation choices. That model, however, has built into it the implication that all will at least reach adulthood. They therefore have a very high probability of reaching old age, and it would be rational to include a prudent amount (if only a prudent amount) for their period of old age.

In the real world, however, some are treated more harshly by the natural lottery. They are born with congenital and genetic problems such that they will suffer from critical, fatal, or permanently handicapping conditions. If a majority of rational adults would spend equally on conditions of infancy, middle age, and old age, it does not follow that it is fair to those who will never reach adulthood. The real ethical issue is what is fair or just. In the same way that I would say to Callahan that completion of the life-span is not the relevant criterion, so I would say to Daniels that prudence is not. The real question is whether justice either permits or requires limits on care to the elderly.

A Justice-Based Limit on Care to the Elderly

I think there is another non-consequentialist argument that supports limits on some care to the elderly, one based more directly on appeals to justice. I agree with Daniels, and with the work of Ronald Dworkin that precedes Daniels,[15] that an ethical health insurance is one that is based on intrapersonal allocational decisions made by those behind a veil of ignorance about their own personal desires, needs, and interests. I would, however, see them further constrained to choose what is fair rather than simply what seems prudent.[16]   In particular, I would see them as obliged by the principle of fairness to deal with the just claims of those who have critical or fatal conditions in infancy.   It is not just a matter of being prudent. It is not a matter of efficiently serving the common good.   Rather, it is a question of which allocation is fair.   Justice requires identifying the worst-off individuals and allocating resources so as to give those persons an opportunity to be as well off as others. I shall argue for certain kinds of health care that give priority to the young.

Age in Deciding Who Is Worse Off

Those committed to justice as at least one of the morally relevant principles in deciding about allocating health care--who see justice as requiring allocations to benefit the least well off--face a critical question: Which patients are really worse off?

Consider two dialysis patients, medically similar, both of whom have a five-year life expectancy if dialyzed and both of whom will die soon if not dialyzed. One is age 40; the other age 60. Can we identify one of them as worse off or do we say that they are equally poorly off? In a hypothetical situation in which there was only one dialysis machine, can we identify who should get it?

If we add the further assumption that we can expect the two to lead equally useful lives during their remaining five years, it should be clear that a utilitarian should be indifferent.   For the non-consequentialist considering egalitarian justice, the problem is more complex.

The Slice-of-Time and Over-a-Lifetime Perspectives

We should consider two different ways of calculating who is worse off. The first, call it the slice-of-time perspective, asks who is worse off at a given moment, say, when the two patients are near death. The second, call it the over-a-lifetime perspective, views well-being cumulated over the lifetimes of the individuals involved. From the slice-of-time perspective these two patients seem equally poorly off.   They are both about to die if they do not get the machine and will live for five years with it.   From the over-a-lifetime perspective, however, they seem to be in significantly different positions. The 60-year-old has had twenty more years of life. From the slice-of-time perspective they are equal. On a per-lifetime basis, the 40-year-old has had much less opportunity for well-being. He would seem to have a much greater claim of egalitarian justice.

Dennis McKerlie, one of the few philosophers who has addressed this problem, concludes (for reasons that seem incomprehensible to me) that the most plausible view is the one that strives for equality in the "simultaneous segments of different lives";[17] that is essentially what I have called the slice-of-time view. He reaches this conclusion in spite of dealing with examples where it seems obviously wrong to insist that people be treated equally in each segment of time. For example, if two equally qualified graduate students are competing for a one-year assistantship that cannot be divided so that the two hold the position at the same time, there seems to be nothing unethical about dividing it so that each student holds the position for one semester. This is true in spite of the fact that at no segment of time are the two treated equally. Over the cumulated time, the net result is equal treatment. That seems to be what should count in this case. I would maintain that that is what equality should require.

Justifying Acute Care and Basic Care Needed for Dignity and Pain Relief

This brings us back to the problem faced by Callahan of why the elderly have a claim for basic medical care, for treatment of acute illness and relief of suffering, and for nursing care for cleanliness and dignity. It seems that the relevant consideration has nothing to do with whether a lifespan is deemed to have been completed. Rather, it seems related to whether it is legitimate to cumulate one's well-being.

I see the problem as related to contemporary debates over the theory of personal identity. A person is one who has continuity of personal identity over a period of time. That continuity of identity requires continuity of awareness of oneself such that one can say, "I am the same person who existed at some previous time."

For some conditions, well-being (or lack thereof) is easily seen as cumulating over time. It makes good sense for people to say that, since they have lived a long time, they have had many opportunities for well-being. In fact, the longer one has lived, the more such opportunities one has had.

By contrast some needs present themselves anew at each moment in time. They cannot be cumulated over a lifetime. There is noncontinuity of personal identity that prohibits the summing up of acute, severe pain over a lifetime. We cannot plausibly say that because one's first eighty years have been relatively pain-free, the acute, severe pain one experiences at age eighty-one gets low priority morally. Acute pain forces radical discontinuity with one's previous life. Life in acute pain is detached from experiences accumulated over the years. Past life experiences seem irrelevant in deciding whether one in acute pain is among the worst off. A similar conclusion seems right regarding significant assaults on personal dignity such as those that come from absence of basic nursing care.

The slice-of-time perspective is appropriate in these cases because people in acute, severe pain or in a state in which they experience significant assault on dignity are entities separate from their life-histories. They are comparable to the child trapped in a well who cries out for assistance. Deciding whether it is ethical to respond is independent of any cool calculation of utility *or* of who is worst off over a lifetime. For those conditions that separate oneself from one's personal identity over a lifetime, the slice-of-time perspective is the correct one in deciding who is worst off. For those conditions such as chronic threat to continued existence, which still leave one recognizing personal identity over a lifetime, the cumulative time perspective is the correct one. That seems to me to explain how we should differentiate kinds of care for the elderly much better than either the "natural lifespan" view of Callahan or the "prudential lifespan" account of Daniels. My conclusion is that for these conditions that permit accumulating over-a-lifetime, age is one relevant factor in deciding who is worse off and therefore a *prima facie*, justice-based reason for allocating scarce resources.

Practical Policy Considerations

Transplants

Having reached this conclusion, we need to return to the two cases with which we began. How does one operationalize a decision rooted in justice to use age as an allocation criterion in the cases of a 68-year-old man needing a heart transplant and a 92-year-old woman who wants by-pass surgery?

Although the man needing a heart transplant may appear to pose a more difficult problem, I believe (for technical reasons) that it is a much easier case to resolve as a matter of public policy. Organs for transplant are scarce in a way that surgeons for by-pass operations are not. We are limited in the case of transplants by the number of organs available. At some point we may reach the situation in which we will decide that certain kinds of transplants are not worth doing even if the organs are available; but for now, with solid organs, the limiting factor is the number of organs.[18]

Moreover, transplant allocation is easier because there is a point system in place that is used for computerized allocation. Points are awarded for various factors, depending on the organ. Some are based on predictors of medical success (such as tissue match) and others on measures of need and other justice-based criteria (such as medical urgency, time on the waiting list, etc.). It is a matter of significant ethical controversy how the utility-based criteria should relate to those oriented to justice.[19] For our purposes, however, what is important is that a multi-factored point scheme is already in place. We could easily add points to the formula based on age.

Based on what has been said here, an ideal point scheme would avoid precipitous cutoffs and would give priority inversely related to age. I have proposed to the United Network for Organ Sharing that an age factor be added to the point formula in which each potential candidate for an organ be given points equal to:

$$[100 - age] \times K$$

in which K is a constant expressing how important age should be in comparison with other factors. I would propose K = 0.05, thus giving a maximum of five points to a young patient and zero to the centenarian. In the practical range of adult patients who would plausibly risk a transplant (say, ages 15-80), the point range would thus be 4.25 down to 1.00 for a differential of 3.25 points based on age. By contrast, in the kidney formula there is a differential of 10 points based on tissue typing; in the heart formula, a differential of 20 points based on urgency. Deciding the relative importance of the various factors is obviously a judgment call. (In my opinion the utility-based tissue-match points are overrated in the kidney formula. They give too much emphasis to efficiency at the expense of justice.) One could adjust the value of K to give age any desired weight in proportion to other factors in the formulas.

By-pass Surgery and Other Procedures

By contrast, the 92-year-old who wants by-pass surgery poses a different kind of problem. We could provide enough surgeons and operating rooms to do as many procedures as we want, but providing surgery for everyone who wants it (including for those for whom the benefits would be very marginal) would be irresponsible. The limit here is from the inevitable competition from the other good things we could do with the time, money, and talent that would go to unlimited bypass.

Here we have no point formula in place, and resources are scarce in a quite different sense than in transplants. I am convinced that not all procedures should be provided and that age is a morally legitimate basis for setting the limits, but devising the policy will take much more work. Using the insurance model for interpersonal allocations, we could ask subscribers (or their agents) to determine what they thought was fair. To the extent that they abstracted from their own idiosyncratic interests and needs, the result would be fair. Still, setting these limits will be somewhat arbitrary. I believe that reasonable people, when asked what is fair, will choose limits that among other considerations, give *prima facie* priority to life-extending care inversely proportional to the age of the recipient. At the same time, for those interventions with the immediacy of acute pain or nursing care needed for dignity, age will not be a factor.

If this is correct, age is--after all--a morally relevant basis for allocating certain kinds of health care. Even if aggregate utility is not an adequate justification for using age as an allocation, the principle of justice can be.

Notes and References

1. Jeffrey Prottas, Mark Segal, and Harvey M. Sapolsky, "Cross-National Difference in Dialysis Rates," *Health Care Financing Review,* Vol. 4 (March 1983) p. 98; Henry J. Aaron and William B. Schwartz, *The Painful Prescription* (Washington, D.C.: The Brookings Institution, 1984), p. 34.

2. "Elimination of Age Over 69," *Federal Register,* Vol. 52, Sept. 1, 1987, p. 33152.

3. For a more developed account of this thesis and an exploration of the alternative moral principles that can be used in making such allocations see Robert M. Veatch, "DRGs and the Ethical Reallocation of Resources," *The Hastings Center Report,* Vol. 16, June 1986, pp. 32-40; and Robert M. Veatch, "Physicians and Cost Containment: The Ethical Conflict," *Jurimetrics,* Vol. 30,

Summer 1990, pp. 461-482.

4. John Rawls, "Two Concepts of Rules," *The Philosophical Review*, Vol. 44 (1955), pp. 3-32; David Lyons, *Forms and Limits of Utilitarianism* (Oxford: Oxford University Press, 1965).

5. See Robert M. Veatch, *The Foundations of Justice: Why the Retarded and the Rest of Us Have Claims to Equality* (New York: Oxford University Press, 1986), for my development of the case for this interpretation.

6. Jerry Avorn, "Benefit and Cost Analysis in Geriatric Care: Turning Age Discrimination into Health Policy," *The New England Journal of Medicine*, Vol. 310 (May 17, 1984) pp. 1294-1300; Nancy S. Jecker, "Disenfranchising the Elderly from Life-Extending Medical Care," *Public Affairs Quarterly*, Vol. 2 (July 1988), pp. 51-68; Nancy S. Jecker, "Toward a Theory of Age-Group Justice," *Journal of Medicine and Philosophy*, Vol. 14 (Dec., 1989), pp. 655-676; John F. Kilner, "Age Criteria in Medicine: Are the Medical Justifications Ethical?" *Archives of Internal Medicine*, Vol. 149 (Oct., 1989), pp. 2343-2346; Eric Munoz, Fred Rosner, Don Chalfin, et al., "Age, Resource Consumption, and Outcome of Medical Patients as an Academic Medical Center," *Archives of Internal Medicine*, Vol. 149 (Sept. 1989), pp. 1946-1950; John F. Kilner, *Who Lives? Who Dies?* (New Haven: Yale University Press, 1990), pp. 77-94; Margaret P. Battin, "Age Rationing and the Just Distribution of Health Care: Is There a Duty to Die?" *Ethics*, Vol. 97 (January 1987), pp. 317-340; Larry R. Churchill, "Should We Ration Health Care by Age?" *Journal of the American Geriatrics Society*, Vol. 36 (July, 1988), pp. 644-647.

7. Daniel Callahan, *Setting Limits: Medical Goals in an Aging Society* (New York: Simon & Schuster, 1987).

8. Ibid., p. 116.

9. Ibid., p. 43.

10. In his sequel, Daniel Callahan, *What Kind of Life: The Limits of Medical Progress* (New York: Simon and Schuster, 1990), Callahan is much more bold about appealing to "the common good" as a criterion for health resource allocation.   He forthrightly acknowledges that certain individuals will be sacrificed, but even here he emphasizes that allocations should not discriminate against whole social groups of people and relief of suffering would still command an important moral priority.   In the new volume, however, Callahan is much more dangerously close to the consequentialist's goal of maximizing the aggregate good even at the expense of the rights of the individual.   In the earlier volume, he suggests that one need not climb into bed with the consequentialists to support an age-based allocation policy. It is that non-consequentialist position I am addressing here.

11. Daniel Callahan, "Natural Death and Public Policy," *Life Span: Values and Life-Extending Technologies*, edited by Robert M. Veatch (San

Francisco: Harper and Row, Publishers, 1979), p. 174.

12. See Norman Daniels, "Am I My Parents' Keeper?" in President's Commission for the Study of Ethical Problems in Medicine and Biomedical and Behavioral Research, *Securing Access to Health Care*, Vol. 2 (Washington, D.C.: U.S. Government Printing Office, 1983), pp. 265-291; and *Am I My Parents' Keeper?: An Essay on Justice Between the Young and the Old* (New York: Oxford University Press, 1988).

13. Daniels, *Am I My Parents' Keeper?* p. 74.

14. Ibid., pp. 58-59.

15. See Ronald Dworkin, "What is Equality? Part 1: Equality of Welfare," *Philosophy and Public Affairs*, Vol. 10 (Summer 1981), pp. 185-246; and "What is Equality? Part 2: Equality of Resources," *Philosophy and Public Affairs*, Vol. 10 (Fall 1981), pp. 283-345.

16. It should be clear that this commits me to a different version of the hypothetical contract than that supported by Rawls and Daniels. I view contractors as discovering a preexisting moral structure, not simply choosing what is prudent.

17. Dennis McKerlie, "Equality and Time," *Ethics*, Vol. 99 (April 1989), pp. 474-491.

18. Bone marrow transplant may pose the first difficult case. If people continue to enter tissue registries as a result of appeals from visible patients needing bone marrow transplants, the availability of compatible tissue could cease to be a limit. Then we will face the situation of thousands of leukemia patients who could be transplanted, some of whom could be elderly or have a low probability of success. Likewise, if we develop the technology to procure kidneys from donors following declaration of death based on heart criteria, we could also have an abundant supply of kidneys.

19. I have raised these issues in Robert M. Veatch, *Death, Dying, and the Biological Revolution*, Revised Edition (New Haven: Yale University Press, 1989), pp. 209-211.

16

Exceptions and the Elderly

Gerald R. Winslow

Introduction

All attempts to ration health care on the basis of fixed categories, such as age, encounter the problem of exceptional cases. If exceptions are granted, because of excellent medical prospects for patients, then the effectiveness of establishing such categories is called into question. If no exceptions are granted, a number of other unhappy results seem inevitable. Among these are demoralizing caregivers and ignoring the unique conditions and personal preferences of elderly patients. So it is no surprise that much of the criticism of age-based rationing centers on the treatment of exceptions.

In what follows, I consider how society should develop publicly debated, publicly approved, and equitably applied rules for rationing that allow for exceptions. I begin with the prism of a case and proceed by considering the need for a public system of norms and the need for exceptions. Finally, I want to make a proposal for a system of rationing that announces the rules but also allows them to be broken when the burdens of proof can be met.

A Prismatic Case

In 1984, Dr. Jefferson C. Pennington was dying of liver failure.[1] His post-necrotic sclerosis of the liver was the result of hepatitis. He had been refused consideration as a liver transplant recipient because of his advanced age. The blanket rule at that time was that no one over 55 could be accepted as a transplant candidate. He was 58.

Nevertheless, with the help of friends, Dr. Pennington was taken to Pittsburgh's Presbyterian Hospital, the workplace of Dr. Thomas Starzl, pioneer in liver transplants. Dr. Pennington was flatly refused admission on the transplant service, but he managed to get admitted as a medical patient because of his bleeding. Through further maneuvering, he was also successful in arranging a meeting with Dr. Starzl. But Dr. Starzl insisted that the patient return home. His age gave him such a low priority that he stood no realistic chance.

Then, as he was preparing to leave the hospital, Dr. Pennington was asked if he still wanted a liver. Someone had died accidentally in Missouri, and the donated liver was too big for anyone on Pittsburgh's waiting list. Dr. Pennington, at six foot three inches, was big enough for the gift. Rather than waste the organ, it was given to him.

When he awakened from the anesthetic, his mind was clear, and his edema gone. Four months later he was whitewater rafting down the Colorado River. Eight months later he was in full surgical practice. At this writing, six years after his transplant, he is 65 and has retired from the practice of surgery. He continues work as a hospital management consultant and is board chairman of Tennessee Donor Services, a regional organ procurement agency.

The Argument Over Exceptions

It is hardly surprising that Dr. Pennington considers age-based rationing "unconscionable."[2] He has enjoyed over six years of productive life because the rule excluding him on the basis of age was broken. He insists that we should make judgments about the allocation of medical resources on a "case-by-case basis." After his own transplant, he met a woman who was 76 when she received her new liver, and who had gone on to years of meaningful life. Dr. Pennington does not deny that difficult rationing decisions are necessary, but he does deny that chronological age, *by itself*, should be a fixed limit.

In this judgment, he is certainly not alone. Indeed, his viewpoint appears to represent the majority of those who have responded to proposals for age-based rationing. For example, the American Geriatrics Society has taken the official position that "Chronological age should not be the sole, arbitrary criterion for limiting particular kinds of medical care. . . . Rationing policies based on age encounter the objection that a profound variability exists among members of the same age group . . . ."[3] And the United States Congress's Office of Technology Assessment, in its report, "Life-Sustaining Technologies and the Elderly," said: "Rationing life-sustaining technologies on the basis of age would clearly result in the deaths of many people who could survive with a quality of life that is acceptable to them.[4]

Even Daniel Callahan, in his first book on the subject, recognized the need for exceptions to age-based limits. In an oft-cited passage, he wrote: "The care of the *physically vigorous elderly person* poses the fewest problems. All levels of care appear appropriate, at least through the first round of illness, and even for those who have lived a natural life span if there is a solid prospect of a few (say, four or five) more years of good life."[5]

Recognizing that such exception-making was bound to be viewed as a denial of his call for age-based rationing, Callahan added: "I make an exception in this case because I do not think that anyone would find it tolerable to allow the healthy person to be denied lifesaving care."[6]

Such willingness to grant an exception might be all that is needed by those who object to a rigid system of age-based rationing. After all, if some personal trait or condition is sufficient to trump age, then age is not the only deciding factor, and might not be even a significant one.

It should also be noted, however, that Callahan's acknowledge-ment of exceptional circumstances was, itself, highly exceptional, very limited, and also apparently short-lived. The only exception-making criterion he mentioned was *physical* vigor. People with other exception-making considerations, such as *mental* vigor, the needs of dependents, or the time needed for the realization of some personal dream, were not encouraged to apply. Callahan also made it clear that an exception for one having completed her natural life-span would be on a one-time basis. Any subsequent appeals for life-sustaining treatment apparently would be denied.

Since the appearance of *Setting Limits*, Callahan has changed his mind about exceptions. In a recent essay, he says that he mistakenly allowed himself, in his earlier work, to be "seduced by our natural inclination to look at individual cases."[7] He now believes that "to be consistent in the use of age as a standard, no exceptions should be made, particularly exceptions based on the conditions of an individual patient."[8] The admission of exceptions, he thinks, would undermine the whole point of having categorical limits.

It can hardly be denied that with exceptions might come chaos and the stubborn endurance of the very problems that drove us to attempt rationing in the first place. Without exceptions, we might build a highly rational and efficient bureaucracy, yet one potentially terrible in its dehumanizing power. It is tempting to reconsider completely the need to establish public norms for setting limits.

The Need for Public Norms

For several years now, writers (including myself) have detailed the need to set realistic and equitable limits on medical care, including some forms of life-saving care.[9]   Our society will never be able to provide every imaginable life-extending treatment to every person in need, regardless of cost or the marginal benefits. Even if most of us agree that excluding people simply on the basis of chronological age should not be one of the rules, we probably can state many other rules that would be virtually non-exceptionable. For example, no one with metastatic cancer and poor prospects for more than a few months of life should receive an organ transplant. But other norms are far more debatable.   For example, should mentally retarded persons be excluded, because of their retardation, from organ transplantation?

We need carefully stated norms if we are to set meaningful and effective limits.   The present system, still pretending most of the time to offer whatever is available if people are really in need, is gradually being unmasked.   But we are, as yet, a long way from having sufficient social consensus on how to proceed.   The initial steps taken in Oregon, and a few other states, are probably a rehearsal for what we must attempt to do nationwide.

It is of great importance that the norms we develop, whatever they are, not only be the result of public debate and public approval but also be publicly announced and understood.   In other words, the norms must meet the requirements of publicity.   The reasons for such publicity are quite obvious.[10]   Public knowledge and understanding of the norms discourage the institution of unfair norms that are incapable of universalization.   Such public understanding helps to ensure the support of society's members and creates valid, mutual expectations.   Publicity also assists people who need to appeal injustices and opens the way to criticism of norms that may be in need of change.

The importance of publicity for health-care limits was recently underscored by Paul Menzel in *Strong Medicine.* Arguing for what he calls the "prior consent model," Menzel says that the limits on marginal health-care benefits can be construed as those to which people, who must live with the limits, have agreed. If no such formal agreement has been struck, we must ask what limits people would have accepted, judging from the way that the community has typically expressed itself. In Menzel's words, "For the guideline-setting bureaucrat. . . the relevant question is the same: Have these patients consented, or would they have, to the sort of policy restriction now being imposed on them?"[11] A major advantage of this model is to reduce the tension between statistical approaches to the aggregate good and expressions of personal autonomy.

One of the effects of Menzel's arguments may be to remind us how far we are from the formulation of clear limits with public involvement and understanding. At the microallocation level (i.e., which individual patients should be selected when resources are scarce), how many members of our society understand how people are selected or rejected for, say, kidney or heart transplants? Or at the macroallocation level (i.e., which health-care programs should be given priority), what is the general public awareness of how decisions are made about what is and what is not covered by third party payors? How do treatments move from the classification of "experimental" to that of "standard" therapy? Or how many, even among those elected officials who are paid to know such things, understand how to compare the costworthiness of, say, a breast cancer screening program with a program for prenatal care. These are, to be sure, immensely complicated matters. They are also highly important both because of the practical effects on peoples' lives and because of what the various alternatives symbolize for our vision of a good and just society.

There appears to be no adequate substitute for pressing toward the day when, as a society, we have faced these questions more openly and established public norms for the allocation of health-care resources. But should such norms be applied without exceptions?

The Need for Exceptions

By "exceptions," I mean divergence from a stated norm, such as "No transplants are allowed for people over 55," which divergence is not, as yet, covered by some other accepted norm. An exception means breaking the stated rules of the day. Dr. Pennington's transplant was an exception. In this section, I list three reasons for exceptions that I consider primary.

The Significance of Individual Differences

Philosopher Stephen Toulmin, in his well-known essay on the tyranny of principles, describes an exceptional case which, tragically, was not treated exceptionally.[12]   The case involved a young handicapped woman who was having trouble with her local Social Security office.   Her Social Security checks were insufficient to pay for her rent, utilities, and food.   So she started a telephone answering service in her home.   The Social Security office learned of the extra income and not only reduced her payments but also demanded the return of some of the money she had received.   The woman, in despair, committed suicide.   A reporter, commenting on the case, concluded that "there should be a *rule* to prevent this kind of thing from happening."[13]

Toulmin thinks that this call for a rule is mistaken--part of the sad, but common, attitude of wanting a rule for everything, including medical care.   What we need is the restoration of an ethics of discretion in which people, who are well acquainted with each other's needs, respond appropriately.   Toulmin preaches warnings about an overly rigid, bureaucratic approach to ethics:

> The delivery of social services has become ever more routinized, centralized, and subject to bureaucratic routine. It should not take horror stories, like that of the handicapped young woman's answering service, to make us think again about the whole project of delivering human services through a bureaucracy. . . . The imperatives of bureaucratic administration require determinate procedures and full accountability; while a helping hand . . . can be truly equitable only if it is exercised with discretion, on the basis of substantive and informed judgments about need rather than formal rules of entitlement."[14]

In these remarks, Toulmin previewed the thesis that he and Albert Jonsen develop, at length, in their book, *The Abuse of Casuistry*, a philosophical and historical analysis case-based moral reasoning.   The authors give an account of why moral reasoning must be concerned with the significant particulars of individual cases.   This is the requirement of Aristotle's *phronesis*, or practical wisdom.   In a passage that captures much of the book's spirit, the authors remind us that "The heart of moral experience does not lie in a mastery of general rules and theoretical principles, however sound and well reasoned those principles may appear. It is located, rather, in the wisdom that comes from seeing how the ideas behind those rules work out in the course of people's lives . . . ."[15]

In so saying, the authors provide the central moral reason for attending to the significant particulars of cases: People differ, and their circumstances differ. If we are to treat each other with respect, we cannot overlook such differences and simply apply the rules. The chorus of negative responses to Callahan's age-based rationing constantly returns to this refrain: The morally significant particulars of individual cases matter too much for us to accept inflexible application of categorical exclusions based strictly on age.

It might be asked why, rather than allowing for exceptions, we should not attempt to establish more and more refined rules. For example, we could say that no one over 80 should have coronary arterial by-pass surgery *unless* the person is physically vigorous in ways that can be carefully measured and documented. Thus, we might have a more precise rule with stated exception-making criteria.

The main trouble with ever-lengthening lists of more and more specific rules is that this approach tends to overlook why cases may be truly exceptional: the complex interaction of countless variables such as a patient's will to continue life, his or her physical condition, the support and attitudes of family or loved ones, and on, and on.

So, for example, Menzel writes that even for terminally ill patients there may be factors that would make a brief and possibly costly extension of life worthwhile. "Why," Menzel asks, "should factors with which we can widely identify, such as the imminent return of a close friend or relative from a far-off part of the world or the quick approach of Christmas with its family reunion, not make a real difference?"[16] Menzel believes that we can arrange institutional policies that favor costworthy care without falling for rigid cutoffs.

Such allowance for exceptions may be dismissed by some as little help for public policy and as insufficiently attentive to the common good. Critiques of immoderate individualism are not uncommon today.[17] However, as Paul Ramsey used to remind us "The good is not common that does not flow back upon all alike . . . ."[18] The constant challenge for today's health-care ethics is to seek socially-responsible balance between caring for individual needs and establishing a costworthy system of health care. Any statistical approach to aggregate health-care benefits should make careful room for artful, expert application of practical wisdom to individual cases.

The Appropriate Use of Expertise

Attention to exceptional cases, with their particular needs, is required not only in order to preserve respect for each patient, but also to preserve the arts of the various health-care professions. It is impossible to imagine that the common good will be well served if we reduce highly skilled, professional nurses, physicians, physical therapists and their allies to bureaucratically controlled automatons. We expect them to be experts. We cannot, at the same time, ask them to perform their arts as if they were novices.

Philosopher Hubert Dreyfus, and systems analyst, Stuart Dreyfus, have done ground-breaking work on how people move from being less than able beginners to being competent and finally expert.[19] For the beginner, attempting to acquire most any skill, the performance is rigid and faltering. The beginner must pay strict attention to the instructions and follow the rules. It is only in dropping the rules that beginners move beyond competence to true expertise.

In *From Novice to Expert*, nurse-philosopher Patricia Benner applies the Dreyfuses' analysis to the art of nursing. Benner shows, in case after case, how expert nurses develop clinical knowledge, rooted in practical experience, that defies textbook description because of the complexity of the circumstances. In Benner's words: "The expert performer no longer relies on an analytic principle (rule, guideline, maxim) to connect her or his understanding of the situation to an appropriate action. The expert nurse, with an enormous background of experience, now has an intuitive grasp of each situation and zeroes in on the accurate region of the problem without wasteful consideration of a large range of unfruitful, alternative diagnoses and solutions."[20] Such expert nurses are guided by very subtle differences in look or feel or a myriad of other conditions that affect perception of the case.

So it must also be for the other health professions. The practical knowledge, embedded in years of experience, makes possible the art of expert professionals. This does not mean, of course, that they are free to practice their art without constraints. Society is not remiss in setting limits on the resources to be expended. But it does mean that health care professionals must have room to grant exceptions to commonly-accepted rules. Asking such experts to retreat to the level of beginners, governed by rigid rules from some bureaucratic institution, will not only demoralize them, it will harm us all.

Exceptions and Progress in Health Care

Progress is, of course, a significant part of our current problem. The price of progress, especially in the case of new medical technologies, can be too high. Still, human beings seem to be designed with curiosity and a desire to extend the limits of knowledge and technique. It is entirely unlikely that, in the spirit of Luddites, society will declare a moratorium on developing new methods of health care. And, without exceptions to current limits, it would often be impossible to discover the true limits of costworthy care.

Consider, for example, coronary arterial by-pass grafting (or CABG). CABG for elderly patients is often listed among the villains of high technology medicine that is not costworthy. But a recent report of CABG in elderly patients indicates otherwise. In a study of 315 such patients (mean age of 69) who had severe, debilitating angina, over 95 percent of the patients survived the procedure and, of these, nearly 90 percent were relieved of angina without further use of drugs. Another 8 percent were able to control angina with use of drugs. The authors of the study conclude that "coronary arterial surgery is an effective treatment for angina in the elderly. This will have consequences for future resource allocation if the elderly are not to be denied effective therapy because of financial rather than clinical restraints."[21]

A single study cannot answer many of the important questions about costworthiness of CABG in the elderly. What were the total costs per patient? How many years of life, if any, were gained? There can be little doubt, however, that for a person who was confined to her home with uncontrollable angina (as was true for 90 percent of the patients) freedom from pain and freedom to move about were no small benefits. We certainly will never know if such interventions are, indeed, costworthy if we never try them.

A Proposal

What is needed, I propose, is a system of public norms for limiting health-care expenditures, that leaves room for professional discretion in the service of individual patients. We cannot continue to pretend that there are no limits to the application of new and expensive health-care technologies. But in the treatment of individual patients there must, somehow, be room to bend the rules.

Help for this proposal comes from Daniel Callahan's recent book,

What Kind of Life. Callahan considers what he calls "categorical" versus "individual" application of limits. He poses this question: "When we have to set limits, . . . is that best done on an individual, case-by-case basis, or by the use of what I call categorical standards?"[22]

By a *categorical* standard, Callahan means a "relatively objective, required public standard."[23]

One of his examples, not surprisingly is the use of age as a limit on some forms of treatment for the elderly. Other examples include a minimum weight for premature infants to receive aggressive life support and a computer protocol for patients with chest pains to determine whether or not they should be placed in a coronary care unit. Such standards would not be intended so much to prescribe in detail how professionals should care for patients as they would be to set the outer limits beyond which care should not go.

Callahan admits that the strict use of such categorical limits would run counter to some of our most cherished values. Why, then, should we override the desires of patients and the long moral tradition of the health professions' commitment to exercise discretion in the patients' best interests? Callahan offers three reasons.

First, given the fact that we simply cannot afford to do everything that might offer curative benefits for every patient, it is more respectful of patients as persons to exclude them by categories than as individuals. Thus we may avoid personally destructive comparisons of the worthiness of various patients.

Second, rationing at the bedside simply does not work. The powerful forces that push in the direction of treating, even in the face of serious doubts about the benefits, tend to overwhelm patients, their families, and health-care professionals alike.

Finally, Callahan appeals to the bureaucratic neatness of the categorical approach. The rules would be subject to debate and capable of the clear application required by public policy. Callahan admits that "Inevitably, categorical standards are unfair to individuals . . . . But the overall balance of fairness and policy clarity can make categorical standards valuable for public programs."[24]

All the talk about the advantages of categorical limits might lead readers to expect only a very rigid approach to their application. Callahan suggests, however, that such categorical limits may be applied either in a *firm* or a *soft* manner. As an example of firm application, Callahan says we might simply set "the age of eighty as the cut-off point for Medicare entitlements for expensive forms of high-technology care--and *make no exceptions.*"[25] The softer way would be to set the categorical limit but then allow for exceptions that meet appropriate criteria. So the limit on eighty-year-olds might be set aside for a patient who likely would, thereby, be given another five years of life in "good condition."

Several questions about the "softer" approach come quickly to mind. For example, if a criterion such as the reasonable likelihood of five more years of life should be applied to eighty-year-olds, why not to seventy-nine-year-olds, or, for that matter forty-five-year-olds? What does the fact that one is eighty add to the application? In the cases of such treatments as CABG or expensive rehabilitation, Callahan says that "only certainty of benefit based on experience of good outcome with certain categories of treatment would justify treatment."[26] But, aside from the fact that health care seldom, if ever, has the luxury of certainty, how would anything like such confidence be available without extensive experience *beyond* the categorical limits?

Despite such questions, we should understand Callahan for what he clearly means (or, at least, what he meant). There are firmer and softer ways of applying categorical limits. Callahan leaves no doubt that he prefers the firmer approach of no exceptions because it is less subject to abuses and more likely to be effective.

But there are better reasons to prefer an exception-granting approach. In addition to those reasons already given, we might add that the likelihood of political success seems far greater if guidelines for limits leave room for professional discretion and the recognition of patients' differences. Even if an age-based limit, such as the one Dr. Pennington encountered, makes sense for some medical interventions, there are ample reasons to doubt the probability of success for a program that would insist on wasting a transplantable liver rather than granting an exception.

Beyond political realities, there are ethical reasons to prefer limits that are open to carefully-considered exceptions. Rules are abstractions from human experience that should be viewed as establishing presumptions in favor of or against specified actions. Once accepted, such presumptions may place a very heavy burden of proof on those calling for exceptions. But when truly exceptional cases occur, the burden may be met and the presumption rebutted.[27] The alternatives of no rules at all or of rigidly-followed rules distort the moral life.

In practical terms, it should be possible to set costworthy limits on what our society currently considers basic health care and then allow for the possibility that professional discernment about a patient's unique condition meets the burden of proof for allowable exceptions. This is not the place to attempt a description of the bureaucratic details for such an approach. In broad terms, it would require that those who wish to make an exception be prepared to explain why such should be granted. And it would require that there be some publicly-accountable method for judging the appeals. In the end, we may discover that such a system will fall prey to the same forces that have led to runaway health-care costs. But before resorting to extremely rigid categorical limits, we should look for ways to account for the diversity and dignity of individual patients. We should hope that an imaginative approach to setting limits would make appeals for exceptions possible without leading to an overly cumbersome bureaucracy.

Conclusion

We are yet a long way from knowing how to set limits to health care without becoming callous. Indeed, we are some way from general public agreement on the need for such limits. As we move toward reasonable and equitable limits, we should guard against the most obvious dehumanizing effects of bureaucratic delivery of care. To do this, we must make certain that our experiments in limit-setting allow room for genuinely exceptional cases.

Notes and References

1.   This story was told as part of an unpublished address given by Dr. Pennington at a national conference on organ transplantation held at Loma Linda University, November 17, 1986.

2.   Telephone interview, August 30, 1990.

3.   American Geriatrics Society Public Policy Committee, "Equitable Distribution of Limited Medical Resources," *Journal of the American Geriatrics Society*, Vol. 37 (November, 1989), p. 1063. This position statement was adopted by the Board of Directors of the American Geriatrics Society, July 1989.

4.   United States Congress, Office of technology Assessment, *Life Sustaining Technologies and the Elderly* (Washington, D.C. U.S. Government Printing Office, 1987).

5.   Daniel Callahan, *Setting Limits: Medical goals in an Aging Society* (New York: Simon & Schuster, 1987), p. 184. Italics added.

6.   Ibid., p. 8.

7.   Daniel Callahan, "Afterword: Daniel Callahan Responds to His

Critics," in *A Good Old Age? The Paradox of Setting Limits*, edited by Paul Homer and Martha Holstein (New York: Simon & Schuster, 1990), p. 311.

8. Ibid. Callahan repeats this argument in his essay for this volume.

9. Gerald R. Winslow, *Triage and Justice* (Berkeley: University of California Press, 1982)

10. Here I am repeating, with few modifications, the points made in my essay, "Rationing and Publicity," in *The Price of Health*, edited by George J. Agich and Charles E. Begley (Dordrecht, Netherlands: D. Reidel Publishing Company, 1986), pp. 199-215.

11. Paul Menzel, *Strong Medicine: The Ethical Rationing of Health Care* (New York: Oxford University Press, 1990), p. 15.

12. Stephen Toulmin, "The Tyrrany of Principles," *The Hastings Center Report*, Vol. 11, Dec. 1981, pp. 31-39.

13. Ibid., p. 32.

14. Ibid., p. 36.

15. Albert R. Jonsen and Stephen Toulmin, *The Abuse of Casuistry: A History of Moral Reasoning* (Berkeley: University of California Press, 1985).

16. Menzel, *Strong Medicine*, p. 198.

17. In addition to Daniel Callahan's works, I am thinking especially of Robert Bellah, et. al., *Habits of the heart: Individualism and Commitment in American Life* (Berkeley: University of California Press, 1985).

18. Paul Ramsey, *Patient as Person* (New Haven: Yale University Press, 1970), p. 258.

19. S. E. Dreyfus and H. L. Dreyfus, "A Five-Stage Model of the Mental Activities Involved in Directed Skill Acquisition," Unpublished report supported by the United States Air Force, Office of Scientific Research, University of California, Berkeley, 1980.

20. Patricia Benner, *From Novice to Expert: Excellence and Power in Clinical Nursing Practice* (Menlo Park, Calif.: Addison-Wesley, 1984), pp. 31-32.

21. J. M. Morgan, et. al., "Coronary Arterial Surgery in the Elderly: Its Effect in the Relief of Angina," *International Journal of Cardiology*, Vol. 23, (June 1989), p. 327.

22. Daniel Callahan, *What Kind of Life? The Limits of Medical Progress* (New York: Simon & Schuster, 1990), p. 202.

23. Ibid.

24. Ibid., p. 205.

25. Ibid.

26. Ibid., p. 206

27. The language of rebuttable presumptions has been developed by a number of moral theologians and philosophers. See, for example, Jonsen and Toulmin, *The Abuse of Casuistry*, p. 328-29, and J. Phillip Wogaman, *A Christian Method of Moral Judgment* (Philadelphia: Westminster Press, 1976).

PART SIX

Personal Autonomy
and Social Responsibility

17

Personal Choice and Public Rationing

Judith Wilson Ross

Introduction

Over the past twenty years, those writing in the field of bioethics have emphasized patients' rights to determine their own medical treatment. Although the right to refuse treatment has received the primary emphasis, this emphasis also supported the belief that patients are entitled to any health-care that they want. Americans like that conclusion.

Although families and patients seldom want useless, futile, or ineffective treatment, they are likely to want treatment that offers potential benefit, treatment that offers even a small chance of maintaining life or restoring them to some social role, whatever that may be. Physicians and patients and their families often join together in this pursuit of hope against all statistical probability. In *Near Death*, a recent documentary filmed in a Boston hospital's intensive care unit, director Frederick Wiseman captured this common situation in which the physician, who believes treatment should not be continued any longer, tries to convince the family (in this case the patient's wife, who is eminently open to persuasion).[1] Except . . . every time she comes close to saying, "All right, no more," she becomes so distressed at the thought of her husband's death that the physician feels compelled to comfort her by assuring her that "we always have hope," which the wife then takes to mean that further treatment might be useful.

Because the physician understandably does not want to discourage patient or family, causing them to give up hope, she or he often compassionately reminds them that "there is always hope." As long as the physician is offering hope, the patient or family is hard-pressed to give up, for disease has not yet shown its ultimate triumph, has not yet won the battle between human and illness. Even when there is no hope for the *patient*, there may still be hope for some *part* of the patient.   For example, a recent case of an elderly man with chronic dementia and multiple other problems found the patient--after an eight-week hospitalization during which he settled into an unarousable state--being given total parenteral nutrition (TPN) because the family wanted "to help heal his decubiti," the only condition that could be reversed.   The physicians were uncomfortable with not providing TPN, not doing what they could to keep him alive, despite describing the man as a "poor, sad, tragic case." Tragic because he was dying? Or because he was being treated not for his own sake but for that of his skin?

Lynn Payer, writing about American medicine in *Medicine and Culture*, comments: "Imagine a medical system in which everyone was brought up reading *The Little Engine that Could*.[2] She was talking about American physicians, but American patients also grew up on that story.   If there is illness, disease, or despair, we Americans see it as something to be overcome. It is foreign to us, not a part of life as we imagine it to be. In our fancy, we will live forever and die quickly.   In the recently articulated concept of "compressed morbidity," we will live a life of complete health, then have a brief period of sickness, and die. Like the "Deacon's One Hoss Shay," perfect for a hundred years, we will one night fall completely apart. Such fancies are understandable but they may not reflect reality for all that.   Trying and wanting are not always enough. It's possible that sometimes the little engine just *can't*.

The legal system, which is thought to have an enormous effect on the style of medical practice in this country, also appears to encourage more rather than less treatment. The threat of malpractice and the rampant fear of litigation among physicians leads to overtreatment because it appears to be legally safer to treat than to stop treating if there is any question that someone--indeed anyone-- might be displeased.   As the legal system prefers that ninety-nine guilty persons go free rather than that one innocent person be jailed, so it seems to prefer that ninety-nine people receive treatment they would not want rather than that one person not get treatment that she or he would want. The Missouri Supreme Court's view of the *Cruzan* case was surely based on such a rationale, given the repeated polls suggesting that only 20 percent or less of the population would want to be maintained in a persistent vegetative state and the very strong evidence that Nancy Cruzan was not among that 20 percent.

Because most forces in the system support more treatment and more kinds of treatment, some writers--Daniel Callahan[3] and William Schwartz[4] come immediately to mind--have argued that specific rationing of treatment is inevitable. Yet the argument for rationing is usually rejected out of hand, as if such a prospect were unimaginable. Even delayed healing, as it turns out, is beyond the pale. In a recent news article discussing the problem of bone fractures that do not heal quickly,[5] physician James Heckman talked about tibial shaft fractures that may take up to three years to heal. He concluded that "such prolonged delays frustrate the patient and the surgeon, and may not be acceptable in this day and age." Waiting up to three years for a broken bone to heal represents significant discomfort and hardship to the patient, as well as frustration for both patient and physician, but to contend that such a wait is one that Americans would not *accept* is quite a remarkable statement. It implies that such matters are solely within our control. If delayed healing is *unacceptable*, then delayed treatment--or no treatment at all--becomes *unbelievable.*

It is worth noting that we can imagine how to ration virtually every other commodity and service in this world *except* health-care. David Eddy has commented that "the word *rationing* has come to symbolize an inhumane attitude and is used only by the most courageous speakers."[6] With respect to health-care, there is almost no discussion of the possibility of restricting or sharply reducing the research funding that ensures more and more expensive technologies becoming available as the years pass. No one suggests that queuing would be acceptable, though it surely exists quietly in health maintenance organizations and in public hospitals. There is no talk about limiting choice of physicians, although prospective provider plans do just that. Our expectations continue to be (as one physician phrased it) for Cadillac care, even if we want to pay only Chevrolet prices. When someone like Callahan actually does offer specific rationing proposals, he is roundly--and often personally--attacked.

The question we are facing, however, is clear: How can we get everyone into our health-care system and, at the same time, keep the costs and the rate of increase of those costs at an acceptable level? Although many urge that we eliminate ineffective and unnecessary care, that reasonable project cannot by itself keep health costs from absorbing all our resources as time passes. There is strong evidence that, if we get everyone into the system, some kind of restriction of services is inevitable.[7] Some kind of health-care restriction is not unknown in the Western world. Indeed, it is widely practiced in other countries.

Rationing and Our Cultural Stories

Why, then, are proposals of rationing so quickly rejected in American culture? Perhaps it is because the problem is not technical but *contextual.* That is, American medicine and the health-care system exist in one metaphor or one narrative, whereas the proposed solution exists in a different and conflicting story. Cultural stories and myths are the ways in which we organize information and give meaning to our lives.[8] Our ability to understand a concept or fact requires that there already be a place for it in our cultural story: that it fit into the story. A new disease like AIDS, for example, was initially incorporated into our cultural story as "plague" (particularly as it connected with sin and punishment), though it has now moved much more closely to the status of infectious disease.[9] We see rationing as "new," and apparently can find no place for such a concept in our story.

What is our story? Is it about personal freedom for personal preferences justified by personal efforts and personal ideals? That is the "autonomy" story that bioethics has emphasized. Is the story one of individualism that does not tolerate any limitations, including the permanent failure of the body? That is the "Little Engine" story of our childhood. Is it about entitlement to the best? We think of ourselves as living in the best country with the best medical system. Certainly we have all known families that insisted upon having "the best doctors in town" when a loved one became ill, even though they had lived their whole lives with an acceptance of *adequacy* as a standard. Or is it a story about control over death and the need for immortality? Rationing has no place in any of these stories, and designing or advocating specific rationing schemes is beside the point if they are our stories.

In order to make rationing understandable to this society's preferred narratives, it would have to occur in the context of an emergency even *greater* than individual medical emergencies (as rationing did in World War II) or it would have to be practiced so selectively that most people were unaffected and its practice could be generally denied. Indeed, to the extent that we accept rationing of health care by ability to pay, that acceptance depends upon most people's not being affected and, preferably, not being aware of it. Oregon's initial success at rationing specific life-saving treatments may derive from the fact that they eliminated organ transplants for a dozen or so people on Medicaid. When rationing measures affect or potentially affect many people whom we recognize as "us," they are unacceptable because they are incomprehensible.

In the absence of emergency or selectivity, Americans are likely to accept--emotionally and politically--less medical treatment only if it occurs within a story that makes specific rationing, implicit rationing, and personal wishes to refuse care contextually understandable.

Let me describe the general problem more concretely.

Recently, a distinguished intensivist gave a public lecture about ethics and economics in the intensive care unit (ICU). His main thesis was that ICUs are often filled with patients who are too sick to be in ICUs. The only benefit patients receive, he argued, is dying *with* rather than *without* ICU care. Given that ICUs account for 10 percent of all medical costs and 17 percent of all hospital costs--one percent of the entire gross national product--he thought it would make some sense to get these patients out of the ICUs.

To the intensivist's eyes, the responsibility lay first with the patients' loving families, who insist upon their father, mother, sister, brother, son, or daughter receiving all of the "everything" that medicine can offer, and, second, with a legal system that insists upon defining the standard of care as everything that has any probability, however remote, of extending life.

A somewhat different view of this typical situation is presented by Jessica Muller and Barbara Koenig in a study they conducted at a California hospital to determine how house-staff decide when to stop recommending treatment.[10] For the doctors in their study, the decision depended upon the residents' concluding that the patient is dying. How do they know when a patient is dying? The physicians themselves describe their job as providing any treatment that can conceivably reverse any abnormal condition until such time as there are no further treatments available. As one resident says, "If we're still fighting, they're not dying." As in the case of the elderly man who received TPN because it was the only procedure left, these physicians make it hard for anyone to say "no more." If there is something left to do, then not doing it means that they or the family members are the "cause" of the patient's death. This *folie à deux* between physician and family is one in which each feeds upon the other's hopes and sense of duty. When nothing medical is any longer possible, according to Muller and Koenig, the patient is understood to be dying. Unfortunately, it must be added, the physicians are then understood to have failed.

If patients are receiving treatment beyond the time in which they would want it, or it could benefit them, or it is cost-effective, or its probable burdens exceed its probable benefits, then it would help if we knew who was responsible for this decision.

Yet, we have physicians saying that they are not responsible; families and patients insisting that they want only the right to die with dignity; and judges and lawyers claiming that the courts are no place for making such decisions.[11] The fact that everyone seems to be pointing the finger at someone else while asserting their own preferences for another, less medically adventurous course of action suggests that there is a much more basic problem in this situation. The problem is, I think, that we are in the wrong story. If treatment decisions are to be made differently, we must get into some other story.

Metaphors and Stories

The controlling metaphor for American medicine is a war in which the health-care professionals are the troops battling death and disease and the patient is the battle ground on which the war is fought.[12] As one physician interviewed by a medical sociologist commented, "I hate to admit it but I had come to view the patient almost as an extension of the apparatus in the room." Another physician in the same study noted that medical practice had become "a contest between me and the disease. The patient was merely an object over which we were fighting."[13]

The controlling story for American health-care is larger. That story focuses on the possibility of immortality and has several parts. First, immortality is achievable because the threat of disease is external. That it comes from outside of us makes it possible for us to see disease as an enemy, as an "other" that means us harm, that we can do battle with, and that we can defeat. It is not internal or a part of us or even a necessary part of the world. Disease is like an alien invader.

Second, immortality is possible because the body is essentially a machine and thus repairable and reconstructible. This makes it possible for us to imagine that there is always something else that can be repaired or replaced to make it right. It may be expensive, but if the body is a machine, it can be put back into satisfactory working order if only we try a little harder.

Third, immortality is an appropriate goal because human destiny is to control nature. This means that we cannot accept less than perfection, less than our ideal, autonomous preferences, because to do so would be both unnecessary and inauthentic. It is what we were born for--to remake the world and our place in it, despite all the public disclaimers about "not playing God." This cultural belief makes stoicism--a sense that some things are to be endured--totally foreign to our natures. Interestingly, Melvin Konner has recently argued that we worry more about risks that we cannot control than those that we actually can.[14] Thus, the risk of lung cancer to the smoker is less worrisome than the risk of cancer caused by toxic waste dumps or preservatives in food, despite the fact that the degree and probability of risk runs the other way. This would mean that as long as disease is perceived as being external, it is not directly in our control and our fear of being out of control is much heightened.

And, fourth, because immortality is the object of our search, death is failure (the patient's, the physician's, or both). This means that death must be postponed at all costs but, if it occurs, someone must take the blame for it. The story of the physician who refuses to let a patient die on his or her shift is a solid part of hospital lore.

If our favorite health-care story is called "Fighting the Enemy," our favorite personal story is called "Writing Our Lives." This story assumes that we can control every aspect of our lives, including *how* and even *whether* we die (the ultimate in personal control). If we are successful in "Writing Our Life," then we will be successful when disease threatens and we must "Fight the Enemy," because "Writing Our Life" assumes that we are in control of what happens to us. And if we are in control, we can successfully combat disease. If we lose at "Fighting," however, the implication is that we have also failed at "Writing." The public movement to obtain death with dignity is actually an attempt to bring "Writing Our Life" into line with "Fighting the Enemy" for, when losing to disease becomes inevitable, control can be retained by shifting the focus of control over the manner of death.

These are the stories that have no room for less medical treatment. "Writing" is about being in control. The empowerment sought by individuals in our society is the power to be--or at least to appear to be--the authors of their own lives. One implication of this belief is that, if I am the author of my life, then my life is a story that has a beginning, a middle, and an end, and that I, the author, get to decide when it is time for the end. The irony is that, if we are to be the authors of our lives, we must stave off disease, and ultimately death, because they impair our ability to author.

That is, since disease is seen as an abnormal state that comes to us from outside ourselves, disease itself is evidence of our failure to be in control. To be sick indicates a victory (at least temporary) for the enemy. Furthermore, the very process of disease imposes a further reduction in our ability to control our destiny because of physical and perhaps emotional or mental impairment.

It is not uncommon for individuals facing serious or chronic illness to say something like, "I have never had to accept limitations before." Such statements seem quite remarkable given the millions of natural limitations that exist for each and every one of us. Despite the restrictions imposed by such ordinary things as physical traits, natural skills and talents, and cultural biases (e.g., against women's and ethic minorities' abilities in certain areas), we still operate under the impression that we do not normally have to accept any limitations unless they are imposed by illness or the government; that we are otherwise in control of our destiny.

Yet, our version of "Writing Our Lives" implies a world in which there is a constant battle between that which would try to control us and that which we try to control, but it is a battle in which we can ultimately triumph. Disease belongs to the external world, the world of a hostile Nature, and is decidedly "not us."

Because disease is "not us," is "the enemy," we need total access to whatever medical science has in order to exert control over the enemy. It is a lifetime's work, of course, and medical technologies are the weapons and tools that keep us in action. Research efforts into new medical technology must continue because we need bigger, more powerful weapons. (This despite the observation that people who can try to cure cancer are the same people that can create environmental conditions that cause cancer!)[15] In our search for new weapons, we are now pursuing the human genome project and the prospects of genetic engineering, our *new* "Manhattan Project," expecting to use the knowledge gained in that project to end disease --just as we expected the development of the atomic bomb to end war.

Controlling Stories and the Problem of Limits

If this is an accurate portrayal of the health-care story in which most Americans are living, then it is clear why denial of potentially beneficial medical treatment seems impossible, unthinkable, and unjust. If we need to fight the enemy in order to maintain our control so that we can be the authors of our lives, we need the resources to conduct the war properly. In time of war, the needs of war take priority. Thus, claims that more funds should be made available if medical care requires an increasing portion of our gross national product are both inevitable and logically sound.

There is a possibility that the current economic pressures on health-care professionals may be changing this shared vision, this *folie à deux*, and physicians themselves seem to be more willing to restrict medical care through implicit rationing. They can do this comfortably, however, only if they restructure their understanding of medicine as fighting the enemy. Otherwise, they must inevitably be derelict in their own sense of personal duty if they provide nothing, or less than is needed to defeat the enemy. The personal, psychological toll for such betrayal would be enormous. Physicians who have difficulty accepting the deaths of patients for whom everything was tried will have far more difficulty if they personally choose--especially on their own initiative--*not* to try everything, or to try nothing.

If patient and physician are unsuccessful in "Fighting the Enemy," the result is death. Many writers have delineated how, for the physician, death is failure. Dr. S. Weir Mitchell, in an early twentieth century novel, has a physician-protagonist who proclaims: "What I personally hate is defeat, by death, by incurable ailments."[16] Muller and Koenig's late twentieth century housestaff seem to share this view. Contemplating a liver transplant for a desperately ill patient, the housestaff see the action as "a potential therapeutic solution to an otherwise insurmountable problem--the death of a patient."[17] Death, in such a situation, is not a probable outcome or an understandable and expected event, but an "insurmountable problem."

If death is problematic for the physician, it is even more so for the patient ensconced in this narrative. If the patient's condition fails to improve, medical language often attributes the responsibility for this to the patient. Thus, for example, the patient "drops his pressure," "spikes a temp," or "fails chemotherapy." Interestingly, chemotherapy does not fail the patient. Nor does the physician fail the patient. "There is nothing I can do" is infrequently heard in the hospital, since there is almost always something more that the physician can do. However, if that something does not help, responsibility for losing the fight begins to fall upon the patient who, technologically powerless, then has only two choices in the "Writing Our Lives"/"Fighting the Enemy" story.

First, the patient can turn to other modes of therapy, non-standard modes that may be able to defeat the enemy by using a different battle strategy. But she or he is not likely to get much medical support for that.

Second, the patient can begin to work on the end of the story; that is, to author the end of her or his life. It is at this point of the story that the public movements for advance directives, assisted suicide, active euthanasia, and death with dignity have focused their work. Although they often present themselves as a counter movement to our medical story, they are firmly *in* that story. They accept that it is time to end the story, but not because no more treatment is possible. It is because they cannot have more treatment and still remain in control of their story. Further treatment means that they risk losing their authorship--which is what is meant by "dignity" in this story--and the end of their life will then be written by someone else and thus be undignified. If we cannot control our life, at least we must control our death to demonstrate that we were worthy of our special status as humans.

If the stories of "Fighting the Enemy" and "Writing Our Lives" do not permit consideration of less treatment, unless it is personally chosen by the author, are there other metaphors or narratives that offer alternatives to our financing and equal access crisis? It must be noted that everyone in the Western world is not having this problem in the same way that it is experienced in the U.S. Clearly, in Canada and many European countries, including Great Britain, all patients do not have access to the same extent of technological intervention that well-insured Americans do, nor do they even want such access. People wait months and even years for hip replacements; very low birthweight infants receive no life-sustaining treatment even though it is recognized that a small percentage might survive mentally and physically intact; dialysis and organ transplants are unavailable for many older individuals; by-pass surgery is provided much less frequently, even for younger patients. This suggests that these people, these cultures, are operating in some other controlling story that permits such restrictions, that provides an understanding of and a place for such limits. A hint to the British narrative is provided by British critic George Steiner who claims that "In this country [Britain] growing old, being sick, and dying is not thought to be a mistake or being an unfairness as in America. Here you can be ugly, old, sick, and it's generally felt that's what life is all about. And that a day which hasn't gone badly is a very lucky day."[18]

Alternative Stories

What might a new American narrative be like? And how might it conflict with our current narrative? The Canadian philosopher Michael Ignatieff suggests that a more useful narrative would, like Steiner's view, be one based on Stoicism.[19] He opines that "cultures that live by the values of self-realization and self-mastery are not especially good at dying, at submitting to those experiences where freedom ends and biological fate begins." It would seem that the American story does not even acknowledge that there is such a thing as biological fate: Limits are for the small-minded.

But the comfort to this bleaker view of life would be Stoicism. Ignatieff suggests that Stoicism, in combination with an "ironic relationship" to our view of selfhood would provide a sharp contrast to "the metaphor that leads us to regard our life as a narrative that we compose as we go along, with a beginning, a middle, and an end. This is a metaphor that convinces us that we are the makers of our lives, when, in fact, chance and contingency and the dull determination of living all combine to push our lives into sequences we neither desire nor intend. To accept death is to accept much more than that we do not write the end of the story; it is also to appreciate that we don't write much of the beginning or the middle either."

Ignatieff offers one alternative that would certainly allow the prospect of specific rationing as long as limitations were not totally arbitrary. It would be a stoic acceptance of limits equally endured.

It is possible that the development of science and the corresponding loss of religious underpinning to our life inevitably makes of death a tragedy. Surely death as tragedy underlies our story; not an early death or a hard death as tragedy, but death itself. We have lost any idea of death as a kind of freeing or as a release of the soul. When anyone dies--young or old, rich or poor, healthy or unhealthy--it is almost always tragedy, never just a sad event, and rarely a welcome release. A different story about death and its meaning is offered by psychiatrist Robert Lifton in his exploration of death as continuity. In his story, life is understood as offering continuity despite death, continuity through offspring, through creative works, through spiritual modes, and through personal transcendence.[20] Lifton attempts to circumvent the problem of death as an end to personal control by creating a different understanding of death. He sees death as the point at which personal control is transformed into personal continuity. These four images that Lifton offers are not foreign to us; they are a part of our cultural tradition, but are too often excluded from the medical environment unless a chaplain or someone from pastoral care is on the scene.   Then it is seen as a "spiritual" issue, not as having anything to do with the medical profession.

Moving to Heaven still offers a viable narrative for those who have available the prospect of an afterlife.   Certainly belief in an afterlife makes it possible to loosen an overly tenacious grip on this one.   Catholicism, for example, though continuing to oppose suicide, has for a very long time accepted that there is no need to combat death at all costs.

"Death as Natural Event" is a story in the making in this culture given our recent enthusiasm for things natural.   Perhaps death would be more acceptable if it   could be characterized as ecologically sound.   As part of a "green" movement, it would gain more support, or at the very least more understanding.   Certainly the power of contemporary medicine's single most negative image-- the body attached to and kept alive by machines--is largely a function of the unnaturalness of the image.   To be reduced to an appendage to machines is far more unnatural (and humiliating) than merely being treated as a machine!   Yet, natural death, like natural childbirth may offer us only a comforting phrase: Even natural childbirth involves pain, and even natural death results in the patient's dying.

The hospice movement is certainly positioned to incorporate appeals to "Death as a Natural Event" as an important aspect of its own narrative.   Callahan's social vision in *Setting Limits* seems also to be based on such a story, that is, that an 80-year life-span is a natural limit or at least a good enough life-span.

But rationing based upon age is not the only criterion that the story of "Death as Natural Event" might support.   Rationing based upon an acknowledgement of natural human limits, incorporating quality-of-life judgments, would offer a more general structure, but is unappealing if there is not some positive quality or benefit associated with the idea of such limits and of the humility that would appear to be associated with cheerful acceptance of reductions in the scale--not only of our lives but our life-styles.

Finally, "Healing the Patient" (as opposed to "Curing the Disease") offers a very different understanding of medicine.   This story flourishes in the humanistic medicine movement and, apparently somewhat independently, in the holistic medicine movement--a movement at least initially organized by patients.   "Healing the Patient" is a narrative that does not necessarily accept direct rationing, but would be amenable to implicit rationing and to less dependence upon medical technology, procedures, and drugs. Such a story would necessarily include a very different understanding of the relationship between body and mind. As our current story sees them as separate, a new story would have to acknowledge their interdependence, and would probably have to relinquish the view of body as machine. Furthermore, it would entail a very different understanding of the kind of education needed by physicians and other health-care professionals.

Whatever story we are to use, however, death would continue to require appropriate social rituals--rituals that we currently lack in the health-care setting. Philip Aries has described several distinct historical views of death and their accompanying rituals: Death as an impersonal event, in which the person understood that his time had come and simply stopped his activities, lay down, crossed his arms, and awaited death; death as a personal event in which the awareness of impending death necessitated a personal accounting of one's life; and death as a familial event, in which death required a resolution of personal relationships.[21] Each of these understandings gives the dying person a specific role and thus a structure for action. The physician, sharing this understanding of the patient's duties, could use her or his skills to help patients fulfill their role.

In our world, death has become a medical event, and the dying patient has a very peculiar role: it is *not to die.* "Don't crump out on me!" the physician yells in frustration and fear. The physician's job is to help the patient *not to die* by providing all possible treatment. If we are to hope that physicians and patients can move into a different story, it must include different roles for both dying person and health-care professional. One cannot remove the ritual need to treat that "Fighting the Enemy" imposes unless it is replaced by some other meaningful ritual.

It is here that stories about caring for the patient could be helpful. In an academic teaching hospital, housestaff often seem to forget (or do not believe) that there is anything they can do for a patient once mechanical or chemical treatment is no longer possible or wanted by the patient. But the dying patient has other wants and needs. He or she wants to be free from pain, wants to suffer as little as possible, wants companionship and touching, wants reassurance that he or she will not be left alone to die alone. There is much to do besides tests and procedures, but our story is so filled with tests and procedures that the other, purely human responses are often overlooked or not even acknowledged. We talk about "withdrawing all treatment from a patient," without remembering that there is something else do to with and for that patient after "treatment" is finished.

The critical factor in our story of disease is, of course, the threat of death, which we see as a personal annihilation. Joseph Campbell has suggested that primitive mythology offers two contrasting views of death.[22] The first is found "among the hunting tribes whose life style is based on the art of killing and who live in a world of animals that kill and are killed. [Here] all death is a consequence of violence and is generally ascribed not to the natural destiny of temporal beings but to magic. Magic is employed both to defend against it and to deliver it to others."

The contrasting view, that of the "planting folk," is that "death is a natural phase of life, comparable to the moment of the planting of the seed, for rebirth." In this second narrative, life and death constitute a cycle, and the task for the living is to find ways of carrying the dead forward in their own lives, thereby providing continuity. Clearly our culture is captured by the former view. We pit our white magic against the black magic of disease. Furthermore, we are more committed to keeping the dead in the past ("let the dead bury the dead"), than to bringing them forward in our present or future. The price of the U.S. version of the hunter's story, however, is more magic and more powerful magic, which relentlessly translates into ever greater medical costs. That is the story we are now paying for. It is a story in which personal choice overwhelms any call for public rationing.

If rationing weakens our fight against death, then a call to rationing must inevitably come up against the demand for more magic, more treatment, more aggressive procedures, more of the only magic we currently know. It is only by finding our connections with a different story, a different mythology, that this conflict can be resolved. The most important purpose of mythology, it has been said, is to carry the individual from old age to death. Our stories do not do this well since they deny death, but there are other stories available to us. It is possible that change is already brewing in our culture. Responses to AIDS, for example, have certainly shown us the strength of the impulse to fight disease at all costs, to pursue not only proven but unproven treatments in the fight against the enemy. But there are other responses that suggest other narratives. The AIDS quilt comes to mind in its attempt to bring the dead forward in our lives. In addition, the growth and acceptance of hospice with its compassionate support of the dying and their families suggests some acceptance of death as a natural event.

Conclusion

Regardless of what the story is, we will have some story at the bottom of our minds that enables us to make sense of what we do and what happens to us. But our story does change. Once, Christians prayed to be preserved from a sudden death. That prayer is still part of the *Book of Common Prayer.* Nowadays, people might be more likely to pray *for* a sudden death. That tells us something: The story has changed. It also tells us that it can change again.

But it is only by thinking consciously about the meaning of illness, the meaning of being a health-care professional, and the meaning of being a patient that we can get hold of the story that currently limits our actions, or can imagine a story that might offer us not only different choices but a different coherence and a different sense of purpose. There are worse choices than starting the discussion on the rationing of health care by returning to a now-lost discussion about the purpose of health-care and about the purpose of health-care professionals. One writer says "caring for sick people." Another says, "serving health, narrowly defined." Neither says "curing disease." Neither says "achieving immortality."

We may think of medicine as war or as assistance (but not salvation) in life's cycle. The implications of these two views of health-care are what the rationing debate is about in this country. As long as we focus on beating that old devil, death, limits are unacceptable. If, instead, we thought of health-care as a way of helping people stay well and of caring for people who become sick, we could begin to consider what might be limited. Perhaps we should begin by renewing our acquaintance with the Stoics, a perspective that would accept access to less and provide an emphasis upon personal control of, at least, our own responses to life's inevitabilities.

Notes and References

1. Frederick Wiseman, producer, director, and editor, *Near Death*, Jan. 21, 1990.

2. Lynn Payer, *Medicine and Culture* (New York: Henry Holt, 1988).

3. See Daniel Callahan, *Setting Limits: Medical Goals in an Aging Society* (New York: Simon & Schuster, 1987); and *What Kind of Life? The Limits of Medical Progress* (New York: Simon & Schuster, 1990).

4. W. B. Schwartz, "We're Already Rationing Medical Care," *New York Times*, October 16, 1989, B5.

5. J. Heckman, as quoted by P. Cotton in "Orthopedic Surgery Turns Attention to Relatively Few Fractures that Fail to Health Over Time," *Journal of the American Medical Association*, Vol. 263 (April 18, 1990), p. 2627.

6. D. Eddy, "What Do We Do About Costs?" *Journal of the American Medical Association*, Vol. 264 (Sept. 5, 1990), pp. 1161-1170.

7. See, for example, M. S. M. Watts, "Health Care in a Dreamworld," *The Western Journal of Medicine*, Vol. 146 (April 1987), p. 471; R. J. Samuelson, "The Cost of Chaos," *Newsweek*, October 2, 1989, p. 52; and D. Callahan, "Rationing Medical Progress: The Way to Affordable Health Care," *The New England Journal of Medicine*, Vol. 322 (June 21, 1990), pp. 1810-1813.

8. Neil Postman, "Learning by Story," *The Atlantic*, December 1989, pp. 119-128.

9. J. W. Ross, "Ethics and the Language of AIDS," in *AIDS: Ethics and Public Policy*, edited by C. Pierce and D. VandeVeer (Belmont, Calif.: Wadsworth Press, 1988), pp. 39-48.

10. J. H. Muller, B. A. Koenig, "On the Boundary of Life and Death: The Definition of Dying by Medical Residents," in *Biomedicine Examined*, edited by M. Lock and D. Gordon (Dordrecht, Netherlands: Kluwer, 1988), pp. 351-376.

11. "Courts are not the proper place to resolve the agonizing personal problems that underlie these cases. Our legal system cannot replace the more intimate struggle that must be borne by the patient, those caring for the patient, and those who care about the patient." Matter of Jobes, 108N.J. 394 (592 A.2d at 451); See also, A. Capron, "The Burden of Decision," *The Hastings Center Report*, Vol. 20, May-June 1990, pp. 36-41.

12. J. W. Ross, "The Militarization of Disease: Do We Really Want a War on AIDS?" *Soundings*, Vol. 72, no. 1 (Spring 1989), pp. 39-58.

13. R. H. Coombs and P. S. Powers, "Socialization for Death," in *Inside Doctoring*, edited by R. H. Coombs and P. S. Powers (New York: Praeger, 1986), p. 270.

14. M. Konner, *Why the Reckless Survive* (New York: Viking, 1990), pp. 125-40.

15. R. S. Sandor, "The Attending Physician," *Parabola*, Vol. 15 (Summer 1990), pp. 38-43.

16. As quoted by Suzanne Poirier, "Literature and Medicine," *Journal of the American Medical Association*, Vol. 262 (Summer, 1990), p. 2382.

17. Muller and Koenig, "*On the Boundary of Life and Death*," p. 364.

18. As quoted by R. Critchfield, *An American Looks at Britain* (New York: Doubleday, 1990), p. 39

19. M. Ignatieff, "Modern Dying," *The New Republic*, December 26, 1988, pp. 28-33.

20.   R. Lifton and E. Olson, *Living and Dying* (New York: Praeger, 1974), p. 76 ff.

21.   P. Aries, *Western Attitudes Toward Death: From the Middle Ages to the Present,* translated by P. Ranum (Baltimore: Johns Hopkins University Press, 1974).

22   J. Campbell, *The Masks of God: Primitive Mythology* (New York: Penguin, 1976), p. 126 ff.

18

Imposing Limits or Changing Attitudes: Strategies for Change

Marilyn Moon

Introduction

The debate over imposing limits on health care for older Americans stems from the economic arguments that we are spending too much on health care and that something must be done that goes beyond the usual tools of cost containment. While ethical and philosophical issues are clearly vital to the debate, economic concerns are also relevant. Moreover, economic incentives provide important mechanisms for influencing use of health services and may offer some solutions to the problem of rising health-care costs.

For a number of reasons, age rationing of health care is not a preferable approach to solving the problems of health-care expenditure growth. Excessive use of medical care by the elderly is often overstated. Certainly a problem exists, but it is neither as critical as some would claim, nor have we tried and ruled out other possible, more moderate solutions. Moreover, the evidence does not support holding the elderly totally responsible for their level of health-care use. We must guard against adopting a cure such as age-rationing that may be worse than the disease. Before seeking such dramatic solutions to the problem, a number of more moderate options should be explored. Many options for changing economic incentives in our system have been suggested; few have yet been adopted.

Terms of the Debate

When are the costs of medical care too high? First, the question needs to be asked, what is too high? In terms of what benchmark? The answers vary depending upon whether we mean unaffordable to society or unsupportable in terms of the benefits received. Unaffordable to society implies that other valuable services or goods are crowded out of peoples' budgets because the costs are too high. This has certainly already happened to some individuals--many of the uninsured, for example, are unable to afford insurance. But on a society-wide level, the term "unaffordable" means that overall spending on health care is too high relative to other goods and services that society wishes to purchase. Health expenses as a share of GNP--now standing at 12 percent--are often cited to bolster claims about the burden to society of health-care spending.[1] But we do not really have a good benchmark by which to judge whether the level is now too high or whether 10 percent or 15 percent or 20 percent would be too high, for example.

Spending is substantially higher than in the 1950s and 1960s, but incomes are also higher and what the health-care dollar will buy has improved. If we spend more on cataract surgery because people live longer, and the surgery is more effective and safer than in the past, who is to say that this is undesirable? An affluent society may decide that additional spending is worthwhile.

A second reason that medical care costs are argued to be too high refers to a sense of value--that the benefits received simply are not as great as the costs paid. This is different from saying health care is crowding out other expenditures. In fact, focusing on whether services are "worth it" is both easier to evaluate and may result in more agreement about spending reductions. Specific procedures or services within the health-care system may not be supportable--because the benefits of the treatment are simply not as great as the costs of the care--and in that sense they are too high. This measure of "efficacy" is different from that of affordability. The problem is to identify ineffective or inappropriate procedures and eliminate them. Such selective reductions pose a daunting task, however, and hence many spending critics look for proxies for inappropriate services. Age rationing of health-care represents one such possible proxy. Daniel Callahan's claim about natural limits on life indicates that at least by his calculus, benefits of health spending are less than cost for the very old.[2]

Layered over the discussion of affordability of health-care costs is the additional complicating factor of the distribution of health-care services and the problems created by unequal access. Individuals who can afford the cost of their own health care or insurance may not like the price tag they face, but they can decide whether or not to purchase the care. They can make their own affordability decision. Those who cannot afford care must rely on subsidies from someone else, and that is where serious discussions of rationing often begin. We simply cannot provide unlimited health-care services to those folks through the public sector--or so the saying goes. But at present this has little to do directly with either efficacy or affordability--and much more to do with a reluctance to share or redistribute resources. As a society, we are implicitly saying that luxury automobiles (or some other spending by individuals) are more important than health care--an individual trade-off that almost no one would make, but which becomes relevant when the luxury good is for the person who would be taxed to pay for health care for someone else.

A final dimension of the affordability question, intergenerational equity, also hinges on the issues of efficacy, redistribution and the size of the government sector. The arguments that we should shift health resources from the old to the young often include claims that investing in children's health care will pay greater dividends to our future than improvements in health care for the elderly. Proponents of this view also point correctly to the paucity of spending on the young versus the old.[3] The imbalance in spending on the old and the young occurs for health expenditures in general, but is even more dramatic when only public spending is considered.

These claims miss some key issues, however. Government spending on the elderly has evolved as part of a deliberate strategy to have a public insurance plan for older Americans while children would be cared for within the family. Consequently, employer-provided insurance generally includes dependent children as a part of health coverage, but not the workers' parents. The lack of coverage of children and lowered health expenditures for them is more directly attributable to problems with private insurance coverage and problems with the American family than to higher government spending on the elderly. Medicaid, the government program that is aimed at low income families, does not cover all poor children, but would a cutback in Medicare for the elderly automatically result in an offsetting increase in spending on children? There is little evidence to believe that such a linkage would occur and more evidence to believe that reductions in Medicare would be used to hold down the level of taxes on Americans in general.[4] Again, the central issue is one of willingness to redistribute resources from those with higher incomes, both young and old, to poor children.

The Factual Evidence

Who is responsible for the high costs of health care? For all types of care and for individuals of all age groups, use of health-care services has risen dramatically over the last twenty years, although health-care spending has grown faster per capita for the elderly than for other age groups. (See Table 18.1)[5] Studies of the growth of spending generally cite a number of contributing factors: health-care price inflation, the aging of the population, technology, and a general increase in the number of services.

TABLE 18.1 Ratio of Health Spending on Older Americans as Compared to Children, 1977 and 1987

	Persons 65 and Over : Children	
	1977	**1987**
Overall Health Spending	6.9:1	7.2:1
Overall Spending on Acute Care	5.4:1	5.8:1
Health Spending in Public Sector	17.0:1	16.9:1
Public Sector Spending on Acute Care	14.6:1	15.4:1

Source: Daniel Waldo, et al., "Health Expenditures by Age Group, 1977 and 1987," *Health-care Financing Review,* Vol. 10, Summer 1989, pp. 111-120.

Inappropriate use of health services and the impact of technology on spending in health-care rate as the most logical candidates for places on which to focus attention. And, it has become fashionable to associate such expenditures with the last year of life. Are we devoting an increasing share of our health resources in vain attempts to forestall death--often through new technology? Certainly, few statistics sound as compelling as the widely quoted statistic of 28 percent of Medicare spending concentrated on the 5 percent of enrollees in their last year of life.[6] This article and other similar research findings are cited by those who believe that a key to controlling health-care spending will be to limit spending on the very old.

But is such rationing the magic bullet we would all like to find to reduce health-care spending in the United States? A careful look at the data suggests that the answer is not nearly so simple. First, if technology is being used extensively in futile cases involving the very old, the share of resources devoted to health care in the last year of life should be rising. The evidence, however, does not support these claims. Anne Scitovsky pursued this question and found that high expenditures were not a new phenomenon; they certainly preceded the introduction of Medicare in 1965, for example.[7] More recently, Lubitz found that between 1976 and 1985,

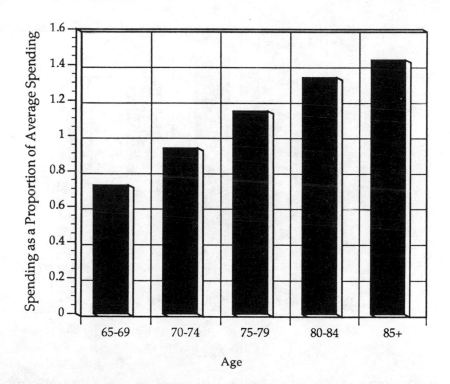

FIGURE 18.1 Medicare spending for all elderly by age, 1986. Source: Health-Care Financing Administration.

a period of enormous cost growth in health care, there was no increase in the share of Medicare resources going to those in the last year of life. The proportion of decedents increased slightly but the proportion of Medicare dollars fell slightly.[8]

Further disaggregation of Medicare data also reinforce this story. If we look first at expenditures by age in Medicare (Figure 18.1), the familiar pattern of more spending on the very old emerges. This pattern seems to support claims by Callahan, former Governor Richard Lamm, and others that perhaps we are foolishly spending resources on the very old in hopes of sustaining their lives just a bit. But, the data show exactly the opposite pattern if we look instead at spending on persons in their last years of life broken down by age (Figure 18.2). In this case, we spend considerably more on younger Medicare beneficiaries who are more likely to recover--a result consistent with reasonable health-care policy. Since life expectancy at age 65 is now about 17 years, spending on the younger old is not

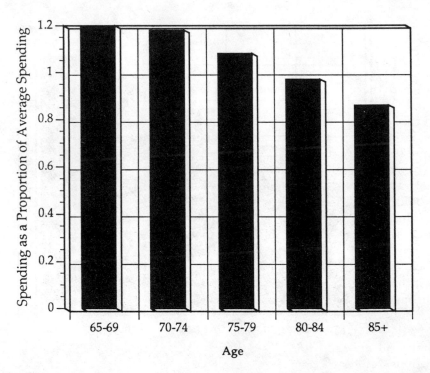

FIGURE 18.2   Medicare Spending for Decedents by Age, 1985.   Source: Lubitz 1990.

necessarily just cheating death for a few months, but rather treating patients with many useful years left.[9]

The findings in figures 18.1 and 18.2 suggest several things. First, physicians do not always know that death is imminent when making health-care spending decisions. And since people often die after being ill or requiring medical treatment, it is only natural to see extraordinary spending on those who die (as well as on those who survive a major illness). The issue more appropriately is whether it appears that we disproportionately spend on those with no chance of survival and whether that contributes substantially to the problem of the growth in health-care spending. Here the evidence is much weaker. There does seem to be a drop-off in spending on the very old as compared to the young in their last years of life, suggesting that at least, on average, decisions are being made to resist heavy acute care expenditures for those with little chance of survival.

Policy Options to Change Attitudes

The problem of health-care spending is less urgent than many tell us. We are not yet at a point where we cannot afford reasonable health care for our citizens, although we may have reached the point where we are not willing to do very much to tax some to help others. Moreover, the facts do not point incontrovertibly to the very old as the main source of high health-care costs. It is, therefore, premature to seek drastic solutions such as age limitations on health-care spending. Not only is that a rather extreme solution, but it would not necessarily save enough to justify the radical change it implies. Nor would it ensure that any savings would be directed at other needy groups.

Instead, five policy options could be pursued that might go a long way to addressing concerns about health-care costs. Changing certain economic incentives might not fully solve the problems, but such efforts could serve to help change people's attitudes about the health-care system. Until the economic incentives are in place to encourage more efficient use of services, we cannot expect individual patients or providers to respond. Modest as some of these proposals are, they are largely untried on a broad scale. Since the problems that lead to calls for age rationing of health care are varied, the options presented here also address different issues and should not be thought of as alternative strategies.

Medicare for Kids

Proposals to reduce spending on Medicare could certainly free up resources. There is no guarantee, however, that the available monies would be redirected to children's health care or other desired social goals. In fact, recent efforts to cut the budget deficit offer a good case in point. The budget for Medicare will be cut more than $40 billion over the next five years, and while there was an effort to raise Medicaid coverage for children, that amount will rise by only about $10 billion. Thus, while some increases in spending might occur among various domestic programs when Medicare is cut, the reductions can just as readily be used to offset cuts in defense spending or increased taxes, for example. Calls to reduce spending on the elderly in order to make resources available to others will only be successful if there are direct linkages between the two groups. Establishing those linkages is a necessary first step to achieve an improved redistribution of resources including inter-generational shifts in public spending.

A system of national health insurance would mean that more for one group could be financed by spending less on another. Countries like Canada or Great Britain do make some explicit choices. The United States is unlikely, however, to adopt such a full scale health program in the foreseeable future. On the other hand, a more modest expansion such as covering all children through the Medicare program might be possible. For example, if revenues to Medicare were increased by an amount sufficient to cover 85 percent of the costs of children's coverage, a strong argument could be made that it would be possible to make up the additional funding requirements by shifting resources away from the elderly to subsidize the young. This would be one way to link the two groups directly.

A direct linkage could offer other benefits as well. The broader the health-care system controlled by the public sector, the broader will be the impact of changes in policy designed to reeducate Americans on the use of health-care services or to control costs. Older Americans with decades of interaction with the health-care system, and in more fragile health than the population as a whole, do not make very good candidates for changing attitudes. Policy changes that affect all Americans equally would more likely be viewed as fairer, and even small shifts in attitudes over time could accumulate into an altered view of the American health-care system. Similarly, constraints on providers that affect only one part of the system encourage providers to shift costs from one group to another and make true cost containment extremely difficult.

The usual argument is that health-care reform should first control costs before trying to expand coverage. Equally strong claims can be made, however, that the process should be reversed; coverage needs to be inclusive in order to make global changes effectively, to prevent costs from merely being shifted from one group to another, and especially to meet concerns about fairness.

Hospice and the Last Year of Life

High tech, expensive care for the terminally ill makes little sense. Yet Medicare policy still treats such care as the "standard" and programs such as hospice as less important and out of the mainstream. To qualify for reimbursement under the hospice benefit, patients must have a doctor certify that the patient has less than six months to live. Moreover, strict guidelines and low levels of reimbursement have discouraged many hospices from participating in Medicare. Such treatment of hospice makes it less available to patients and keeps it as a "stepchild" of the Medicare program.

When added to Medicare, hospice was viewed as a benefit expansion and therefore the rules were made restrictive enough to prevent it from costing additional federal monies. But such a rationale is penny wise and pound foolish over time. The view of hospice as a standard alternative to health-care is one that advocates of de-emphasizing high-tech care ought to espouse. But when the Medicare program restricts its role and limits its expansion, patients' attitudes are also likely to reflect this vision.

The Medicare Catastrophic Coverage Act would have expanded hospice by eliminating the lifetime limits on the number of days that would be covered. The Congressional Budget Office estimated the cost for that policy change as just $1 million per year--certainly not a rampant expansion.[10] Hospice is not an "add-on" likely to attract people who would abuse it. Patients in need of hospice care are unlikely to enter the program too early; on the other hand, restrictive policies may dissuade patients from entering a hospice program at all when they know that, at some point, benefits could be cut off if they are "unlucky" enough to live longer.

The budget summit of 1990 added an additional benefit period for hospice if a doctor recertifies the patient. This change largely eliminates the problem of benefits expiring but does not ease the other restrictions.

Eliminating the cost-sharing now required under hospice might also encourage further use. Cost sharing is a tool used to discourage excessive use of services. Instead, by treating hospice not only as a reasonable alternative but also as one to be encouraged, attitudes about the use of life-prolonging technology might also be influenced.

Another approach to change patient and provider attitudes would be to promote hospice or similar activities to be offered alongside other care in a hospital setting. This "quasi-hospice" approach could put alternative treatments into the mainstream and perhaps change attitudes of providers as well as patients. By offering such services in a more traditional setting, an individual is not making such an absolute commitment to one type of care. Patients in a "low-tech" wing might receive more nursing and social services in place of the technology, for example. Deductibles and co-insurance might be waived for this type of hospital stay to encourage use of such services.

The bottom line is that if the patient's choice is to forego treatment that would likely do little to meaningfully prolong life, the patient ought to share in the Medicare savings that could be generated. Positive economic incentives of this sort might undermine the attitude of "why not try the treatment since there is no cost to me." A careful analysis of the potential costs of alternative, lower-tech care needs to be assessed against the possible savings from foregoing high technology. At a minimum, it makes little sense to restrict access to hospice and it may actually prove to be cost-saving to promote it.

Effectiveness Research

While the potential cost savings from eliminating unnecessary care may not prove to be the magic bullet that will solve all the problems, effectiveness research is an area where, over time, current investment would pay considerable dividends. But the research alone is not sufficient. To make full use of any findings, a number of other steps would also need to be taken.

First, the results of effectiveness research must be widely disseminated. There is a considerable amount of encouraging evidence that when practitioners are aware that certain procedures are not desirable or effective, those procedures fall in volume. For example, recent evidence on caesarean section for delivery of babies has led to a decline in caesarean births in the United States. This may be due to improved physician awareness or to patient awareness; in either case, the dissemination of information can change behavior.

Further, we need to increase our skepticism about the introduction of new treatments and new procedures. Generally these have been introduced in the United States without careful trials or tests of effectiveness. And once treatments are in the mainstream of care, it becomes difficult to discourage their use. Again, economic incentives might be used to change behavior. Reimbursements under insurance for new or experimental procedures could be lowered until their effectiveness had been determined.

While established procedures that cannot be shown to be effective also could be reimbursed on a lower level, this more dramatic step might need to be postponed until public attitudes about health care begin to change. Giving up accepted procedures would likely be a much tougher policy to achieve. If severe cost pressures continue, however, reimbursement restrictions on ineffective procedures represent a better approach than using proxies such as age limits. This is not to say, however, that such limitations would be simple to enforce or popular with patients.

Constraints of these sorts also need to be system-wide before they will be truly effective. If we want to discourage ineffective or inappropriate procedures, we cannot rely on Medicare and Medicaid (the public programs for the aged, disabled and poor) to discipline the whole system. Again, bringing more people under a public system is one approach. Short of that, the government could exert some system-wide control. Private insurance may be difficult to oversee, but it is subsidized in the United States through the tax system. Limits on the deductibility of insurance that fails to offer disincentives for ineffective care could be developed, for example. True changes in attitudes will only follow if Americans are convinced that these controls represent good *health* policy rather than merely ways of holding down federal spending.

Physician Payment Reform

The recently enacted physician payment reforms in the Medicare system will increase reimbursement to physicians for office visits while decreasing payments for procedures such as surgery and interpretation of tests.[11] Such a change in approach sends the right message about what is important in the health-care system--further shifting emphasis away from high technology and back to more basic care.

Physician payment reform will likely be more successful if it is adopted by other payers as well as Medicare.   If Blue Cross/Blue Shield and commercial insurers move in this direction, payment reform is likely to change physicians' incomes across specialties and activities.   There will be fewer opportunities to game the payment system, and the traditional bias favoring surgeons, anesthesiologists, ophthalmologists, pathologists and radiologists might shift toward primary care physicians.

While physicians might not change their behavior dramatically, at least the financial incentives will offer less of a bias for performing one more procedure or taking one more CAT scan, for example.   While payment reform is likely to be a necessary part of changing attitudes by patients and providers, it may not be sufficient to spur the change.   Tougher controls on volume may be one logical step.   Medicare's physician reform legislation of 1989 included Volume Performance Standards as a crude first step in this direction.   No one has yet developed a satisfactory scheme for achieving such controls, but this represents a promising area for further experimentation.

In addition, further careful analysis about whether the new payment system goes far enough in the desired direction is necessary.   Monitoring of the new payment system must also build in explicit mechanisms for changes in technology.   The reforms in Medicare and changes in other third-party payment plans must be viewed as an ongoing activity rather than casting in stone another mechanism that will quickly become dated.

Voluntary Moves to Limit Care

Until very recently little attention has been paid to efforts by individuals to make their own feelings known about the type of care they wish to receive in case of terminal illness or irreversible medical situations such as coma or Alzheimer's disease.   Do-not-resuscitate orders, living wills and durable powers of attorney show great promise as ways in which individuals can voluntarily seek to limit care.   These activities establish individuals' rights to control certain life-extending measures or to specify an advocate to act on their behalf.   Again, lending credibility and support to such activities can help promote their use.   Patients needs can be met, physicians' reluctance to make such decisions and saving society's use of resources on care may all be accomplished without the need for requiring limits.

Interest in these types of instruments to control the care that individuals received may reflect changing attitudes about the use of high technology health-care in at least some situations. Nonetheless, more needs to be done in this area to help individuals clarify the implications of their choices in living wills or durable powers of attorney, and in making sure that professionals and institutions honor patients' wishes and that the legal system recognizes the validity of such actions.

Conclusion: What the Future Holds

To draw direct conclusions about the future from the past risks making a number of dangerous assumptions. In the past 30 years, health care in the United States has become increasingly expensive and oriented to high technology. In general, advances in technology have been cost-increasing and not cost-saving. But there is nothing to dictate that this fact must always be true. For example, technology that makes surgery easier or unnecessary (replaced by other treatments) could indeed save resources--especially if payment systems reflected these changes as well.

Moreover, there are at least some signs that Americans are becoming less enamored with technology--at least in some areas. We have had only about one generation of Americans whose lives have been prolonged with complicated machines. Intensive care units similarly are a relatively new phenomenon, and the children of those first "beneficiaries" of this technology often decry "being kept alive by a machine." Although it is too soon to know whether there will be a response to voluntarily cut-back on such care, it is certainly a possibility. At any rate, there is no compelling evidence that the situation is getting worse.

In sum, although we may need more drastic measures in the future, there is no need to rush to judgment. Age rationing should be one of the issues discussed, but we should also consider less dramatic, but perhaps effective alternatives in the meantime. A debate on the drastic measures should not serve to postpone other more incremental changes in our health-care system. To the extent that these incremental policies reinforce change in attitudes toward the health-care system, they would also help ease any tougher decisions that must be later adopted.

Notes and References

1.   U.S. Department of Health and Human Services, Public Health Service (PHS),   *Health United States*   1989 (Washington, D.C.: U.S. Government Printing Office, 1990).

2.   Daniel Callahan, *Setting Limits: Medical Goals in an Aging Society* (New York: Simon & Schuster, 1987).

3.   Jack Meyer and Marilyn Moon, "Health-care Spending on Children and the Elderly," *The Vulnerable,* edited by John Palmer, Timothy Smeeding, and Barbara Torrey (Washington, D.C.: Urban Institute Press, 1988).

4.   Actually, one area where trade-offs between the old and the young in health-care spending may have occurred is in Medicaid.   Some have argued that the rapid growth in long-term care benefits under that program that have largely benefited elderly persons have precluded expansions on the acute care side that might have benefited children.

5.   Daniel Waldo et al., "Health Expenditures by Age Group, 1977 and 1987," *Health Care Financing Review,* Vol. 10 (Summer 1989), pp. 111-120.

6.   James Lubitz and Ronald Prihoda, "Use and Costs of Medicare Services in the Last Two Years of Life," *Health Care Financing Review,* Vol. 5 (Spring 1984), pp. 117-131.

7.   Anne Scitovsky, "The High Cost of Dying: What Do the Data Show?" *Milbank Memorial Fund Quarterly,*   Vol. 62 (1984), pp. 591-608.

8.   James Lubitz, "Use and Costs of Medicare Services in the Last Year of Life, 1976 and 1985," *Health Care Financing Administration,* May 11, 1990.

9.   U.S. Dept. of Health and Human Services, Public Health Service (PHS), *Health United States*   1989 (Washington, D.C.: U.S. Government Printing Office, 1990).

10.   U.S. Congressional Budget Office, "The Medicare Catastrophic Coverage Act of 1988." Staff working paper, photocopy, 1988.

11.   U.S. Congress, House, Ways and Means Committee (Overview of Entitlement Programs) *1990 Green Book* (Washington, D.C.: U.S. Government Printing Office, 1990).

19

Old Age and Euthanasia: A Theological and Personal Perspective

John C. Bennett

Introduction: The Context of Old Age

I shall begin with the topic of old age and turn later to the controversial issues raised by euthanasia. Old age is not a time in which people are chiefly waiting for the most appropriate form of euthanasia. Old age is a time of life which for many can include a long period of rich, satisfying, and creative life. Recognizing this fact is the place to start.

Old age includes many years. As we think of it conventionally, it begins when we are 65 and ends when a few of us are 100. It is often said that we are "young-old" between 65 and 75. But from my experience as a member of the retirement community of 300 persons for 15 years, I would put the beginning of an "old-old" period somewhat later. Certainly it does not typically begin before 80. And I am impressed by the liveliness of many people far into their eighties if they keep their basic health and live in a favorable environment and community. In a society in which so many members are less privileged either in regard to health or in regard to environment and community, I may be describing a minority. But if that is true, how far is age the cause of functional weakness? I do not claim to know the answer, but the question must be raised and many other factors are certainly involved. Economic opportunities and access at various stages of life to health care are among them. I should admit that I have a vested interest in a more than usually favorable view of the possibilities for old people, as I am 90.

Of course there are limits of strength, of fresh initiatives, and of planning for the future for those who are in their eighties. One of the saddest of our experiences is to know many neighbors who are struck down by long-continued, debilitating diseases or by sudden strokes and heart attacks with permanent effects. But when we are generalizing about human possibilities and hopes we should avoid dogmatism about limits earlier than I am suggesting.

Today there is much talk about a "natural life-span." Daniel Callahan, who brings important, pioneering guidance for our thinking about old age in his books *Setting Limits* and *What Kind of Life?*, makes much use of that phrase. In doing so he courageously faces many realities. One of his major interests is the enormous and growing cost of medical care for society, and he seeks to limit the care intended chiefly to lengthen life after one has lived through the natural life-span. His second book strongly suggests that most people can achieve what has most value for them during that period, and that for them the meaning of their lives does not depend upon their living a little more and then a little more even though they may have very great desire to do so. He finds the end of the natural life-span in the late seventies or early eighties. Optimistically, we might take 82 as the end to mention. After such an age, Callahan emphasizes that medical care should be intended not to lengthen life but to prevent or reduce suffering, and to preserve a desirable quality of life.[1]

In *Setting Limits*, Callahan does allow for exceptions. But he does not mention them until late in the book.[2] It seems that he does not want to blunt his main argument until he has presented it fully. In that later passage, he speaks of "physically vigorous elderly persons" and for them he says: "All levels of care are appropriate, at least through the first round of illness and disease, and even for those who have lived a natural life-span if there is a solid prospect of a few (say, four or five) more years of good life."[3] I do not see that he integrates this exceptional status for such fortunate people, which would surely be claimed by many, into his system. His main purpose is to lessen the excessive amount of medical care which now goes to those who because of age cannot expect improvement of life. One of his most important sentences is this: "A disproportionately large portion of health care goes to the elderly dying."[4]

After admitting that, at some point, age should be a basis for limiting the use of expensive medical care, if the length of time of the expected benefit is short, I want to raise a question which is not being raised by those who emphasize the concept of a natural span of life. Why should we now assume that the length of this span is static for the majority? Should we not consider the possibility of lengthening the expected life-span by improving the health care received by all people before they are 65, beginning with prenatal care? Not only medical care is essential. In a 1968 article on the allocation of health-care resources, Professor James Childress anticipated much that is being said now. He shows that medical care is less important than many other factors in peoples' long-term health, including many factors in the environment and community in which people live and especially in their style of life. He refers to such habits as exercise, sleep, and the avoidance of tobacco or alcohol. He makes reference to the startling contrast between the health history of two states, Utah and Nevada, where the populace tends to have vastly different health habits.[5] Medical care may be crucial in such areas as the immunization of children and providing cures in various crises. But many other factors can be even more important in the lives of people if they are to achieve a natural span of life that is a few years longer than Daniel Callahan suggests.

I do not want to detract attention, however, from the shocking fact that about 35,000,000 people in our country have no health insurance and many more have no insurance against catastrophic illness. They inevitably postpone too long their visits to doctors because of expense. A fifth of children are among those who have no reliable access to medical care. Our society treats its elderly citizens better than its children. Older Americans have political clout whereas neither poor children nor their parents have that clout. A large part of our population, when they begin at 65 the last stage of a natural life-span, are already victims of our unjust medical system or lack of system.

I need to raise another question with Callahan. He says that, after the natural life-span, medical care should be used to prevent or reduce suffering and to maintain a desirable quality of life rather than to extend the length of life. I believe that idea gives good guidance, the more so the fewer years a person can benefit from very costly therapy. Yet it is difficult to draw the line when a particular operation is needed to remove the causes of intense suffering. I learn about so many elderly neighbors whose suffering has been cured by heart operations which have become almost routine. I wonder where as a matter of policy the line should be drawn. In these cases the operations do extend the length of life but the urgency of them comes from the pain that calls for remedy. I fully accept Callahan's emphasis on limits to curative medicine. My questions deal only with the difficulty of deciding when a natural life-span ends and of deciding in detail about particular therapies used chiefly to limit suffering.

The major question which I wish now to address is whether or not euthanasia is an acceptable solution when the limits of medical care have been reached.

Changing Theological Attitudes Toward Suicide

We cannot discuss the legitimacy of some forms of euthanasia without reexamining the traditional rejection of all suicide because of theological principles.   There is often an element of suicide in both passive and active euthanasia.   Consider, for example, the signing of an advanced directive of the sort that we, in California, call "Durable Power of Attorney for Health Care."   An agent may thus be authorized, under some conditions, to make decisions against keeping a patient alive.   Such authorization of what amounts to the hastening of death may involve what some would consider to be conditional, assisted suicide.   What is more, many cases of active euthanasia, though they may not have the legal support of the currently accepted advanced directives, implement the will to commit suicide. (Later I shall discuss the relation between passive and active euthanasia.)   Such actions run counter to the traditional rejection of suicide in our culture.

Shakespeare expressed this traditional view of suicide when he had Hamlet say: "O, that the Everlasting had not fixed his canon against self-slaughter."[6]   Thomas Aquinas, the great Roman Catholic theologian, said that "suicide is the most fatal of sins because it cannot be repented of."[7]   One can hardly exceed that statement in its absoluteness.

One of the greatest Protestant theologians of this century, Karl Barth, is hardly less extreme.   He wrote the following about suicide:

> Suicide even according to nature is a horrible aberration.   From the standpoint of religion suicide is a manifestation of the most extreme and arbitrary self-assertion. . . .   The suicide wants to be lord over life and death.   Therefore this sin directly violates the very majesty of God governing our life.[8]

I believe that this absolutistic denial of all suicide, which has in the past caused the churches to deal cruelly with the memories of suicides and with their families, no longer has the intuitive support of most people who read such words of condemnation. In this regard, it may be helpful to report on three theologians who, when they speak in general terms, repeat the traditional condemnation of suicide but, when they deal with particular cases, abandon it. I shall report on Karl Barth himself, on Father Bernard Häring, who has for two generations been one of the most influential Catholic moral theologians, and on Dietrich Bonhoeffer who is known to us as one of the Christian martyrs of our time who also produced great writings on theological ethics.

Barth, only a few pages after he gives the traditional view of suicide, says the following:

> Who can say that it is absolutely impossible for the gracious God himself to help a man in affliction to take this way out. In some cases perhaps a man can and must choose and do this in the freedom given him by God and not therefore in false sovereignty, in full self assertion, but in true obedience.[9]

Bernard Häring makes a concession in this way:

> [R]egardless of the sin of suicide taken objectively, we cannot and may not judge the subjective guilt of anyone who takes his own life. In many cases an acute mental disturbance is present. In fact we may assume this to be the case in those instances in which persons known to lead a virtuous life take their own lives in a fit of melancholy or under some degree of compulsion."[10]

Bonhoeffer allows for the possibility that a person may quite rationally take his own life for the sake of others. He says the following:

> If a sufferer from an incurable disease cannot fail to see that his care must bring about the material and psychological ruin of his family, and if he therefore by his own decision frees them from this burden by this unauthorized action, and yet here, too, a condemnation will be impossible.[11]

Do we not see signs here of theology being changed?

Professor James Gustafson, one of the major current ethical theologians in this country, summarizes the results of this change in the following way: "Yet there are probably few persons in our society who are prepared to make a strong moral condemnation of a person who takes his or her life."[12] He gives his own view by saying: "suicide is always a tragic moral choice: It is sometimes a misguided choice. But it can be a conscientious choice." He adds: "We must consent to its being done--justifiably, tragically, mournfully."[13]

In a 1981 symposium on "Ministry With the Aging," I wrote the following sentence: "It seems to me that suicide committed by the dying may at times be the most defensible form of positive euthanasia; it is based on the consent of the person involved and often the motive is concern for others."[14] The book had considerable use but I have never heard a negative word about that sentence.

Before leaving this subject of suicide, I want to warn against the misuse of what I have said. We should emphasize the enormous difference between suicide during a period of terminal illness and suicide that comes from youthful despair. There is sometimes an epidemic of such youthful suicides. I once heard Arturo Rubenstein, the great pianist, say in a television interview that he tried to commit suicide when he was 22 but that when he was 90 he thought that he was the happiest man in the world. This should serve as a good warning.

Suicide is also a temptation that should be resisted as a matter of character when it appears to be a quick solution of or escape from a tormenting problem, when living in mature life with such a problem may create or strengthen the virtues of loyalty to responsibilities, courage, and endurance. Even in the case of a long illness, often painful and always frustrating, suicide would often prevent experiences of spiritual growth. I learned this from an experience in my own family. One of its members, very close to me, suffered for two years from a struggle against cancer. She transcended that experience in a wonderful way until the last weeks and remained herself in her relationships. She was an inspiration to others. I often thought that she combined what I call pain and frustration with an unusual form of blessedness. Such experiences probe life's depths. By contrast, illness is very different when in its loss and suffering we see the body surviving the self.

Passive Euthanasia

Passive euthanasia, in contrast to active euthanasia or direct killing of the patient, involves the decision not to initiate therapy that would prolong life, or the removal of life supports in order to allow the disease to take its course. There are many forms of passive euthanasia decisions such as the removal of a respirator, allowing the patient to die of another disease such as pneumonia, or stopping artificial feeding. Sometimes a directive, "Do not resuscitate," is written in case heart failure should occur; such a directive is authorized by a doctor with the consent of patient or agent or family. The conditions for such decisions would be a terminal illness that is irreversible with the prospect of early death whatever is done, uncontrolled suffering, an irreversible, comatose or vegetative condition which has already been long continued.

There is a persistent debate as to whether there is any moral difference between passive and active euthanasia since both have the same purpose: the hastening of death. When one has gone through the process of deciding that either passive or active euthanasia is justified, I doubt if there is any fundamental moral difference between the two kinds of acts themselves. I would suggest, however, that there are at least three differences related to them that may affect the choice. First, there is a psychological difference that may have moral overtones in our minds. There are fewer inhibitions against allowing a disease to run its course toward death when obstacles have been removed than against direct killing. Passive euthanasia also carries less likelihood of publicity and, under our current legal system, is usually not considered to be acting against the law. Second, it is possible that a society that allows active euthanasia to become almost a routine matter in relation to some kinds of disease would reduce a highly desirable inhibition against killing. The results of a more permissive law and policy in the Netherlands need to be studied. Finally, I suggest that passive euthanasia depends for its methods on the particular conditions of the person affected and is less likely to be abused by being applied by a state or any other agency to a group of people.[15]

States differ in the extent to which their laws permit passive euthanasia. Some states allow it but insist that the person involved must have left a directive for it as was the case in Missouri when the Cruzan case came to that state's supreme court. Some states forbid the abandonment of artificial feeding, and this is often supported on moral and religious grounds as feeding is an essential part of caring. A number of states, following the lead of California, are making available a variety of advanced directives such as "living wills" (or "directives to physicians") and "Durable Power of Attorney for Health Care." Persons are thereby encouraged to make preparation for life and death decisions. Such advanced directives are good examples of what should be done in all states to provide clarity and to firm up the legal basis for passive euthanasia.

In 1990, the U.S. Supreme Court faced, for the first time, the

issues involved in passive euthanasia. Its decision in the case of
Nancy Cruzan was tragic so far as she was concerned. But the
majority and minority opinions throw light on what the court may
permit in the future. Even though Nancy Cruzan was in her
twenties, the issues discussed are important for all persons, old or
young.

Most of us know the basic facts of the case, but I shall touch on
a few of them. After an automobile accident in her early twenties,
Nancy Cruzan was in an irreversible vegetative condition for over
six years. She was kept alive by a tube for artificial feeding in her
stomach. Her parents asked a court to allow the tube to be
removed. A lower court agreed to this but the Supreme Court of
Missouri by a 4-3 decision refused permission for the tube to be
removed. She had not left in writing what she wanted to have done
in such an unexpected situation. What young person would do so?
Close friends did report that she had said that she would never
want to live under the kind of conditions to which she was now
condemned, and her parents were sure that this was the case. (The
U.S. Supreme Court went out of its way to praise the parents, and
there was no question about their integrity or about their acting out
of love.)

The Missouri Supreme Court acted on the basis of an
assumption that needs to be challenged. They assumed that the
state's interest was in the preservation of human life as such and
did not want to be limited by concern about any quality of life. It
is true that we would not want the state to make many
authoritative judgments about qualities of life. But is there not one
quality of life on which all other desirable qualities depend: the
capacity for consciousness and for conscious human relations?

The U.S. Supreme Court denied permission to remove the tube.
The main reason stated was that the Missouri court had the right to
take its action because the incompetent's wishes as to the
withdrawal of treatment was not proved by clear and convincing
evidence. The four in the minority did not have any more
knowledge of the wishes of Nancy Cruzan than the majority. Did
they have the right to be guided in part by their realization that
they would not want to live and they would not want their own
loved ones to live as Nancy was forced by the court to live? Surely
this was involved when Justice Stevens said: "The constitution
requires the state to care for Nancy Cruzan's life in a way that
gives appropriate respect to her own best interests."[16]

I have given this attention to the Cruzan case not only because
of the court's decision about the fate of Nancy Cruzan, which was

most unfortunate, but also because the opinions of the justices give clear support to passive euthanasia under other conditions. The majority in this case said that the Missouri Supreme Court had the right to insist on there being clear and convincing evidence concerning Nancy's real wishes. Chief Justice Rehnquist, in the majority's opinion, said that few cases of this sort had come before the Quinlan case fifteen years ago and that since then cases involving the right to refuse life-sustaining treatment have burgeoned. He said the following about the present situation: "The principle that a competent person has a constitutionally protected liberty interest in refusing unwanted medical treatment may be inferred from our previous decisions." Later he wrote: "but for purposes of this case, we assume that the United States Constitution would grant a competent person a constitutionally protected right to refuse life-saving hydration and nutrition."

This seems to me to be a radical statement, as some states have not permitted this very thing--the refusal of hydration and nutrition. Nancy Cruzan was not competent at the time and had not given directions about this when she was competent. Justice O'Connor in her opinion seemed to express an implied regret concerning the fate of Nancy Cruzan, when the justice wrote:

Few individuals provide explicit oral or written instructions regarding their intent to refuse medical treatment should they become incompetent. States which decline to consider any evidence other than such instructions may frequently fail to honor a patient's intent. Such failures might be avoided if the state considered an equally probative source of evidence: the patient's appointment of a proxy to make health-care decisions on her behalf. . . . As is evident from the court's survey of state court decisions, no national consensus has emerged for this difficult and sensitive problem. Today we decide only that one state's practice does not violate the Constitution; the more challenging task of crafting appropriate procedures for safeguarding incompetents' liberty is entrusted to the 'laboratory' of the states . . . in the first instance.[17]

Already California has provided a good report from that laboratory. I add one more point: Always it will be difficult for young people to see the need to appoint proxies or surrogates; but it should be less difficult to expect persons to do this as they approach old age.

(Most readers know that six months after the U.S. Supreme Court had acted, Nancy Cruzan was allowed to die. As I have said, the Supreme Court had emphasized its view that Missouri had the right to decide the case as it had done. The change came within Missouri. Nancy's parents went to the judge who had earlier rendered a favorable decision with the testimony of three more friends of Nancy that she had said to them, in effect, that she did not want to live under the conditions of a living death. The judge permitted the removal of the feeding tube. The difference this time was that the state's Attorney General, who had taken a hard-line position earlier, decided not to appeal this judge's decision.)[18]

Active Euthanasia

What should we think of active euthanasia, the direct killing of a person whose death would be a relief from a long period of intense suffering or from a degenerative disease that prevents a person from having a future with hope for any positive qualities of life or any positive relations with others? His or her condition may not have reached a point where passive euthanasia would be possible. Yet, he or she may be in that situation described earlier by Bonhoeffer as a "sufferer from an incurable disease [who] cannot fail to see that his care must bring about the material and psychological ruin of his family."

I confess that I discuss active euthanasia with less confidence than I discussed passive euthanasia. Passive euthanasia now has a public history. It is now out in the open. Cases of active euthanasia are known to us but often they are known confidentially. The law only condemns it. Its practice may lead to indictment for murder--the only relief from which may be a jury's refusal to convict or a judge's reduction of the penalty in light of the real human situation. Still, if what I have said about suicide has any validity, it is difficult to believe that all arrangements for active euthanasia are indefensible.

I have already said that passive euthanasia and active euthanasia are not in themselves morally different. They have the same intention, the hastening of a person's death. The differences between them are that some of the by-products of active euthanasia may be more problematic. I shall repeat one of my reasons for this because of its importance. If active euthanasia is institutionalized and becomes frequent, it may weaken the general human inhibition against killing. I am not so much concerned about the so-called "slippery slope" in *medical* care. I am more worried about the inhibition against killing that now seems to be eroding widely in our society--the kind of worry that is stimulated by viewing the local evening news in many American cities.

Such concerns should not cause us, however, to oppose active euthanasia on principle. When active euthanasia is the only relief from intense and relentless suffering or from a darker and darker future, I hope that active euthanasia may become legally possible with protections against its abuse. Those who support it emphasize the fact that it can more quickly end the suffering that justifies it than can passive euthanasia.

I am still impressed by a petition to the legislature of New York that was signed by 120 of the Protestant ministers of New York City in 1947.[19] The petition asks the legislature for a legal amendment "that would permit voluntary euthanasia for incurable sufferers, when authorized by a Court of Record, upon receipt of a signed and attested petition from the sufferer, and after investigation by a medical committee designated by the Court." The reason that I have been impressed by that petition is not only the number of signers (of whom 51 were Episcopalians--no fringe group!) but by the fact that the letter that went out to collect signatures was signed by Harry Emerson Fosdick, Henry Sloane Coffin, W. Russell Bowie and John Howard Lathrop. Those names are better remembered by me than by the younger people, but they represented the finest leadership of American Protestantism.

I am not familiar with the full history of what happened in regard to active euthanasia between 1947 and the effort to put a "Humane and Dignified Death Initiative"[20] on the ballot in California in 1988. (This latter attempt had only 120,000 signatures though the main idea received a large majority in the polls.) I do not know that there was a continuous large scale effort after 1947, but the miracles of medicine in greatly extending the length of life have, in recent years, greatly increased openness toward both passive and active euthanasia. People may say that the practice of euthanasia is taking the place of God. But a measure of that already happened with the extension of life through the miracles of medicine. Euthanasia counteracts some of the results of modern medicine's power.

For two generations, one of the greatest American teachers of Christian ethics was the late Paul Ramsey of Princeton University. He was always quite conservative about life and death issues. But in his powerful book, *The Patient as Person,*[21] published in 1970, he speaks of two situations that may call for passive or active euthanasia: cases of patients in "deep and irreversible coma" and "a kind of prolonged dying in which it is medically impossible to keep severe pain at bay." In what follows, and in a note, he indicates that he is still making up his mind in regard to pain. He raises the question whether it is always possible to control the most severe pain. It is often assumed that the means of doing this may weaken the patient and thus hasten death. Such means, since they are not intended to kill, should not come under the heading of euthanasia. Ramsey has no doubt about what should be done in the comatose situation. Then he raises the question whether allowing these exceptions may weaken the medical profession's "impulse to save" and he concludes that this would not be the case. He makes the judgment that in these extreme situations "we have correctly located the point at which the crucial moral difference between omission and commission [or passive and active euthanasia] as a guide to faithful actions has utterly vanished." To me, it is very important that Ramsey, in view of his dominant assumptions, did come to sanction active euthanasia in some situations.

Professor Daniel Maguire in his illuminating book, *Death by Choice*,[22] reports on a study of Dr. R. H. Williams of the University of Washington based on a poll of the Association of Professors of Medicine which found that 87 percent of those responding favored negative euthanasia (what I call passive) and that 80 percent said that they have practiced it. He quotes a related study that showed that 90 percent of fourth-year medical students interviewed favored negative euthanasia but only 15 percent of doctors quizzed favored positive or active euthanasia. It would be hard to guess how much this difference was a matter of personal conscience and how much of it resulted from a recognition of the legal situation. A full discussion of the issues on their merits may eventually change both convictions and the law.

Conclusion

I believe that active euthanasia can at times be supported religiously and morally as a matter of conscience. Great difficulties will remain for institutions to sanction it, and there is great need to change the legal situation. I have not emphasized the support for either active or passive euthanasia that might come from their relevance to the very important public problem of the costs of medical care. I will leave that discussion to others. Rather, I have emphasized concern for the dignity and quality of life of individual patients, and their freedom from the fate of a living death imposed upon them by doubtful dogmas or the law. I am concerned about them and about the anxieties, the hard decisions, and the suffering of their families.

Notes and References

1. Daniel Callahan, *Setting Limits: Medical Goals in an Aging Society* (New York: Simon & Schuster, 1987), and *What Kind of Life: The Limits of Medical Progress* (New York: Simon & Schuster, 1990).

2. Callahan, *Setting Limits*, p. 184.

3. Ibid.

4. Ibid., p. 21.

5. In this matter Childress makes use of the ground-breaking work of Victor Fuchs, *Who Shall Live? Health, Economics, and Social Choice* (New York: Basic Books, 1974).

6. *Hamlet*, Act 1, Scene 2. Shakespeare knew of another feeling about suicide in the conflict between Laertes and the priest who refused to give Ophelia a full Christian burial. He said to the priest: "I tell thee, churlish priest, a ministering angel shall my sister be, when thou liest howling." Hamlet, Act V, Scene 1.

7. Thomas Aquinas, *Summa Theologica* ii-ii 64.5.3. (Various editions.)

8. Karl Barth: *Church Dogmatics*, Vol. III, 4 (Edinburgh: T. and T. Clark, 1961), p. 404.

9. Ibid., p. 410. Before making this statement, Barth says that suicide is not unforgivable as "this cannot be said of any isolated will or act of man, and therefore not even of the last," p. 405.

10. Bernard Häring, *The Law of Christ*, Vol. 3 (Chester Springs, P.A: Mercier Press, 1966), pp. 199-200.

11. Dietrich Bonhoeffer, *Ethics*, edited by Eberhard Bethge, translated by Neville H. Smith (New York: Macmillan, 1953), p. 126.

12. James Gustafson, *Ethics from a Theocentric Perspective*, Vol. 2 (Chicago: University of Chicago Press, 1984), p. 187.

13. Ibid., p. 215.

14. William M. Clements, editor, *Ministry With the Aging* (New York: Harper and Row, 1981), p. 150.

15. Richard A. O'Neil, "The Moral Relevance of the Active/Passive Euthanasia Distinction," in *No Rush to Judgment*, edited by David H. Smith and Linda M. Bernstein (Bloomington: The Poynter Center, Indiana University, 1978), pp. 177-202.

16. I have taken this and other quotations from the opinions of justices from "Excerpts From Court Opinions," *The New York Times, National Edition*, June 26, 1990, p. 12.

17. Ibid.

18.   Ronald Dworkin, "The Right to Die," *The New York Review of Books,* Jan. 31, 1991, p. 14.

19.   This is primarily a local effort. I have a copy of the petition to the Legislature of New York and a list of all the signers. They come chiefly from the following denominations: Episcopal, Baptist, Presbyterian, and Unitarian.

20.   There is an account of the effort to get the initiative on the 1988 California ballot in Allan Parachini, "The California Humane and Dignified Death Initiative," *The Hastings Center Report* (Special Supplement: Mercy, Murder, and Morality: Perspectives on Euthanasia), Vol. 19, January/ February 1989, pp. 10-12.

21.   Paul Ramsey, *The Patient as Person* (New Haven: Yale University Press, 1970), pp. 161-164. His reference "The crucial moral difference between omission and commission" indicates that he is thinking of both passive and active euthanasia.

22.   Daniel C. Maguire, *Death by Choice* (New York: Schocken Books, 1975), p. 116.

20

Ethics and Aging:
Callahan and Beyond

James W. Walters

Introduction

In a positive review of Daniel Callahan's *Setting Limits: Medical Goals in an Aging Society,*[1] *Time* magazine called the author "arguably the nation's leading medical ethicist." In 1990 Callahan published a second book on allocation of health care, *What Kind of Life: The Limits of Medical Progress.*[2] Because of the importance of these books, the first half of this paper, particularly, is devoted to a critical assessment of Callahan's basic argument. I then turn to my development of a constructive proposal.

Callahan's Views

Callahan generally views the problem of health care in economic terms. However, more fundamentally, he laments society's miscon-struing of the value of old age (continued self-indulgence) and our misconception of medicine's purpose (promotion of longevity).

Callahan's proposed solution is two-fold. Formally, he calls for a broad--and probably protracted--debate on the issues. Substantively, he advances key proposals which the book elaborates. He is hopeful that a consensus will develop in support of his vision of limits.

There are two core ideas in *Setting Limits.* Fundamental to the argument is Callahan's notion of a "natural life-span." This period consists of about 80 years during which an individual may be expected to have essentially lived out his or her life's potential--experiencing education, travel, culture, and the like. After fourscore years, an individual and society should recognize that resources ought to be directed to younger citizens as opposed to life extension of the elderly. Following on the heels of the natural life-span, is the author's suggestion of a "tolerable death." Persons after 80 years of age--accepting their growing frailty and mortality--should be willing to accept gracefully a death which is not welcome but is at least tolerable, given society's other needs. In terms of social policy, such a death means that governmental programs will no longer fund any modalities of life extension (from expensive transplants to antibiotics), but will make dying as comfortable as possible. The second volume, *What Kind of Life*, applies Callahan's perspective on medical limits to general society, arguing that America already has a sufficiently good level of health care and that funds saved from a disallowance of development and use of high-technology medical advances should be diverted to other pressing national goods, such as public school education.

If such a stance toward health care were adopted in our nation, three primary benefits would accrue: First, society would save money, or at least it would avoid the further burgeoning of medical expenditures; second, death would be accepted as a part of life's rhythm and a greater intergenerational equality of resource allocation would be realized; and third, medicine would no longer be a search for immortality, but would be understood more realistically as helping to avoid premature death and alleviation of pain.

A Critique

Theological Considerations

In profound writing on health, old age and death, the taking of religious positions can hardly be avoided; and particularly in Callahan's writing they are not far below the surface. Because of the importance of basic presuppositions of faith in *Setting Limits*, I will first comment on the book through the spectacles of a theologian before donning those of a bioethicist.

In his concluding chapter, Callahan quotes the ancient Greek poet, Pindar: "Do not yearn after immortality. But exhaust the limits of the possible." *Setting Limits*, finally, is an exegesis of this text. And the interpreter of the text, if one did not know better, might be seen as a Calvinist whose God had foreordained the limit to human existence as being roughly fourscore years--an age "relatively impervious to technological advances." However, since Callahan's background is Roman Catholic, perhaps an undergirding natural law is surfacing in his advocacy of the central concept, "natural life span."[3] Regardless, one thing is certain: The author is no Wesleyan interpreter of the text. For one of John Wesley's most profound teachings was Christian perfection--the belief that through diligent Christian living, perfection of character is attainable. Wesley did not clearly distinguish the possible from the unattainable. And those in the Wesleyan tradition--Americans within the Methodist churches, other American denominations influenced by Wesley's followers, and countless Americans who carry on the spirit of Wesley--are inclined to be more optimistic about human progress than Callahan appears to be.

Callahan appears in both books to have an accepting view toward life's negative side--including death. An underlying theme throughout these books and in earlier work[4] is a strong suspicion of technology. For example, Callahan sees "slavery to the promise of high-technology medicine" as a modern addiction. This is contrary to his advocacy of modest goals for medical care. And Callahan means medical *care*-not medical cure. Society owes all citizens a decent minimum of medical treatment, but not necessarily the curing of heart disease in middle age, only for the patient to die later of Alzheimer's. A basic tenet of the theology advocated by Callahan is gratitude by the old for the life of fulfillment which they have lived, and a willingness to allow resources to be diverted to those who have not realized such fullness.

Acceptance of the limitation on medical resources for the elderly inevitably leads to acceptance of one's mortality and death. Death is but a part of a larger view of life--the "cycle of life" as Callahan would have it. A death coming after a full life is a "loss," a time for expression of "sadness," but it is not an evil. Such thinking may be merely good American pragmatism. Or it may have its origins in Eastern thought, where much more organic views of human involvement in nature prevail. The author's footnotes do not tell.

Regardless, Callahan is in direct opposition to much of Protestant theology on acceptance or denial of death. For example, Swiss theologian, Oscar Cullmann, in his Ingersoll lecture at Harvard in 1955, contrasted the death of Socrates with that of Jesus. Socrates, with complete composure and peace, saw his impending death as liberation. Jesus, however, cried that the cup of death might pass him by, seeing death as "this greatest of all terrors."[5] The pervasiveness of this sentiment in Western thought is illustrated by Dylan Thomas' well-known exhortation to "rage against the dying of the light."[6]

If the sin of humankind is worship and misuse of medical technology, salvation lies in a universal recognition of the malady, calling it by its right name, renouncing it and swearing that from henceforth medicine will live by more temperate goals. Its proper aims, says Callahan, are two-fold: avoidance of premature death and alleviation of pain. However, our sinless state is future and humanity must not be unduly pushed. So entrenched is our attachment to life extension that Callahan recognizes that adoption of his vision would be immoral if adopted before a societal change of attitude toward death.

Callahan's vision is akin to a religious hope. He hopes that discussion and debate will bring all parties to see the truthfulness of this vision of a society which provides basic minimal health care for young and middle aged and makes possible a good quality of life for the elderly, with octogenarians gratefully receiving only comfort care in their illnesses. Even if Callahan's vision is appropriate (and I happen to think his *philosophy* has much going for it), an expectation of ecumenical sharing of vision in this increasingly pluralistic country is comprised more of hope than realism.

A separate but related aspect of ecumenical hope, is Callahan's desire to see an advance beyond superficial pleasure-seeking among the aged population and a turn toward grappling with life's deeper meaning. In the name of intergenerational equality, he calls for the old--if not all society--to take advantage of the current crisis in health care and address issues of life's basic meaning. He suggests that "transcendent" meaning may be found in a willingness of the elderly to pass on their wisdom to the young and allow limited resources to be utilized by those whose lives are primarily future. A widespread acceptance of such selflessness is desirable among all citizens, but in Callahan's vision it is demanded only of the financially destitute.

Ethical Considerations

In *Setting Limits*, Callahan courageously bares his soul in grappling with an immense problem which we will be facing for years to come. Although I have reservations about the solution offered, I praise the author for the intellectual bravery and moral fortitude in laying out a proposal to initiate the debate.

The financing of health care in America is in crisis. Relative to the rest of the economy, health-care costs have doubled in the last 25 years. Yet, health statistics are no better for this country, which spends nearly 12 percent of its gross national product on health care, than in Great Britain which spends little more than half this percentage.

Urgent questions are being raised about the value of our entire health-care system: prenatal treatment, preventive treatment, high-technology treatment, treatment for the 35 to 40 million uninsured, and finally, treatment for the elderly. The latter health-care challenge, of course, is Callahan's basic focus in *Setting Limits*. And although Callahan deals with broader health care issues in his *What Kind of Life*, his path-making proposals in *Setting Limits* are not withdrawn and remain controversial. In light of Callahan's published response to his most severe critics,[7] he is still persuaded that budget-impacting savings can be achieved by placing mandatory limits on life-extension treatments funded by Medicare. An over-arching question is whether it is wise to see both the problem and solution so single-mindedly in terms of the elderly poor.

Many specific questions can be raised about the original proposal:

- Is there any such thing as a "*natural*" life span?
- Since society has increased the life span some 30 years in the last three centuries and this is deemed a good, what are the moral and medical warrants for contentment with fourscore years?
- If the natural life span is to include fulfillment such as education, travel, and culture, might not some privileged persons encompass this goal by, say, 40, and many underprivileged never?
- Can medicine focus on quality-of-life issues for the pre-octogenarians without increasing the likelihood for an aborted longevity?
- What is so valuable in our common life that coercing some persons to forfeit their last several years of life is warranted?
- If unlimited life-extension modalities will always be available to the wealthy, can a democracy bear to encourage the dying of the aged poor in the name of economics?
- Is it possible to affirm the "inestimable value" of the old and simultaneously call for a non-voluntary foregoing of extant, even moderately priced, life-extension modalities such as antibiotics?

Callahan's proposal is nothing, if not bold. Now I hold no brief against bold actions--Roosevelt's New Deal, Johnson's Great Society, Gorbachev's *perestroika*. But is Callahan's natural life span in this league? Let me briefly develop three substantive points, playing on the notion of Callahan's boldness: Callahan's proposal is *unreservedly* bold, it's *unnecessarily* bold, and it's *uncharacteristically* bold.

Unreserved boldness. Callahan, like many health-policy analysts, cites the percent of the gross national product (GNP) which the United States is spending on health care--nearly 12 percent currently. This is double what it was a single generation ago. With the prospects of a continuing barrage of medical technology and a burgeoning elderly population, the percentage could continue its climb. It is assumed that this is unacceptable because of other goods--beyond health--which deserve their share of the financial pie. As Callahan indicates, we could get to the point where we would be spending so much on health that there would exist precious few other goods to pursue with our healthy bodies. But I do not see that we are approaching such straits that elimination of life-extension to the aged poor is needed.

True, the United States is spending a greater percentage of its GNP on health care than any other country. In many ways, this is lamentable. For we do not have the results in vital, international health indices to warrant such expenditures. Callahan is right to state in *What Kind of Life* that the U.S. "desperately" needs a universal health-care insurance which guarantees a decent minimum of care for all.[8] And he candidly recognizes that if his vision of health care for America were implemented, it probably would cost more--at least initially. He continues to believe, however, that great savings can come from limiting treatment to the elderly and that the current percentage of GNP spent on medical care is excessive.

Is 12 percent of GNP for medical services too much? Perhaps. But there is no referendum or consensus stating what percentage is the ideal figure. What matters is where national priorities are placed. Today over 6 percent of the GNP is spent in preparing for war. However, attitudes are changing. Increasingly society is recognizing that all our bombs make us no safer. As John Mueller points out in his *Retreat from Doomsday: The Obsolescence of Major War*,[9] war, a well-accepted if not popular manner of settling national disputes a century ago, is now coming to be seen very differently, and the superpowers are progressively moving away from war as a legitimate option. If we can spend over $300 billion annually on defense, is it not possible that that figure may be reduced as we enter the *post-nuclear* age envisioned by former President Reagan? And, if truly warranted, could not some of the "peace dividend" be given to health care?

My point is that there may be several ways of rationalizing or raising more money for health care without having to balance future needs against the lives of the destitute old.

A crucial aspect of Callahan's argument is paradoxical. On the one hand, he argues for societal refusal to pay for life-sustaining treatment--even antibiotics--for an 80-year-old patient who wants to live but has a relatively minor life-threatening illness. At least, such is the proposed approach for an average octogenarian. But in his *Setting limits*, 1986, he allows for an exception: If an elderly person is physically vigorous, during at least the first round of illness, that person is entitled to all levels of medical care if there are decent prospects for four or five more years of good life. This would be the case even if the person is over the natural life-span limit. "I do not think anyone would find it tolerable to allow the healthy person to be denied life-saving care," admits Callahan.[10] The public may not have changed its mind, but Callahan did. In a 1990 piece, the author recanted:

> I was myself seduced by our natural inclination to look at individual cases. That was a mistake, and my critics were quite right to point that out. I would now say that, to be consistent in the use of age as a standard, no exceptions should be made, particularly exceptions based on the conditions of the individual patient; the whole point of a categorical standard is to avoid having to make judgments of that kind.[11]

Few ethicists would deny that age should have some bearing in determining the extent of medical treatment available. For example, most all of us would agree that a 95-year-old should not have an equal chance at a heart which could be successfully transplanted into a 20-year-old. But to make age the exclusive criterion, and then to take it consistently to its logical conclusion is philosophic purity, but whether it is good social policy is another issue.

Interestingly, despite Callahan's boldness in rationing, he is against active euthanasia, or assisted suicide:

> If one believes that the old should not be rejected, that old age is worthy of respect, that the old have as valid a social place as any other age group, and that the old are as diverse in their temperaments and outlooks as any other age group, an

endorsement of a special need for euthanasia for the old seems to belie all those commitments.[12]

Callahan, like most American moralists and clinicians, opposes active voluntary euthanasia. However, interestingly, allowance of a person who is terminally ill to choose time and type of death appears less threatening to our moral ethos and society's stability than the natural-life-span/tolerable-death proposal.

Uncharacteristic boldness. Daniel Callahan has long been reluctant to let go of societal myths--even taboos--because he so highly values their social utility. A sustaining myth in the West is individual self-determination: Each citizen is free to pursue life as he or she sees fit. It seems uncharacteristic for the author to make a proposal which appears to be diametrically opposed to this fundamental democratic notion.

A related problem with the life-span model is that another worthy myth--one which is under continual assault from the Right-- would be dealt a severe blow. I speak of the notion of *human equality*--regardless of wealth. Under Callahan's proposal the poor would suffer de facto discrimination. Those without a rich uncle would have to accept a societally imposed "tolerable death," while all the non-poor may purchase the latest technology our free enterprise medical system has devised. In sum, this myth-destroying proposal is not vintage Callahan.

Callahan's seminal *Setting Limits* contains two essential agendas-- one is a call for discussion and debate building toward a new *philosophy* of aged life; the other is a call for a new *social policy* for aged life. Much of what I have said concerns the latter's social policy, because I find it basically flawed.

However, I heartily applaud the call for our society to grapple with the question of values--the basic, common values which may continue to undergird civilized living *and* dying. Modernity does lend itself to superficiality. Even if the young and middle-aged may live with little thought of life's final meaning, it is a particular tragedy for such lack of thinking to continue to the grave. The idea of a common appreciation for a life cycle, including varying roles for life's different stages, is appealing--as opposed to the idea of the old merely living for just one more round of tennis. However, I am a bit uncomfortable with a clarion call for altruism on the part of the old, with so little said about similar needs for persons at other stages of life. All in all, the call for the old (and I hope all others as well) to think more substantively about our inner selves and how we relate to the broader society is loud and welcome.

A Constructive Proposal

Beyond my appreciation for and qualms about Callahan's basic project, I now turn to a constructive argument. First, I suggest that we implement new procedures within current law and within the contemporary social ethos which further Callahan's philosophy of old-age realism. We need to be much more comfortable with death as an inevitable component of our mortal life together. Second, I will contend that genuine respect for sentient human life demands that elements of our current ethos be questioned; and further I argue that we openly debate changes in today's law which would allow people more choice regarding their final days and their type of death, and save other human lives. It is imperative that changes in views of life and death be deliberate and consensual, because this topic cuts close to the marrow of many people's self-identity.

New Procedures Within Current Understandings

We need to exercise unprecedented creativity in devising and implementing medical procedures which allow persons a more timely death than is now often the case.

Consider a proposal on nursing-home patients recently devised by Robert Marsh, a Glendale physician who chairs his hospital's ethics committee. Marsh questions California regulations which he believes mandate excessive acute treatment for ailing nursing home residents. Marsh believes that transfers to acute hospitals of nursing home patients should be the exception. Further, he contends that upon admission each nursing-home resident (or surrogate) should be presented with the need to decide the type of care to be given when the patient enters a terminal illness.[13]

Another area needing reform is use of do-not-resuscitate orders (DNRs). DNRs are designed for certain very ill patients. The writing of such instructions generally is at the physician's discretion. Regulatory agencies are beginning to require that hospitals have policies on DNRs. However, current literature shows considerable apprehension among physicians about discussing DNRs with patients. This is lamentable and shows what some studies have demonstrated-- that often patients are more accepting of their terminal condition than are their physicians. Discussion of DNRs could be part of the admissions procedure for patients with designated illnesses. It can be hoped that hospitals will go beyond the mere letter of the congressional Patient Self-Determination Act, a measure which as of

December 1991, mandates that all hospitals receiving Medicaid or
Medicare broach the subject of advanced directives to all admitted
patients.[14]   A new medical ethos is needed which, at the very least,
calls for physicians of seriously ill patients to initiate discussion of
what type of care is desired if the patient should lapse into a semi-
comatose state.

California has been a leader in recognizing the legitimacy of
citizens deciding in advance about their medical treatment for
terminal illnesses.   Examples are the "living will" and the Durable
Power of Attorney for Health Care (DPAHC).   The latter document
allows persons to name a surrogate and to declare the guidelines for
their medical care when they can no longer decide.   Although this
document has been available since 1984, its recognition has been
belated and is still minimal.   State agencies and professional groups
could do much more in making use of the DPAHC.   The document
is a God-send to persons concerned about the type of medical care
given or withheld in their waning weeks--or years.   Further, because
most citizens oppose heroic measures which result in minimal
quality of life, use of the document would spare families emotional
pain and society would conserve valuable medical resources.[15]   Now
that the federal government is requiring that hospitals discuss
advanced directives with patients, the use of these instruments and
its resulting benefits should dramatically increase.

Reevaluation of mandatory emergency care for ailing nursing-
home patients, greater openness about DNRs, and more extensive use
of advanced directives are merely three instances of measures which
can be taken within the current law to give individuals more control
over their dying days.   However, as new medical technologies give
physicians increasing control over vital life processes, our ideas
about what constitutes intrinsically valuable human life are being
slowly altered.   And as views shift, the laws concerning life and
death which rest on these views, need reevaluation.

An Emerging Ethos and the Need for
New Legal Formulations

An old ethos holds that if life is human, it is, per se, valuable
and sacred.   And so we spoke--and many still speak--of "human
beings" rather indiscriminately as possessing a moral status not
approached by other lives.   (This is essentially the stance of the more
strident pro-life groups.)

However, for several reasons such talk is increasingly difficult when precise language is desired:

- We live in the era of Koko, the great ape of Northern California who possesses a 1000 word vocabulary, and who so mourned the accidental death of his adopted kitten "All Ball" that he was given another.
- Our medical technology can physically sustain a Karen Ann Quinlan or a Nancy Cruzan; but the value of such heroics is questionable and widely criticized. Thus, the American Medical Association in 1986 declared the ethical permissibility of withholding or withdrawing even artificial nutrition from permanently comatose patients.
- Scores of parents in the last few years have requested that their anencephalic newborns be used as organ sources so that some good might come from their personal tragedies. But because these higher-brain absent newborns do not meet the technical definition of death in the U.S., other salvageable babies die.
- Add one more to these vignettes: the hundreds of thousands of early fetuses which are aborted each year in this country by women who decide--for a host of reasons--that they will no longer sustain the growing human life within them.

Assisted Suicide or Voluntary Active Euthanasia

The point of the above examples is merely that previously serviceable concepts and categories are no longer adequate. Or, if they are, they require revised, updated warrants. A pressing question in any discussion of ethics and aging is that of voluntary active euthanasia. Should a nursing-home resident, for example, faced with encroaching Alzheimer's disease, have the option of assistance in taking his or her own life? This is the nub of the issue, since attempted suicide itself is not an illegal act. Further, the idea of active euthanasia or assisted suicide brings to the fore society's moral views of the planned, purposeful killing of oneself when one's deterioration necessitates assistance in perpetrating the act. Should assisted suicide be viewed as a moral option and legalized in this country?

The first thing to be said is that the morality of assisted suicide in individual cases is a related but quite different issue from the legality of the practice. I can quite easily envision circumstances which would make assisted suicide not only right but obligatory. On the other hand, I have reservations about legalization of assisted suicide.   My reservations are utilitarian in nature and specifically concern what society might be saying symbolically to itself about its valuation of individual existence.   Of course, any law allowing assisted suicide could and should be carefully hedged and nuanced; but my questions concern the implicit message any such law would send throughout the popular culture.

Any society--indeed civilization itself--exists on the basis of shared views on a myriad of subjects both great and small. Throughout the preponderance of human history our pre-scientific forebears' societies were bonded by common belief in many strange and clearly erroneous concepts.   The pioneering British anthropologist, Sir James Frazer, particularly underscored the nature of the faulty reasoning from which taboos and magical beliefs arose. However, to A. R. Radcliffe-Brown it is the accidental consequence of these beliefs which constitutes their essential function--the forming of a stable, orderly society.   Radcliffe-Brown's point is best made by relating his tale of Confucian beliefs:

> In China, in the fifth and sixth centuries B.C., Confucius and his followers insisted on the great importance of the proper performance of ritual, such as funeral and mourning rites and sacrifices.   After Confucius there came the reformer Mo It who taught a combination of altruism--love for all men--and utilitarianism.   He held that funeral and mourning rites were useless and interfered with useful activities and should therefore be abolished or reduced to a minimum.   In the third and second centuries B.C. the Confucians, Hsun Tze and the compilers of the Li Chi (Book of Rites), replied to Mo It to the effect that though these rites might have no utilitarian purpose they none the less (sic) had a very important social function.   Briefly the theory is that the rites are the orderly (the *Li Chi* says "the beautified") expressing of feelings appropriate to a social situation.   They thus serve to regulate and refine human emotions.   We may say that partaking in the performance of rites serves to cultivate in the individual sentiments on whose existence the social order itself depends.[16]

Perhaps Radcliffe-Brown is merely a conservative Briton who is fearful of modern pluralism.   However, Clifford Geertz sounded a related concern in a lecture series at Yale's law school earlier this decade.   He spoke of man's laws as "webs of signification he himself has spun." The primary question, argues Geertz, "is whether human beings are going to continue to be able, in Java or Connecticut, through law, anthropology, or anything else, to image principled lives they can practicably lead."[17]

As a complex modern society, America, of course, has much greater diversity than found in primitive peoples. What cohesiveness we possess comes not from magical tenets and less and less from religious views, but increasingly through our laws. In the sixties laws against segregation helped bring equality to the races; in the seventies all women gained the right to legal abortions; in the eighties regulations were made and laws interpreted which further widened the gap between the haves and the have-nots. The question which dogs me regarding assisted suicide is this: If our society approves of this measure, would this action make us a better society? Yes, it would allow more freedom to thousands, perhaps tens of thousands of citizens who desire an earlier than natural exit from a debilitating life. But what effect would such legislation have on the other 250 million Americans whose views on day-to-day life and its value are formed in manifold ways? If each case of assisted suicide would follow the usual pattern--a gruesome, terminal illness brought to a merciful end in an unending sleep--the impact on society's life-valuing could well be beneficial. However, what of the inevitable cases of people who decide that life is not worth living when they lose ambulatory ability or other functions generally seen to be tolerable losses? What will publicity of these cases say to the handicapped about themselves? What will they say to the teenager who is depressed about school grades and sees a bleak future? To the drug user who is contemplating his suicidal lifestyle?

Such questions as these are important, but they are not sufficient to stymie adoption of assisted suicide if a strong case exists for it. But to my knowledge, such a strong case does not presently exist. The acute physical pain from some cancers and other illnesses can be alleviated and generally eradicated by use of analgesics--although in severe cases large quantities of pain medication will induce a deep stupor and may hasten death. The emotional pain of debilitating old age is sometimes alleviated by an accompanying senility.

Particularly tragic is the mentally alert old person whose friends have died, who is neglected by family, and whose body is falling apart. Another problematic category is that of persons who see themselves as possessing marginal personal value and who desire an early exit from life to conserve resources for other healthier lives. I know of no satisfactory answers to such personal tragedies. In regard to the first category, there are alert persons whose lives do become net liabilities and who have a strong moral case for suicide. And if suicide is not possible because of circumstances, then, by extension, assisted suicide could be a moral option. Although assisted suicide is illegal, in extreme cases it may well be morally obligatory, involving civil disobedience. Regarding patients who desire resources to be spent on the more able-bodied, the money spent for debilitated elderly persons is not yet a significant percentage of the health-care budget; thus guilt for present macro-allocation of the health-care budget should not weigh heavily on the dying. In sum, neither alert, physically debilitated patients nor finance-conscious patients constitute such urgent circumstances that immediate national adoption of assisted suicide is indicated.

My position on this topic may be clearer if distinguished from that of James Rachels, a philosopher whose book *The End of Life*[18] is an eloquent argument for active euthanasia or assisted suicide. Rachels contends that the essential issue is not whether active or passive euthanasia is morally acceptable; both are concerned with the question of the means to be used to achieve an already determined end--namely, death. In regard to a particular patient, the basic moral question is: Is this patient's life worth living? If the answer to this question is no, then the secondary concern of means is attended to. Because Rachels sees that some patients, and relevant others, view the subject's life as not worth living, and because he holds that such a decision is a morally licit one, he, of course, argues for the morality of active euthanasia.

I accept Rachel's reasoning as valid, given his implicit presupposition of individual autonomy. However, if one gives equal weight to the principle of community or societal well-being, the appropriateness of active euthanasia is not so self-evident. If a strong case exists for assisted suicide which takes fully into account the notion of community, I am not aware of it.

I believe that a moderately good case for a restricted right to assisted suicide does exist and that it consists of at least two separate points: first, a basic respect for a sentient individual's right to determine how his or her final weeks of life will be spent, culminating in a type of death one has chosen or at least accepted; second, the recognition that the majority of society now views assisted suicide in certain circumstances as humane and decent.

As I have mentioned, I believe that much more can and should be done, short of assisted suicide, to allow more humane deaths. However, still there would exist the hard cases which only assisted suicide would address. Nevertheless, for reasons previously argued, I do not see these cases as constituting a compelling need for a national law allowing assisted suicide. Yet, because of the moderate argument for assisted suicide and because of the hard cases, I favor a socially progressive, homogeneous nation such as the Netherlands experimenting with a policy of assisted suicide. In this country, a progressive and homogenous state such as Oregon or Washington could profitably debate legislation permitting assisted suicide. If one or more of these states votes to allow assisted suicide, a comprehensive study of consequences should be done before widespread acceptance.

Conclusion

Regardless of how the debate and vote go on   assisted suicide, this is a less troubling possibility than is Callahan's proposed mandatory withholding of life-extending treatments from octogenarian patients.   Our very contemplation of these two measures suggests the challenges in ethics and aging which modern society presents. Again, we can thank Daniel Callahan for flinging open the door on this debate.

Notes and References

1. Daniel Callahan, *Setting Limits: Medical Goals in an Aging Society* (New York: Simon & Schuster, 1987).

2. Daniel Callahan, *What Kind of Life: The Limits of Medical Progress* (New York: Simon & Schuster, 1990)

3. For a discussion of this possibility see Anthony Battaglia's chapter in this volume.

4. See *Science, Ethics and Medicine*, edited by H. Tristram Engelhardt and Daniel Callahan (Hastings-on-Hudson, N.Y.: Hastings Center, 1976).

5. Oscar Cullmann, *"Immortality of the Soul or Resurrection of the Dead?"* in *Immortality and Resurrection: Death in the Western World: Two Conflicting Currents of Thought*, edited by Krister Stendahl (New York: Macmillian Company, 1965), p. 15.

6. Dylan Thomas, "Do Not Go Gentle Into That Good Night," *Collected Poems of Dylan Thomas* (New York: New Directions, 1953), p. 128.

7. See the final chapter of *A Good Old Age? The Paradox of Setting Limits*, edited by Paul Homer and Martha Holstein (New York: Simon & Schuster, 1990).

8. "We desperately need a universal health insurance plan, one that makes a decent level of health care available to all." Callahan, *What Kind of*

9. John Mueller, *Retreat from Doomsday: The Obsolescence of Major War* (New York: Basic Books, 1989).

10. Callahan, *Setting Limits* p. 197.

11 Daniel Callahan, "*Afterword*," in *A Good Old Age?*, edited by Paul Homer and Martha Holstein (New York: Simon & Schuster, 1990), pp. 311--312.

12. Daniel Callahan, S*etting Limits*, p. 197.

13. Personal correspondence with Dr. Marsh.

14. Patient Self-Determination Act, Sections 4206 and 4761 of the Omnibus Budget Reconciliation Act of 1990.

15. For further discussion of the effects of using California's Durable Power of Attorney for Health Care see the essay by Lawrence J. Schneiderman in this volume.

16. Alfred R. Radcliffe-Brown, *Taboo: The Frizzier Lecture*, 1939 (Cambridge: Cambridge University Press, 1939), pp. 32-33.

17. Clifford Geertz, *Local Knowledge: Further Essays in Interpretive Anthropology* (New York: Basic Books, 1983), p. 182 and 234.

18. James Rachels, *The End of Life* (Oxford: Oxford University Press, 1986).

Contributors

Anthony Battaglia, Ph.D., Professor of Religious Studies, California State University, Long Beach, California.

Charles E. Begley, Ph.D., Associate Professor of Management and Policy Sciences, School of Public Health, University of Texas, Houston, Texas.

John C. Bennett, D.D., S.T.D., L.L.D., President Emeritus and Reinhold Niebuhr Professor of Social Ethics Emeritus, Union Theological Seminary, New York.

Daniel Callahan, Director, The Hastings Center, Briarcliff Manor, New York.

Emily Erwin Culpepper, Th.D., Director of Women's Studies and Assistant Professor of Women's Studies and Religion, Religion Department and Women's Studies Program, University of Redlands, Redlands, California.

Jeanie Kayser-Jones, Ph.D., Professor, Physiological Nursing, School of Nursing and Medical Anthropology, Department of Epidemiology and Biostatistics, School of Medicine, University of California, San Francisco, California.

The Honorable Richard D. Lamm, L.L.B., Director, Center for Public Policy and Contemporary Issues, University of Denver, Denver, Colorado, and Former Governor, State of Colorado.

Paul T. Menzel, Ph.D., Professor, Department of Philosophy, Pacific Lutheran University, Tacoma, Washington.

Marilyn Moon, Ph.D., Senior Research Associate, The Urban Institute, Washington, D.C.

Donald J. Murphy, M.D., Medical Director, Senior Citizens Health Center, Presbyterian/St. Luke's Medical Center, Denver, Colorado.

Edmund D. Pellegrino, M.D., Director, Center for the Advanced Study of Ethics, and John Carroll Professor of Medicine and Medical Humanities, Georgetown University, Washington, D.C.

Michael D. Reagan, Ph.D., Professor Emeritus, Department of Political Science, University of California, Riverside, California.

J. Wesley Robb, Ph.D., Professor Emeritus, School of Religion and School of Medicine, University of Southern California, Los Angeles, California.

Judith Wilson Ross, M.A., Associate, Center for Healthcare Ethics, St. Joseph Health System, Orange, California.

Edward L. Schneider, M.D., Dean, Department of Gerontology, Andrus Gerontology Center, University of Southern California, Los Angeles, California.

Lawrence J. Schneiderman, M.D., Professor, Department of Community and Family Medicine, and Department of Medicine, University of California, San Diego, California.

Bethany Spielman, Ph.D., Istructor, Center for Biomedical Ethics, University of Virginia, Charlottesville, Virginia.

Robert M. Veatch, Ph.D., Director and Professor of Medical Ethics, Kennedy Institute of Ethics, Georgetown University, Washington, D.C.

James W. Walters, Ph.D., Professor of Christian Ethics, Loma Linda University, Loma Linda, California.

Gerald R. Winslow, Ph.D., Professor of Ethics, Department of Religion, Pacific Union College, Angwin, California.

Index